Narratives for a New Belonging

TENDENCIES: IDENTITIES, TEXTS, CULTURES

Series Editor: Peter Brooker

Other titles in the series are:

Deconstructing Ireland: Identity, Theory, Culture
Colin Graham

Cruising Culture: Promiscuity, Desire and American Gay Literature
Ben Gove

Race and Urban Space in Contemporary American Culture
Liam Kennedy

Memory, Narrative, Identity: Remembering the Self
Nicola King

Fundamentalism in America: Millennialism, Identity and Militant Religion
Philip Melling

Narratives for a New Belonging

Diasporic Cultural Fictions

Roger Bromley

Edinburgh University Press

For Anita, Carl and Catherine

© Roger Bromley, 2000

Edinburgh University Press Ltd
22 George Square, Edinburgh

Typeset in Melior
by Hewer Text Ltd, Edinburgh, and
printed and bound in Great Britain
by MPG Books Ltd, Bodmin

A CIP Record for this book is available from the British Library

ISBN 0 7486 0951 2 (paperback)

Contents

Acknowledgements

This book began life as an inaugural professorial lecture at Cheltenham and Gloucester College of Higher Education some years ago and I am grateful to colleagues there for encouraging me to develop those initial ideas. More recently, I have had the opportunity to test some of the arguments in a number of institutions, including Lillehammer College, Norway, the University of Lüneburg, the University of Karlsruhe, the University of Münster, the University of Vienna, University College, Northampton, the University of Hull and the University of Birmingham, and thanks are due to those who invited me and to staff and students who responded with a number of valuable suggestions.

The Faculty of Humanities at Nottingham Trent University has proved to be an extremely stimulating and inspiring place to work in over the past few years and I am fortunate to be surrounded by a range of outstanding and supportive colleagues bursting with ideas. Of particular value has been the comradely research environment provided by Viv Chadder, Deborah Chambers, Stephen Chan, Neal Curtis, Alison Donnell, Mike Featherstone, Sandra Harris, Richard Johnson, Eleonore Kofman, Ali Mohammadi, Parvati Raghuram, Tracey Skelton and Estella Tinck-nell. Chris Rojek, John Tomlinson and Patrick Williams have always shared ideas, time, and information in ways which have been more helpful than they can ever imagine.

In the wider world, mention must be made of the work of Stuart Hall, Homi Bhabha, Paul Gilroy and Victor Burgin, without whom this book could not have been written, Bruce Woodcock who supplied some vital material at a critical time, and Stephen Slemon for making me aware of Fred Wah's *Diamond Grill*. Peter Brooker, long-time friend as well as long-suffering and patient series editor, has been exemplary in the ways in which he has helped to shape the manuscript, and Nicola Carr has been an efficient, prompt, and supportive editor at Edinburgh University Press. There must have been times when both of them came close to giving up on me and I thank them for their forbearance when pressures of work and bouts of ill-health made completion difficult. That completion has been possible owes an enormous debt to Glynis Fry who worked with enormous speed, precision, and skill to convert my longhand scribble into a legible script. I am also grateful to Jeffrey Fry for his assistance, and to Dilys Hartland who has been a model copy-editor. By their capable administration, both Terry McSwiney and Glynis Fry have made my role as Director of the Graduate School a relatively easy one. My long-distance son, Carl, has frequently sent me valuable material from New York for which I am indebted. Finally, my wife Anita, my daughter Catherine, and the rest of my family have always offered a loving and companionable space for the constant renewal of my own belonging.

Series Editor's Introduction

Contemporary history continues to witness a series of momentous changes, altering what was only recently familiar ideological, political and economic terrain. These changes have prompted a new awareness of subjective, sexual, ethnic, racial, religious and cultural identities and of the ways these are constructed in metropolitan centres, regions and nations at a time when these spheres are themselves undergoing a period of critical transition. Recent theory has simultaneously encouraged a scepticism towards the supposed authenticity of personal or common histories, making identity the site of textualised narrative constructions and reconstructions rather than of transparent record. In addition, new developments in communication and information technology appear to be altering our fundamental perceptions of knowledge, of time and space, of relations between the real and the virtual, and of the local and the global.

The varied discourses of literature and media culture have sought to explore these changes, presenting life as it is negotiated on the border-lines of new hybridised, performative, migrant and marginalised identities, with all the mixed potential and tension these involve. What emerge are new, sometimes contradictory perceptions of subjectivity or of relations between individuals, social groups, ideologies, and nations, as the inner and public life are rewritten in a cultural environment caught up in religious and political conflict and the networks of global consumption, control and communication.

The series *Tendencies: Identities, Texts, Cultures* follows these debates and shows how the formations of identity are being articulated in contemporary literary and cultural texts, often as significantly in their hybridised language and modes as in their manifest content.

Volumes in the series concentrate upon tendencies in contemporary writing and cultural forms, principally in the work of writers, artists and cultural producers over the last two decades. Throughout, its consistent interest lies in the making and unmaking of individual, social and national identities. Each volume draws on relevant theory and critical debate in its discussion *inter alia* of questions of gender and sexuality, race and ethnicity, class, creed and nation, in the structuring of contemporary subjectivities.

The kinds of texts selected for study vary from volume to volume, but most often comprise written or visual texts available in English or widely distributed in English translation. Since identities are most often confirmed or redefined within the structures of story and narrative, the series is especially interested in the use of narrative forms, including fiction, autobiography, travel and historical writing, journalism, film and television.

Authors are encouraged to pursue inter-textual relations between these forms, to examine the relations between cultural texts and relevant theoretical or political discourse, and to consider cross-generic and intermedia forms where these too bear upon the main concerns of the series.

Peter Brooker
University College, Northampton

The Third Scenario

One of the central tasks confronting those seeking to develop narratives for a new belonging is the deeply embedded presence at all levels in Western culture of authorative, and authorising, texts which foreclose alternative ways of thinking and seeing. The alternative is always forced to occupy a subordinate – and secondary – space and is tolerated, patronised or suppressed, depending upon the level of its challenge to the hegemonic:

> Contemporary global understandings remain attuned to historical narratives that naturalize a particular, territorially oriented view of sovereignty, reinforce it with a political economy story that disparages precommercial systems of livelihood and exchange, and substitutes myths of evolutionary development for histories of violent confrontation and usurpation. (Shapiro 1997: 17)

The principal focus of this book is on cultural fictions which, in Barthes's phrase, speak 'outside the sentence' (Barthes 1976: 47) – texts which are written from the affective experience of social marginality, from a disjunctive, fragmented, displaced agency, and from the perspective of the edge. Excess, dream and fragment shape these fictions in an attempt to produce an act of reinscribing, of revising and hybridising the settled discursive hierarchies, by constructing a third space beyond existing political, social and cultural binaries: it is a space of revaluation.

In *New Left Review*, Stuart Hall argues that 'the issue of cultural identity as a political quest now constitutes one of the most serious problems as we go into the twenty-first century', and this book will make use of the issue of cultural identity and the concept of a 'border' metaphor, which advocates the adoption of the viewpoint 'of people moving in and out of borders constructed around co-ordinates of difference and power' (Hall 1995). Almost all of the fictions are by, and concern themselves with, those for whom categories of belonging and the present have been made unstable as a consequence of the displacement enforced by post-colonial and/or migrant circumstances. Language, home, memory and marginalisation are recurring problems throughout the texts analysed and the book focuses upon the ways in which the fictions speak of, from and across migrant identities and develop narratives of plurality, fluidity and always emergent becoming. Many of the texts also seek to renew severed links between the conflicted, diasporic 'self' and the collective, to shape a critically imagined solidarity, a healing, out of discursive rupture.

Several of the chapters use Bakhtin's concept of the dialogical as one means of challenging the oppositional presumptions of border, division, exclusionary thought and absolute difference. The dialogical is an inclusive, never finalised interactivity, an opening up and a breaking down; it is also a resource in a communal, many voiced storying. Combined with this use is also an awareness of the ways in which, although almost all the texts referred to use either a coloniser's language or that of a dominant social order, this language has been dislocated and acted upon, violated even, so that, in Marlene Nourbese Philip's terms, 'the historical realities are not erased or obliterated' (Philip 1993: 85). Transformation and textual negotiation are key features of the uses of language identified in 'border' writing; this is also true of its narrative practice. By using concepts of syncretism and hybridisation, the book examines the ways in which the indeterminacy of diasporic identities is produced by a continuous process of transculturation, of cultural translation.

Although the principal concerns of the book are with memory and silenced, or absent, histories, as well as transnational (and transgressive), cross-cultural and discursive border crossings, many of the writers and film-makers are also sensitive to the fact that borders are *within* persons and communities, as well as in discourses and geopolitical spaces. Each textual journey over multiple ethnic, linguistic, cultural, national and political–economic borders has to be articulated with the historical and contemporary journey of the exile, immigrant and refugee. Even, or perhaps particularly, when the experience addressed is that of those born in the 'migrated space', the narratives construct journeys of displacement, alienation, pain, loss and, perhaps even in the end for some, of opportunity. The subject of address, the object of representation, unvoiced and invisible, the 'othered' border crosser met, and continues to meet, that hostility reserved for the stranger who comes today, and the discriminatory and exclusionary legislation shaped for the stranger who stays, or might stay, tomorrow. In the words of bell hooks: 'We could enter that world but we could not live there' (hooks 1984: 1).

While this will be shown to be true in many respects, the book will also argue that the urban centres of the US, Canada and Britain (the primary locations of the narratives to be analysed) have been transformed by the processes of a local–global dialectic in which once-migrant groups have syncretised the so-called 'host' cultures and have unsettled commonsensical ideologies of race, nation and identity by forming new diasporic 'cityscapes'. Migrants, that is to say, have not been merely passive travellers but have actively transformed the worlds into which they have entered As Salman Rushdie has asked in *Satanic Verses*:

> How does newness come into the world? How is it born?
> Of what fusions, translations, conjoinings is it made?
> How does it survive, extreme and dangerous as it is? (Rushdie 1992: 8)

Some attention will be paid to the historical context of these fusions, translations and conjoinings, but the main emphasis of the book is on the contemporary: particularly, but not exclusively, on fictions produced in the 1990s. Changes in the world since 1989 have refocused attention on the displaced person, the migrant and the stranger; people dispossessed and separated from their identity and their history (not that these can ever be seen as stable or essentialist). This experience has to be seen in the context of a new global economy characterised by complex, inter-acting and disjunctive transnational flows. The conjunction of this historical moment with both the emergence of a diasporised generation of 'hyphenated' writers (Asian-American, Black-British and so on) and the theoretical developments of post-modernism and post-colonial theory have prompted this book as a means of exploring in a systematic way the dialectic of belonging and not belonging in the context of what Hall has called 'new ethnicities: identities that are *somewhere-in-between*' (Hall 1987).

Informed by the theoretical writings of Said, Bhabha, Spivak, Hall and Gilroy among others, the book considers the ways in which fictions can be seen as participating in new cultural strategies referenced, in many instances, by the dimensions of class, gender, sexuality and ethnicity. The fictions concentrated on are 'borderline' narratives, works of re-combination and 'hyphenation', texts of incomplete signification and hybridity: in-between spaces. The essence of the work is the cultural analysis of struggles to go beyond the boundaries and to exceed the limits of racialised, colonised and national identities. They are not simply narratives about contestation and difference, but achieve their very textualisation through constructions of difference and contestation; it is an aesthetic and a political issue.

My work on the nature of belonging has led me to believe that the key questions are best posed at the boundaries of nations, cultures, classes, ethnicities, sexualities and genders – at the boundaries because this is where the 'taken for granted' of identity formation is most put at risk. As borderline/boundary identities – identities at risk – seem to represent a positive, if unsettling, phenomenon by opening up the possibilities of new affiliations, I have chosen to examine a range of cultural narratives –

primarily, though not exclusively, literary – which raise the issue of what the world looks like from the margins and the borderlands. They are, mainly, narratives which give space and voice to the excluded and the dispossessed in an attempt to find new ways of responding at a time when conventional and current stories seem to be running out. These narratives are seen as cultural resources.

Each narrative is a fictional exploration of the complexities of belonging and identity, the shifting and cross-cutting cultural experience of diaspora and relocation. The book discusses particular post-colonial and minority writings – narratives of the excluded – as a way of seeking to understand the complex cultural territory in which the dominant and the subordinated within societies interact, struggle and negotiate their differences. Each text is generated out of a particular, but significantly different, migrant or post-colonial condition, and each text is concerned with the denial of identity, both within the marginalised community (in the case of women) and by the dominant culture. The narratives are mostly produced by women and shaped by what might be called bi-culturalism in the sense that they are born of two worlds (or more), expressions of marginalisation which emerge from migrant experience and cultural border zones: plural and fractured voices, multiple personalities struggling with placelessness and the rootedness of old, hollowed-out belongings. That the narratives are mainly produced by women is not surprising at this juncture, as the 'worlds' they are challenging are almost exclusively male dominated and designed primarily for fulfilment in terms of the human as envisaged by men occupying positions of power; the women are doubly exiled.

Form is a crucial issue because these texts are often working against authorised and authorising paradigms. They are multi-lingual, polyvocal and varifocal, inter-textual and multi-accented; the relationship between dominant and subaltern is destabilised. The location of each narrative is a cultural border zone, always in motion, not frozen for inspection: a liminal landscape of 'changing meanings in which seemingly distinct human cultures encounter one another's "otherness" – in conditions of profound inequality – and appropriate, accommodate or domesticate it through language' (Kolodny 1992: 13). However, these layered and hybridised discourses are writing very much against the idea of a melting pot or mosaic, of a simple 'rainbow' merging, and, if anything are sites of cultural resistance and refusal, empowering critical difference. Instead of a melting pot identity, what emerges is what Gloria Anzaldúa in *Border-lands/La Frontera* calls 'the new *mestiza*': a process of synchresis.

The new *mestiza* copes by developing a tolerance for contradictions, a tolerance for ambiguity. She learns to juggle cultures. She has a plural personality, she operates in a pluralistic mode – nothing is thrust out, the good, the bad and the

ugly, nothing rejected, nothing abandoned. Not only does she sustain contradictions, she turns the ambivalence into something else. (Anzaldúa 1987: 79)

In some of the texts, the figures are literally of mixed race or bi-racial, but
in many instances the mix is cultural, as is the border. They are
narratives that help us to think a twenty-first century, 'marked by
borrowing and lending across porous national and cultural boundaries
that are saturated with inequality, power, and domination' (Rosaldo
1989: 217).

The fictions are, for the most part, constructed around figures who
look in from the outside while looking out from the inside, to the extent
that both inside and outside lose their defining contours. They are figures
with hyphenated identities, living hybrid realities which pose problems
for classification and control, as well as raising questions about notions
of essential difference. The in-between zones are shifting grounds,
threshold spaces, and displacement and migration have led to a struggle
for space where identity is endlessly constructed, and deconstructed,
across difference and against set inside/outside oppositions. Techniques
are used which achieve a certain aesthetic distance, a holding back, but,
at the same time, the 'inwardness' of violation and displacement is
historically framed. The narratives are involved in a process of endless
locating and undermining: belonging is always problematic, a never-
ending dialogue of same with other.

Trinh Minh-ha argues that the challenge of the hyphenated reality lies
in the hyphen itself: the *becoming* Asian-American by bringing it into
story, finding voices and forms against repression, forgetting, racist
legislation, exclusion, self-hatred and stereotypes, and other arrested
forms of representation. In a sense, the texts I am describing are written
against the givens of representation, in fluid narrative modes in which
becoming remains active and intransitive. Becoming always exceeds its
own limits, fixtures and closures – even to the point of suicide as in
Woman Warrior and in *Bone*. The narratives use both the dominantly
constructed orders of discourse and the unsettling, undercutting and
subversive orders of dream, the unconscious and the 'mad'. There is
considerable reversing, doubling, repetition and displacing as ways of
establishing 'interstitial' ground against the grain of hegemonic binary
thinking. What these narratives demonstrate is that, 'cultural syncretism
takes place both at the margins and between the margins and a changing
mainstream' (Shohat and Stam 1994: 237). Additionally, they are texts
'which metaphorise the public sphere even when apparently narrating
private stories' (ibid.: 230). It is important to remember this as some of the
fictions I shall be examining have been criticised for confining themselves to the domestic and the private at the expense of wider social and
political issues.

Each narrative is involved in a process of reclaiming, of travelling back to an endlessly receding origin or identity, a point ultimately of no return, which is seen as diacritical and strategic – a strategy for producing a cultural framework for the possibility of emergence; the capacity to move across existing frontiers and to cut across fixed allegiances. The narratives are inter-generational (sometimes covering four generations) and deal constantly with crisis and emergency, as metaphors of the cracks and gaps, the splits and the sunderings, which accompany any attempted return to denied identity and cultural heritage. In fact, the very tracing of the 'return', the act of remembering, undermines the very notions of identity and ethnicity, originary and initial subjectivities. The space of writing is the space of an activity in which everything takes on a collective value (by refuting the extremely attractive propositions of individualist cultures); all the pre-existing, already-there belongings and definitions have to be interrogated in order to be exceeded.

What I would argue is distinctive about our 'contemporary' is the increasing prominence of the literature of what Stuart Hall has called the third scenario, an emergent discourse. This third scenario is a non-binarist space of reflection and its struggle in the politics of location. The dilemma we experience is of both attempting to situate this scenario and also refusing to confine it to a knowable location. It is not a liberal, multicultural space in which several cultures are juxtaposed with their essentialised frontiers intact – the space of demographic plurality – but 'diaspora identities . . . which are constantly producing and reproducing themselves anew, through transformation and difference' (Hall 1990: 402); the borderline negotiations of cultural translation. The third scenario is a performative location, readily disarticulated and rearticulated, constitutive and positioning, not enclosing and excluding.

The third scenario is the inter-cultural site of borderline writings, that boundary 'where "presencing" begins' (Bhabha 1994: 9), that aspect of the contemporary which has seen the culturally contingent 'frontiers' of modern nationhood open up to a potentially new internationalism with a 'transnational and translational sense of hybridity', in Bhabha's phrase. Bhabha uses a particularly salient quotation from Walter Benjamin which speaks precisely to what I am trying to describe: 'translation passes through continua of transformation, not abstract ideas of identity and similarity'. The phrase 'continua of transformation', with its element of untranslatability, is an appropriate way of talking about the political conditions of the present, and the narratives I am working with are attempting to produce analogical cultural forms of this continua of transformation, not out of abstractions but from the lived migrations and survivals (Derrida's sur-vivre – living on the borderlines) of the contemporary which detonate any comfortable idea of the present as a simple continuum. The fictions engage with and renew the past, refiguring it as a contingent 'in-between' space, a space of innovation which interrupts the performance of the present which has cleansed, erased, expelled and buried difference, except as a species of exotica or 'otherness', as the indispensable and endlessly renewed condition of the continua of transformation.

Bhabha argues that the 'non-synchronous temporality of global and national cultures opens up a cultural space – a third space – where the negotiations of incommensurable differences create a tension peculiar to borderline existences' (Bhabha 1994: 218). This third space, Bhabha suggests, is not necessarily a position in itself but is something which allows other positions to emerge, and is yet another formulation of the phenomenon I have already introduced as a way of establishing a critical discourse for analysing borderline writings, a rapidly increasing contemporary cultural form in film and literature. Our contemporary, with its discontinuities, rifts and fissures is, in Benjamin's terms, 'that moment blasted out of the continuum of history' (quoted in Bhabha 1994: 8).

BEYOND THE BOUNDARY: POST-NATIONAL PERSPECTIVES AND THE SEARCH FOR A MULTI-LOCATIONAL IMAGINATION

Throughout, this book is informed by the assumption that it is possible to speak of a 'world culture', a culture of interactive diversity shaped by what Gilroy in *The Black Atlantic* calls 'inter-cultural and transnational formations'. Emphasis is placed on cultures of 'encounter' and the possible condition of belonging simultaneously, mentally, psychologically and experientially, to a diversity of cultures. An attempt is made to theorise culture in ways which are not primarily national, and to explore identity in ways which do not bind it to nationality. This is partly done by using a concept which is becoming increasingly central to contemporary cultural studies: that of diasporic communities. The founding issue of the journal *Diaspora* included a valuable statement of what it understood by the concept of diaspora which I have found useful as a guiding principle in some of the chapters which follow. The editor, Khacha Tölölyan, argues that the journal must pursue:

[T]he traces of struggles over and contradictions within ideas and practices of collective identity, of homeland and nation. *Diaspora* [the journal] is concerned with the ways in which nations, real yet imagined communities, are fabulated, brought into being, made and unmade, in culture and politics, both on the land people call their own and in exile. (Tölölyan 1991: 3)

Fabulation is, among other things, a narrative activity; which is why I have chosen to examine the diasporic and transnational through the lens of cultural fictions. Migration has been seen as the quintessential experience of the twentieth century, from south to north and from east to west. The outcome of this movement of peoples, this displacement and deterritorialisation, has been the formation of diasporic communities and the development of diasporic identities: 'the fissured identities and hybridities generated by colonial dislocation' (Loomba 1998: 180). However, even if cultural diaspora-isation is acknowledged as a major contemporary phenomenon (and it is not only contemporary, of course), and its value as a resource in theorising post-coloniality is recognised, there is still a vast amount of analytical and empirical work which has to be done in order to understand the very significant differences between the experiences of diaspora. For example, the movement of populations brought about by the division of India and Pakistan, the migrations from Latin America to the United States, or the guest-worker phenomenon of Turkish people in Germany, have all resulted from distinctively different histories. It cannot be assumed, either, that simply being within a particular diasporic community confers an automatic and common shared identity, as the dimensions of class, gender and sexuality also have to be addressed. The question is also raised as to who is located within that community, and by whom. As Shohat reminds us, it is important to 'discriminate between the diverse modalities of hybridity, for example forced assimilation, internalized self-rejection, political co-optation, social conformism, cultural mimicry, and creative transcendence' (Shohat 1993: 110). In varying degrees, all of these different modalities figure in the fictions which are examined.

Even if diaspora is a global phenomenon, and although – according to George Lamming – 'the exile is a universal figure', cultural analysis has to begin again with the localised forms and internal conflicts of specific diasporas – as, for example, the Chinese in California, African-Caribbeans in London, Vietnamese in Norway, Indonesians in Australia, or South Asians in Canada. It is also important to remember, as Loomba points out, 'that large numbers of people in the Third World have not physically moved, and have to speak from "where they are", which is also often an equally ideologically or politically or emotionally fractured space' (Loomba 1998: 181). Equally significant is the fact that 'hybridity', or even diasporisation, is not simply a condition of metropolitan First World countries but also occurs in Third World cities. Although the reality of diaspora is one of the most visible and salient features of a globalised world, it has to be noted that the most prominent analytical model for understanding it is drawn from post-colonial theory. This, of course, gives priority to colonialism (perhaps not surprisingly, as 85 per cent of the non-European world was colonised by European powers by 1914) but it is not theoretically adequate for exploring the movement of peoples from east to west, or south to north, within Europe, or even those migrations within the American continent. It is also a theory which has mostly been elaborated from an Anglocentric perspective, and also from within originally white settler communities.

Nevertheless, I would argue that the concept of diasporic communities is one way of helping us to think beyond nationality as the necessary locus for models of analysing cultures. As Tölölyan has said: 'Diasporas are emblems of transnationalism because they embody the question of borders', and even if diasporised intellectuals in the First World have been prominent in its conceptualisation, this does not invalidate the idea of the 'diasporic community' as the focus of a post-national model of belonging. There is already some important work in this area: Avtar Brah's *Cartographies of Diaspora* on South Asian women and young people in Britain; Paul Gilroy's *The Black Atlantic* on the African-Caribbean diaspora in Britain and the US; Ien Ang's theorisation of the Chinese diaspora; Stuart Cunningham and Tina Nguyen's work on the media of the Vietnamese diaspora; and Hamid Naficy's study of Iranian television in Los Angeles.

The concept of diasporic communities will only be of value if it is not simply used as yet another extension of the tendency in cultural studies to 'speak of the subaltern'. As Stuart Cunningham and Tina Nguyen point out:

For the most part, media studies treatments of diasporic identity have concentrated on issues of representation *by* mainstream media *of* ethnic and racial identities. Not surprisingly, the conclusions reached in the numerous studies of this kind is that western mass media operate as prime filters of a hegemonic discourse 'othering minority cultures and identities' . . . [N]ecessary as these researches are, they are not sufficient to understand the productive construction of new hybrid identities and cultures by the active processes, simultaneously of maintenance and negotiation, of an original home and a newly acquired host culture. (Cunningham and Nguyen 1998: 2)

The concept of 'diasporic identity' has enabled us to go beyond the rather tired formulations of cultural imperialism ('prime filters of a hegemonic discourse') and to address, for example, media use within diasporic communities as both a localised and post-national set of practices. As Cunningham and Nguyen remind us, this productive construction, and not passive consumption, is always a matter of maintenance and negotiation. By going beyond the discourses of boundary it is possible to understand these 'new hybrid identities and cultures', which impact not only upon the diasporic but also upon the members of the 'host' society to such an extent that in time the notions of 'diasporic' and 'host' may be rendered existentially and analytically redundant. At present, they are used merely as terms of convenience, of transition. These new constructions remind us that identity is a matter of 'becoming' (negotiation, perhaps) as well as 'being' (maintenance, perhaps).

It is this double sense of identity, a characteristic of the diasporised, which produces a reconfiguration which I see as being based upon two valuable concepts of Michel de Certeau: strategy and tactic. A strategy, de Certeau argues, has the capacity 'to transform the uncertainties of history into readable spaces' (de Certeau 1984: 36). A conception of the post-national has to understand those strategies of the diasporised which have created these new 'readable spaces', and to begin to make them 'theoretically' legible. De Certeau also sees that the kind of knowledge generated by strategy is 'one sustained and determined by the power to provide oneself with one's own place' (ibid.). This relates to the struggle by the diasporised to achieve, in Hall's words, a 'centring of marginality', to provide their own place for their 'being'. A tactic is 'a calculated action determined by the absence of a proper locus', a matter of 'becoming' in a place where no centres remain and where no prior claim is made to any base. The post-national forces us to rethink our concept of the local as a site of both the strategic and the tactical, of both a settled, achieved community and a space of improvisation: 'They can represent themselves; they must not be represented', to paraphrase Marx on the peasantry. This process of representation is complex, uneven and conflicted.

In Hall's words, migration may be a one-way trip, but many of those who inhabit the 'transnations' of diasporic communities maintain links with their land of birth or origin and with other diasporised members both within, and beyond, the country of migration; these multi-locational attachments and, in some cases, travelling back and forth, help to constantly refine and revise the diasporic experience as always being in motion. Hybridity is the condition of belonging to 'an inter-continental border zone, a place in which no centres remain' (Gómez-Peña 1992–3: 74). Living diasporically has led to complex processes of identity building and an active engagement in a series of dialogues simultaneously conducted at local, national and transnational levels, but at the same time impoverishment and racism can also lead to excessive boundedness and local confinements.

In the words again of de Certeau: 'Other regions give us back what our culture has excluded from its discourse' (1984: 50); in other words, the difference of another cultural or discursive regime can be used to disclose the specificity and contingency of the present and of the culture of the Western nation-state. A lot of work has yet to be done in understanding the terms 'other' and 'our' in the de Certeau quotation.

This is not to say that we can just dispose of the nation-state as an exhausted late eighteenth-century formation, or focus exclusively on the diasporic communities as we also have to concern ourselves with the dominant European self-understanding which, Derrida has argued, has led to a failure in ethical discernment, precipitated by its moral geography. Having taken itself, Derrida says, 'to be a promontory, an advance – the avant-garde of geography and history . . . [it has] never ceased to make advances on the other' (quoted in Shapiro 1997: 194).

While it is probably true, in some respects, to say that these 'advances on the other' have ceased in their explicit imperial form (although globalisation is mainly a Euro-American phenomenon), it is also important not to consign Europe to oblivion as, in guilt-trip fashion, we celebrate global creative diversity. A fairly lengthy quotation from Derrida might help here, and it might also act as a transition to a brief consideration of what I am calling 'the post-national':

On the one hand, European cultural identity cannot . . . be disposed . . . into a myriad of provinces, into a multiplicity of self-enclosed idioms or petty little nationalisms . . . It cannot and must not renounce places of great circulation or heavy traffic, the great avenues or thoroughfares of translation and communication and thus of mediatization. But, on the other hand, it cannot and must not accept the capital of a centralizing authority that, by means of trans-European cultural mechanisms . . . would control and standardize, subjecting artistic discourses and practices to a grid of intelligibility. (in Shapiro 1997: 194)

For Derrida, this aporia in the midst of European cultural identity between 'self-enclosed idioms or petty little nationalisms' and a centralising 'grid of intelligibility', can help to form the basis of an ethical sensibility in the encounter with alterity (both within and without Europe): 'ethics, politics, and responsibility, if there are any, will only ever have begun with the experience and experiment of the aporia' (in Shapiro 1997). The presence of the diasporic community (alterity) within the 'host' society dramatises the aporia and stages the possibility of an ethical encounter in a post-national context: the diaspora has, literally and metaphorically, taken place in, from and because of the places of circulation and has travelled through the avenues or thoroughfares of translation and communication. As Michael Shapiro has pointed out:

The encounter between two subjects is not between two 'I's, but two 'we's, and each 'we' is a narrative construction, a textually bounded 'we' whose boundaries can be attenuated with an acceptance of the ambiguities and paradoxes imminent in the stories through which the collective self is lent coherence. (Shapiro 1997: 194)

In other words, our models of subjectivity are historically framed and culturally bounded; what I will be arguing for throughout is an analytical process which goes beyond an understanding based upon either the self-enclosures of national–provincial cultures or Derrida's imperialising and dirigiste 'grid of intelligibility', recognises the historical and contingent nature of the cultural within the nation-state, and brings about an attenuation of boundaries.

So far, I have spoken of diasporic communities from a positive perspective, taking what might be called the liberal view. There is, however, also an illiberal view which is why I have introduced the question of ethics, politics and responsibility. I want to think of the nation-state from the point of view of *sovereignty* – 'the sovereign *nomos* is the principle that, joining law and violence, threatens them with indistinction' (Agamben 1998: 31). According to Agamben, the sovereign is 'the point of indistinction between violence and law, the threshold on which violence passes over into law and law passes over into violence' (ibid.: 32). The German poet Hölderlin defined the *nomos* – which I understand to mean the legally encoded field, or sphere, of governance/government – as rigorous mediation, with mediation as the process of distinguishing.

If sovereignty is the space of 'indistinction', it follows that the nation-state (itself a historically and politically specific configuration) is predicated upon the concept of distinction (between violence and the law), and that citizens of a nation-state have symbolically identified with this distinction and vested all mediation, indistinction and the power of distinguishing, all ambiguities and paradoxes, in the figure of the sovereign. The nation is premised upon the link between localisation and ordering, and this link always implies a zone (or territory) that is excluded from the law and that takes the shape 'of a free and juridically empty space' in which the sovereign power no longer knows the limits fixed by the *nomos* as the territorial order. This 'territorial' order is what constitutes belonging for the citizen of the nation. The issue of citizenship is crucial here. The outsider, the migrant, the visibly different are seen as being beyond/outside localisation and territorial ordering, threatening indistinction because he or she is not symbolically identified with, or by, the rigorously mediated power of distinguishing which is the 'national' ground. Strangers threaten because they lack the vestments of the local or national territory – colour, language, accent, religion, cuisine and so on. The more the 'localised' have invested in the 'sovereign' nation and drawn 'power' from it, the more densely mediated, or overcoded, their lives become and a kind of territorial fundamentalism is produced – very often an effect of powerlessness.

This excluded zone beyond the line is metaphorically seen by the localised – the civil-ised – as a state of exception (a temporary and spatial sphere in which every law is suspended) occupied by the diasporised. This is particularly crucial because the state of exception is not external to the *nomos* but included in it, on the condition, so to speak, that it is a threshold, a space of liminality, which is never occupied (other than by the sovereign). So, by analogy, the localised citizen who is defined by the 'law' and is delimited, and takes his or her identity as if freely chosen, by not having access to the state of exception, sees the diasporised (and perhaps now the 'underclass') as inhabiting a forbidden, but also desired, space. At the very centre of the localisation-ordering link is the very condition of its own dissolution, its own virtual rupture.

The migrant confronts the 'localised' with those very ontological anxieties – of temporariness, of transience, of instability, of contingency and the arbitrary, of 'not sameness', of having sacrificed the desirable (the dread signs of the internal 'other') – which have been consigned to, and invested in, the national-sovereign. The more deeply territorialised, the more total the identity investment, the more threatening and destabilising is this threat of 'ontological anarchism', these manifestations of alterity (of race and ethnicity, but also of gender and sexuality). Racism, misogyny – and its instrument rape – and homophobia are all forms of territorial cleansing.

To the localised, then, the diasporised occupies the state of 'nature' and the state of exception (which the 'native' has 'voluntarily' ceded) and thus imperils the sovereign power (the nation incarnate) which is the locus of the very impossibility of distinguishing between outside and inside, nature and exception, violence and law, *physis* and *nomos*. The state of exception is not so much a spatio-temporal suspension as a complex topological figure in which not only the exception and the rule, but also the state of nature and law, outside and inside, pass through one another. It is this topological zone of indistinction which had to remain hidden from the eye of justice, and the lived identities and mindsets of the localised. The diasporised (like the deviant) bring into transparency and visibility, make 'readable spaces' of, the possibility of *indistinction* because they are perceived as coming from outside the localised and ordered – the sovereign *nomos* – and bearing several visible markers of difference, of alterity. The diasporised are experienced as breaking the constitutive link between the localisation and ordering of the old *nomos* and the system of reciprocal limitations and rules of the *ius publicum Europaeum*. (We only have to think of the ways in which Australian Aboriginals, North American Blacks and Hispanics, Turks in Germany, and African-Caribbeans in Britain are criminalised out of all proportion to their numbers because they are vilified and envied as dwellers in a free and empty space, figures of excess and transgression within zones of indistinction.)

In contemporary Europe, and to a greater extent perhaps also in the United States, the state of exception has in recent years transgressed its spatio-temporal boundaries, overflowing outside them, and is starting to coincide with the 'normal' order in which everything again becomes possible because everything is exposed in its contingency. For the most deeply rooted territorial, localised and ordered, this state of affairs has to be projected and rationalised as they cannot tolerate the thought that *everything again becomes possible*. The extreme form that this 'explanation' takes is, of course, ethnic cleansing (as well as anti-Islamic ideology): the removal of all exceptions (and tangible reminders of the unbearableness of exception), of all conditions of

possibility which challenge the necessary and the localised – the
'nationed'.

As Agamben argues, what is happening in the former Yugoslavia, and
in the processes of the dissolution of traditional state organisms in
Eastern Europe, is not a re-emergence of the natural state of struggle of
all against all, but rather as the coming to light of the state of exception as
the permanent structure of juridico–political delocalisation and dislocation: a new *nomos* of the earth – post-national, rather than new national
and state localisations. It is why the Right in Britain fear being 'swamped
by alien cultures', or, at a trivial but sinister level, speak of applying
'cricket loyalty' tests to Asian immigrant families. For obvious and
already apparent reasons this post-national *nomos* will not be achieved
without large-scale and often bitterly fought-over transformations.

One of the main questions posed in the 1998 UNESCO World Culture
Report is 'How do multiple cultures co-exist in an interactive world?' and
in the concluding section of this introduction I want to summarise some
of the main points made in the Report as a way of thinking about future
directions for cultural analysis in the context of 'the contemporary
globalisation of economic, political and social life [which] has resulted
in even more cultural penetration and overlapping, the co-existence in a
given social space of several cultural traditions, and in a more vivid
interpenetration of cultural experience and practice' (UNESCO World
Culture Report 1998: 16; hereafter WCR). Cultural analysis needs to
inform and help give shape to new social and governing arrangements
which will facilitate the development of cultural diversity and the
shaping of contact zones between cultures and beyond national boundaries.

In his contribution to the UNESCO Report ('Cultural policy options in
the context of globalization') Nestor Garcia Canclini analyses three key
changes:

- The recomposition of national cultures through the advance of globalisation
  and regional integration.
- The predominance of the mass communication industries over traditional,
  local forms of production and circulation of culture.
- The new conditions generated by these changes for democratisation and
  multicultural cohabitation. (WCR: 157)

Canclini goes on to trace the development of thinking about cultural
policies from the 1970s and 1980s – within the horizon of the nation-state
– through to the 1990s with globalised productions circulating in
transnational communication networks and being consumed as messages of what Canclini calls a multi-locational imagination generated by
a system with many centres but no longer any specific national cultural
belonging: deterritorialised cultures. To what extent this multi-locational

imagination will simply be absorbed by globalised productions (another stage of cultural imperialism), or will resist, transform and exceed them is one of the challenges facing those involved in the shaping of oppositional, and alternative, diasporic identities. As John Tomlinson and others have shown, cultural imperialism was never as effective, totalising or extensive as has often been claimed nor was its transmission of values ('messages') received as passively as once was thought (Tomlinson 1991).

Cultural understanding and analysis have to adapt to this ability to move flexibly between numerous centres on every continent in a way which combines the distinctively local with a global capability: 'Transfrontier relations are becoming more decisive than national representativity, and multi-cultural alliances more important than identification with particular culture' (WCR: 162).

Everyone who speaks of globalisation warns of its macrosocial tendencies, its propensity for homogenisation, and its segregating and stratifying potential in the midst of 'the asymmetrical inter-dependence of the world system'. At the same time, there are positive aspects of integration and of new forms of multi-culturality, as well as complexities and counter-trends (heterodox and horizontal) which could mean that 'new forms of citizenship, consumption and sociocultural interaction are taking shape in these interstitial practices' (WCR: 169).

In other words, can new patterns of post-national exchange and communication (not always the same thing as globalisation by any means) be – under the impact of diasporic experiences – multi-directional and articulated with local and regional heterogeneity?

Diasporic communities which have contributed to an experience of intense and complex hybridisation and heterogeneity may offer useful models for exploring cultural practices which 'move on from the separatist exaltation of difference ['ethnic' or 'host'] . . . to the shared acknowledgement of the different and the heterogeneous in symbolic searchings capable of inter-cultural communication' (WCR: 170). Can multi-cultural repertories be sustained to a point where they are no longer the ethnicised practices of diversity but the very core of post-national cultural experience, not an afterthought but epicentral? Can there be such a thing as a public interest on an international, and post-national, scale?

Having a significantly different future means developing *post*-national spaces which can respond politically and culturally to the weakening of national local cultures and confront multi-national globalisation in a process which is able to understand and impact upon 'the cultural, aesthetic, financial and political implications of transcultural brokering' (WCR: 178), so as to ensure that the redistribution of power in culture and communication does not simply lead to the hegemonic filters of a new cultural imperialism, but that 'transcultural brokerings' take place at the 'crossroads for articulating different landscapes, histories, genres, styles of perception and performance' (ibid.: 190), an intersection which is transnational and cosmopolitan, as well as being based upon the fluid movement of 'proximate' human beings.

I will conclude with a comment from Catherine Stimpson and Homi Bhabha (also in the UNESCO Report) which has agenda-setting characteristics:

> There can be no understanding of the global without understanding it as the ways in which different 'local' sites are co-ordinated; yet there can be no understanding of any 'local' without understanding the global of which it is a part. The challenge is, however, *from a given location*, do we create forms of understanding that can grapple with the situatedness of local knowledge and its more global implications? (WCR: 185; my italics)

As Appiah's model of 'rooted cosmopolitanism' argues, each of us can have roots in a specific location and yet dwell in the world at large. What follows is a study of a range of cultural fictions situated in a given location, and frequently from within a national framework for the purposes of analytical convenience. However, they are always situated with reference to their diasporic nature and to a process of, if not precisely denationalisation, then delinking from the givens of hegemonic nationalities or cultural nationalist models of identity (*British* Asian or Chinese *American*, for example) which prioritise and privilege the dominant category unproblematically. There are far larger, and much more important, struggles than those involved in the battle for control over stories, but, as Said has argued, the power to narrate is not a negligible aspect of cultural politics: 'The power to narrate, or to block other narratives from forming and emerging, is very important to culture and imperialism, and constitutes one of the main connections between them' (Said 1993: xiii). The stories which form the subject of this book demonstrate the ways in which narrative can become a fundamental resource, not in connecting culture and imperialism, but in disconnecting and fracturing hegemonic relationships by giving shape to utterances which are outside the sentences of power and control.

1

Sliding against the Masks of Newer Selves: Hyphenation and the Mestiza – *Jasmine*, *The Woman Warrior* and *Borderlands*

One of the principal issues that recurs throughout this book is that of binarism, with the corresponding oversimplifications that result from the insistent polarities of either/or, self/other, black/white and so forth. This binarism has been instrumental in establishing those essentialising norms of identity which, whether in terms of sexuality, class, gender or 'race', have marginalised and oppressed increasing numbers of people. There is also the need to be aware of the dangers of homogenisation, of collapsing a number of discourses into one, and of the tendency to construct a single, new other – the colonised or the marginalised – to replace now-discredited versions of the other. We need to avoid the by now conditioned reflex of using 'colonisation' as a catch-all metaphor for a range of distinctively different oppressions. Western cultural critics, in particular, as well as those working within Western institutions, could unwittingly run the risk of adding yet another 'distinct cultural invariant' to what Samir Amin calls 'Eurocentrism' (1989).

Since 1989, with the collapse of bureaucratic socialism in Eastern Europe, the end of a bi-polar power system, and US President Bush's announcement of a 'new world order', there has been an increasing sense of a fundamental political, social, economic and cultural impasse, a breakdown in ways of thinking the future. The focus in this chapter is on particular narratives as 'goods to think with and as good to think with', but before examining these narratives as cultural resources for new possibilities, of new belongings, I want briefly to look at two recent works of political analysis as a way of framing my argument. Francis Fukuyama's *The End of History and the Last Man* (1992) is already an international best-seller and an immensely influential, if deeply controversial, book; the other, Samir Amin's *Eurocentrism* (1988), is not widely known beyond academic and political activist circles. Both propose a historical and philosophical setting for the twenty-first century from radically differing perspectives.

Fukuyama argues that a consensus concerning the legitimacy of liberal democracy as a system of government has emerged over the past few years and that this liberal democracy may constitute the 'end point of mankind's ideological evolution . . . the final form of human government', and as such constitute the end of history (Fukuyama 1992: xi). He is using history in the Hegelian sense as a 'single, coherent, evolutionary process, when taking into account the experience of all peoples in all times' (ibid.: xii). It is this evolutionary process that has ended, according to Fukuyama, leaving liberal democracy as the only coherent political aspiration that spans different regions and cultures around the globe. He constructs a universal, directional history that guarantees an increasing homogenisation of all human societies, regardless of their historical origins or cultural inheritances. All countries undergoing modernisation, he asserts, 'must *increasingly resemble each other*' (ibid.: xiv; my emphasis), that is, follow the pattern of a unitary nation-state, economically rational (liberal capitalist) and predicated upon the existence of global markets and the spread of a universal consumer culture.

The driving force of this directional history is what Hegel analysed as 'the struggle for recognition', or Plato's third part of the soul – *thymos*, or 'spiritedness' (ibid.: xvi). I shall be examining narratives that are very much concerned with value, recognition and self-esteem, and it is interesting to note that Fukuyama argues that 'the propensity to feel self-esteem arises out of the part of the soul called *thymos*' (ibid.: xvii); and that Hegel had asserted that, with the coming of the American and French revolutions, history comes to an end because the longing that had driven the historical process – the struggle for recognition – has now been satisfied in a society characterised by universal and reciprocal recognition. No other arrangement of human social institutions is better able to satisfy this longing, and hence no further progressive historical change is possible.

The homogenising and universalising process that Fukuyama describes as necessary for the establishment of 'a world made up of liberal democracies' involves an imperialism that is economic, political, social and above all cultural. I say above all cultural, because capitalism's need for surplus and unequal accumulation means that standardisation can only ever be achieved through cultural imitation at a consumerist level; economically, politically and socially the peripheral nations will remain fundamentally unequal.

The idea of central and peripheral nations is developed in Samir

Amin's *Eurocentrism*, in which he argues that Eurocentrism 'is a culturalist phenomenon in the sense that it assumes the existence of irreducibly distinct cultural invariants that shape the historical paths of
different peoples' (1989: vii). It is this notion of 'distinct cultural invariants' that the narratives examined in this chapter challenge at the level
of structure, trope and word, as well as in the terms of gender, ethnicity
and sexuality.

Amin shows how Eurocentrism is anti-universalist yet presents itself
as universalist through its claims that imitation of the Western model by
all peoples is the only solution to the challenges of our time. He does not
oppose this Eurocentrist paradigm – the primary ideological construct of
capitalism – with a universalist Marxist alternative, because this, he
argues, also understood Europe as the model for everything. Both liberal
capitalism and its Marxist alternative inhabit the same cultural impasse
confronted by what Amin considers to be fundamentalist, provincial and
'inverted Eurocentrisms' (1989: vii).

Any critique of the core of the Eurocentric dimensions of capitalist
culture has to be produced, on the one hand, at the level of the
fundamental transformation of economic, political and social practice;
but if, as Lyotard says, 'narration is the quintessential form of customary
knowledge' (1984: 28), cultural narratives that transgress and subvert
ideas of essentialism, invariance, and transhistorical constants are also
of crucial value in the search for a new theory of culture – fluid, dialogical
and transnational. A mode of analysis is needed that locates specificity,
difference and historical particularity but does not remain located within, or enclosed by, either provincial cultural models or cross-cultural
generalisations; instead, it recognises aspirations for boundary crossing
collectivity in the diasporic and the nomadic. Against mimicry, these
narratives offer, in unresolved, arbitrary and contradictory ways, decentering, deterritorialisation and, in Amin's phrase, 'delinking' – the
unharnessing of cultural narratives from the Eurocentrist paradigm and
its culturalist distortions. Liberation struggles, whatever forms they take,
will challenge the end of history and the eternal West, but narratives
enable us to hypothesise, speculate and write against the grain of
prevailing empires of truth and value.

It is not surprising perhaps, given that North America and its adjacent
Americas are the principal source of the current form of the cultural
phenomenon of Eurocentrism, that the transgressive, boundary narratives I will consider have been written within its immediate domain. In
each text, to a greater or lesser extent, assimilation to a Europeanised or a
Euro-Americanised version of cultural identity is an ever-present option
or challenge – to be fully 'human' is to be Westernised (a Eurocentrist
term of approval). To propose an 'otherness' that is not simply marginalised, minoritised or celebrated for its right to irreducible difference –

culturally evasive and relativist – is to work towards a concept of transnational value that marks 'a rupture with everything that submission to the law of international value implies; in other words, it implies delinking' (Amin 1989: 123).

GIVING VOICE TO CONTINENTS

The word rupture is an appropriate way of describing the narrative condition of the texts under scrutiny: Maxine Hong Kingston, *The Woman Warrior* (1975, 1981); Bharati Mukherjee, *Jasmine* (1989, 1991); and Gloria Anzaldúa, *Borderlands/La Frontera* (1987). Each text concentrates upon a figure on the boundary, at the crossroads (a 'chiasmic' figure), on the frontier. In a literal sense, the crossing never takes place, because the 'other side' is precisely that – the site of the minoritised/marginalised figure's 'othering'. What does happen is that, with all their ambivalences and unresolvedness, the narratives open up conditions for the possibilities of – in Anzaldúa's words – 'the new *mestiza*'. A *mestiza* is a person of mixed origins; but what I shall try to argue is that these narratives work both with origins and with progeny – a proleptic condition of a new belonging: mixed, ambivalent, ambiguous, post-essentialist. The narratives work along what Rosaldo calls 'cultural border zones [that] are always in motion, not frozen for inspection' (1989: 217). 'Othering' is a method of preservation, a homogenising, a freezing for inspection. Rupture is the key trope for the kind of narrative that confounds/confronts 'othering'.

To return to a point raised in the Introduction, Gloria Anzaldúa says, in *Borderlands*, 'The new *mestiza* copes by developing a tolerance for contradictions, a tolerance for ambiguity . . . Not only does she sustain contradictions, she turns the ambivalence into something else' (1987: 79). In a sense, each of the narratives operates by turning ambivalence into something else while, at the level of form, remaining ambivalent and contradictory – on the boundary. It is this characteristic which marks the texts as post-colonial, post-imperial and post-nationalist, while each one's condition of emergence, its *emergency*, is marked by the indelible traces of empire, colonisation and cultural nationalism.

Another 'dislocated' writer, Marlene Nourbese Philip – born and educated in Trinidad and Tobago, now living in Canada – provides us with a valuable means of imagining and imaging a 'new belonging'. In her poem, 'She tries her tongue; her silence softly' (1993), she installs an extract from *The Practical Guide to Gardening*:

It is important, when transplanting plants, that their roots not be exposed to the air longer than is necessary. Failure to observe this caution will result in the plant dying eventually, if not immediately. When transplanting, you may notice a gently ripping sound as the roots are torn away from the soil. This is to be expected: for the plant, transplanting is always a painful process. (59)

Each of the narratives in question *is* a transplantation, as well as being about transplantation; and roots, old soil, and new soil are all changed by the process – the 'plant' is not simply assimilated to the new soil, rerooted. The rerooting is also a rerouting, hence the proliferation of journey metaphors throughout the texts. Above all, each narrative constructs 'a painful process' of arrival and departure, flight and return (mentally, if not literally), rupture and explosion, decentering and delinking, rape and disfigurement, the losing of tongues and the loosening of tongues, reterritorialisation and deterritorialisation. The transplanting is never final but always in process; the gently (and not so gently) ripping sound is continuous; and the tearing away of roots never finally completed. Above all, each narrative is marked by tropes of excess. For each writer, this is not simply a matter of theme but an urgent formal challenge – how to construct such a transgressive narrative, the journey from periphery to centre, from Third World to First World: across codes, across references, and across heavily policed zones of identity. It is a journey against certain fixed notions of origin, against supposed authenticity, and, above all, against irreducible cultural absolutes. Another imperative is, in Marlene Philip's terms, for the writer to use language in such a way 'that the historical realities are not erased or obliterated', given the pressure of imperial cultures to erase and obliterate the 'realities' of the 'other' in all ways except those in which they are constituted in their colonised 'otherness'. As Philip says, '[T]he language as we know it has to be dislocated and acted upon – even destroyed – so that it begins to serve our purposes' (85). Dislocation is a significant trope in each text.

The narratives all use a memoir or autobiographical form and are written in English, although for Gloria Anzaldúa this is not an adequate description, as she punctures and traverses her primary use of English with Castilian Spanish, North Mexican dialect Spanish, Tex-Mex, and Nahualt – a way of revealing that the actual physical borderland, the US–Mexican border, is also a junction of languages, a juncture of cultures and an intersection of psychological, sexual and spiritual borderlands that has no specific territorial signified. This interference/interreference enables her to write about identity, as D. Emily Hicks points out in *Border Writing: The Multidimensional Text* (1991), in ways that come close to Deleuze and Guattari's notion of deterritorialisation.

Each narrative is both an individual story and, explicitly, a cultural narrative – bi-cultural or varicultural, in each instance. The bi-culturalism is rehearsed throughout as the primary site of narrativity, with discontinuous frames to mark the contrapuntal codes/references as a way of unsettling ideas of origin, centre, authenticity, and the representational – all features of the culturalism discussed earlier. I mention these issues, especially the explicitness of the cultural narrative, because, as Raymund A. Paredes says (Payne 1992: xxvii), 'the quintessentially modern literary figure [is] the solitary observer, immune to involvement in anything he [sic] surveys'.

For reasons of gender, ethnicity or sexuality (or a combination of any or all of these) the primary figure in each narrative is excluded, initially, from the fullness and wholeness of identity and language, except in so far as these are imposed partially and prescriptively. Each text is a descripting/description, an unwriting laterally placed alongside the ostensible telling. Many marginalised people have found themselves – in an echo of patriarchal and slave culture – denied the power to name, and are renamed (as was their landscape) by the European stranger or through religious hegemony. In *Jasmine* (1989), the eponymous figure is variously Jyoti, Jasmine, Jazzy, Jase and Jane – all are the namings of others/males. The woman, doubly colonised in this text, as so many black females are, is screened from her own body (throughout the narrated time she is pregnant), as it becomes a site of exploitation and profoundly anti-human use; she is abducted, brutalised and raped by the sailor upon whom she depends for passage from the Third World to the First World. The enclosed nature of that passage, the confinement and violation in the impoverished and dirtied hotel room, the blood of the murdered sailor (a sacrificial exchange for the woman's blood), and, later, the circumscription of her body by pregnancy – all trace out the dangers and impurities confronting the boundary crosser, the 'othered' travelling to the construction site of their othering. The narrative makes space for her body and her voice, but not without extensive violence.

In 'A Four Hundred-Year-Old Woman' Bharati Mukherjee says:

I was born into a class that did not live in its native language. I was born into a city that feared its future, and trained me for emigration. I attended a school run by Irish nuns, who regarded our walled-off school compound in Calcutta as a corner (forever green and tropical) of England. My country – called in Bengali *desh,* and suggesting a homeland rather than a nation of which one is a citizen – I have never seen. It is the ancestral home of my father and is now in Bangladesh. Nevertheless, I speak his dialect of Bengali, and think of myself as 'belonging' to Faridpur, the tiny green-gold village that was his birthplace. (1991: 24)

Desh has become for her a merger of Faridpur and Manhattan, but she resists the hyphenated ascription Indo-American or any other form of cultural ghettoisation. She regards herself as an immigrant whose investment is in the American reality, as an American writer. On the surface this sounds like a simple matter of assimilation, of yielding to the dominant culture. It is, actually, a refusal of nostalgia and exoticism, a claim to be 'as American as any steerage passenger from Ireland, Italy or the Russian Pale' (25). What she does not question is the ways in which American has come to be identified with a particular, hegemonic (white) form of identity; this is an issue taken up by some of the other writers discussed later in this book. As a writer her literary agenda 'begins by acknowledging that America has transformed *me*. It does not end until I show how I (and the hundreds of thousands like me) have transformed America' (25). This agenda, continuous and presumably never-ending, is a challenge to the culturalist phenomenon – with its assumption of the existence of irreducibly distinct cultural invariants – of Eurocentrism for which the United States is now the prime medium, but it does not address matters of power or gender.

Mukherjee acknowledges that there are parts of herself that remain Indian (a contestable category from a critical perspective) and – in a memorable and, for my analysis, definitive phrase – there are 'parts that slide against the masks of newer selves' (26). The fluidity of sliding and the variability of masks mark so much of these new kinds of narrative of displacement: narratives of process and becoming, of renewing and reclaiming. She says that it is her duty to 'give voice to continents' but also to redefine the nature of American and what makes an American. For Fukuyama, Eurocentrist America gives voice to continents by homogenisation and universalisation, but for him the nature of American is an unproblematic given, a natural category. Mukherjee's 'material' is transformation, not preservation; her stories are 'about the hurly-burly of the unsettled magma between two worlds' (27). The hurly-burly is a collocation, a figure of commotion and confusion; a matter of structure, not just theme. Unsettled describes the larger project that I am trying to locate, as does magma with its suggestion of varying strata, amorphousness and liquidity. Given the United States's current global hegemony, her theme 'the making of new Americans' has a bearing on the issues raised earlier in connection with Amin's *Eurocentrism*. The crucial point is whether these 'new Americans' melt into the prevailing ideological constructs of liberal capitalism or actively engage in delinking. I speak metaphorically, but narratives can arguably have a function in making a space for that critical distance necessary to the breaking of the post-1989 ideological gridlock.

Bharati Mukherjee speaks of being 'aware of [herself] as a four-hundred-year-old woman, born in the captivity of colonial, pre-industrial, oral culture and living now as a contemporary New Yorker' (27), but she does not place that colonial, pre-industrial, oral culture in the context of contemporary New York – a centre/periphery polarisation based upon unequal development in which the history of one is dependent upon the history of the other.

The epigraph to *Jasmine* is a quotation from James Gleick's *Chaos*: 'The new geometry mirrors a universe that is rough, not rounded, scabrous, not smooth. It is a geometry of the pitted, pocked, and broken up, the twisted, tangled and intertwined' – a timely reminder in a period of renewed provincialism (nationalism) and 'ethnic cleansing' that, systemically, the world is inter-dependent and that round and smooth categories like self, ethnicity and nation have become pitted, pocked and broken up, and that narratives are needed that articulate the twisted, the tangled and the intertwined.

Jasmine begins in an astrological framework (and with a sentence that links the medieval with the post-modern), a moment of cultural fatalism that the narrator describes as 'lifetimes ago' – seventeen years from the point of narrating, but 'ideological' lifetimes in her sliding selves and fluid masks. The chapter ends with the narrator's refusal: 'I know what I don't want to become' (5). The negative actually contains a positive, but it rejects the specificity and detail of the astrologer who proposes an absolute closure, an ending at the very beginning.

The opening chapter locates a fundamental ambivalence that operates throughout the narrative. The astrologer foretells her widowhood and exile, a prophecy designed to contain her and determine her: 'what is to happen will happen'. The prediction removes all possibility of agency; in foretelling it forecloses: 'Bad times were on their way. I was helpless, doomed. The star bled' (4). It is a system of gendered patterning: 'Go join your sisters', the man with the capacious ears commanded. 'A girl shouldn't be wandering here by herself' (4). The wandering enables Jasmine to defy not the facts of the prophecy but its design and intention to render her less than human.

In the last section of the chapter the narrator is swimming and makes a discovery:

Suddenly my fingers scraped the soft waterlogged carcass of a small dog. The body was rotten, the eyes had been eaten. The moment I touched it, the body broke in two, as though the water had been its glue. A stench leaked out of the broken body, and then both pieces quickly sank. That stench stays with me. (5)

The chapter is constructed around two 'memory' events: the astrologer's prediction and the dead dog in the water. The girl is encircled. She chooses to remember the dismembered body that her touch had broken in two – a touch that announces the leaking and broken body of the narrative that follows and predicts the dangers to her own body as its ownership and use are contested throughout the text (named by men) shuttling between identities. The 'glue' that holds her body together is the water that enables her to travel from Amsterdam to Florida, her identity distorted by illegal documents, her body dismembered by the grotesque Half-Face, the trawler captain. The stench of the dog is overlaid by the new memory of the stench of the captain's blood after she has murdered him.

The death of the narrator's father, gored by a bull; of her husband, by a bomb meant for her; and her killing of the sea captain are all 'fragmentations' of the patriarchal body, necessary regressions and sacrifices. Like the dismembered dog, each death focuses on a violation of the body; it explodes, breaks up the completed, finished product. The narrative is, hence, opened up in a way that allows the woman's body (in her 'original' culture designed and destined to be isolated, alone, fenced off from all other bodies as female: negated) to be translated from her repressed beginning to a point where signs of its unfinished character, of its growth and proliferation, are foregrounded; its protuberances, offshoots and convexities are made apparent. The ever unfinished nature of the body is made visible: conception, pregnancy and death throes are all shown.

Analogically, the narrative itself has a similar 'body', and unfinished nature, of growth and random proliferation, an amorphousness that refuses the shapings of others. Jasmine grows and changes but her child is, narratively speaking, never born: the deferment, the retardation, the unfinalisability are critical. Her banker partner is shot and becomes wheelchair bound, a neighbouring farmer hangs himself; Iowa, the Middle West, a landscape of fertile pastures, becomes a place of decay and death, of endless repetition, a terminus. Her partner Bud and the neighbour, Darrel, have become immobilised: their belonging has been too long.

The narrative shifts, slides, moves synchronously and laterally, overlaps and intertwines; it braids 'feudal' reference with electronic discourse; it splits, dissolves, scars and pries open the sealed and discrete – it leaks India into Iowa, and Iowa into India. Her assumed surname, Ripplemeyer, neatly sounds out her ambivalence, both ripple and mire. The narrative is mobilised by an image of revisiting – the woman travelling in time and space is more than Jasmine, and other than Jasmine, the Third World woman: '[W]hich of us was raped and raped and raped in boats and cars and motel rooms?' (127). She meets 'monstrous' America, 'liberal' America, and 'middle' America – each one locked into its own limits. In Clearwater, Florida, the narrator has an experience the ambivalence of which helps to situate her for the next phase of her journey from rape, through a brief stay in a 'Third World' compound, to East Coast America:

In one of the department stores I saw my first revolving door. How could something be always open and at the same time always closed? She had me try

out my first escalator. How could something be always moving and always still?
(133)

These questions staple the remainder of the narrative together and are
their staple form. Their undecidability becomes her medium: the undocumented living in the fluidity of American character (in Florida she
mimics an American voice and an American walk as a strategy of
'documentation') and the American landscape. She jumps 'tracks', distancing herself – her widowhood disguised in T-shirts and cords – from
Indians living in America but retired behind ghetto walls. The text, with
its fractures, spirals and syncretisms, avoids the cultural and linguistic
ghetto of closure and coherence, of teleology and astrology: '[N]othing
was rooted anymore. Everything was in motion' (152).

I have concentrated almost exclusively on the transformations of the
narrator, limited though they are by the need for 'assisted' passage: 'I
have had a husband for each of the women I have been. Prakash for
Jasmine. Taylor for Jase. Bud for Jane. Half-Face for Kali' (197). However,
there is another 'other' figure in the text, Du Thien, the Vietnamese
refugee boy adopted by Jane and Bud. He is 'the brightest boy in the
camps. The boy who survived' (155). His survival, like Jasmine's, is
based upon adaptation. His electronic obsession becomes him: he *is* the
circuits he reshuffles, combining new functions. His genius is for
scavenging, adaptation, appropriate technology. Finding himself in
America, he founds himself through 'recombinant electronics', by altering 'the gene pool of the common American appliance'. The 'American'
could not survive in Vietnam; the Vietnamese American lives out his
'hyphenisation' by constantly changing shape; his name, Du, *sounds out*
many possibilities – due, jew, do, dual, a personal pronoun in German,
zoo:

At school they say Du's doing so well, isn't he, considering. *Considering what?* I
want to say. Considering that he has lived through five or six languages, five or
six countries, two or three centuries of history; has seen his country, city, and
family butchered, eaten filth in order to stay alive; that he has survived every
degradation known to this century, *consider all those liabilities*, isn't it amazing
that he can read a Condensed and Simplified for Modern Students edition of *A
Tale of Two Cities*? . . . Du's doing well because he has always trained with live
ammo, without a net, with no multiple choice . . . Once upon a time, like me, he
was someone else. We've survived hideous times. I envy Bud the straight lines
and smooth planes of his history. Until Harlan. Always, until Harlan. (214)

The litany of excess in the first half of the quotation, the hyperreality, has
become the condition of numberless people in the 'periphery' – a condition of fissure and rupture and unending violence. This has superseded
the 'realism' (narrative and political) of 'straight lines' and 'smooth
planes', which are now the fairy tale of 'once upon a time'. The 'real'

is grotesque, another order of fairy tale: '[W]e've hurtled through time tunnels. We've seen the worst and survived. Like creatures in fairy tales, we've shrunk and we've swollen and we've swallowed the cosmos whole' (240).

Du and Jasmine share this provisionality; they are figures of continuing metamorphosis, sojourning awhile in various spaces, not living in one place. The episodic and the interstitial *is* their condition. They are not living in the world as such, but the world that they make up, invent, as a condition of survival, is living in them. Both are explosive, volcanic: tornadoes and rubble-makers. Bud, the banker, 'enters' their world, fascinated by the exotic and erotic, simultaneously guilt-ridden, as it is a world generated by capitalism's need for surplus in imperial markets; he is shot by Harlan, a local victim, bankrupted by the same economic process.

Both Jasmine and Du have only partial affiliations, disinterested identities, tactical belongings. At one point the narrator says: 'How many more shapes are in me, how many more selves, how many more husbands?' (215). The gendered and ethnicised others write back, script their own otherness in flight and fluidity, temporariness and the transitional. Both leave Iowa for California, separately. Travelling west to another boundary, beyond which is 'their' East, they arise from nowhere and disappear into a cloud. Jasmine leaves Bud and goes away with Taylor, in love but also seeking another form of 'glue' to prevent her body from breaking in two, another means of transformation: 'greedy with wants and reckless from hope' (241).

Hope has motivated the narrative, recklessness shaped its condition:

Adventure, risk, transformation: the frontier is pushing indoors through un-caulked windows. Watch me re-position the stars, I whisper to the astrologer who floats cross-legged above *my* stove? (240)

The ambivalence of the opening chapter returns, staging the 'known' of astrology with the unknown risks and illusions, perhaps, of agency: 'Watch me re-position the stars'. The frontier is, remember, *pushing*, not being pushed *by* the subject. Du and, to a certain extent, Jasmine overcome what Deleuze and Guattari call the paranoiac impulse to reterritorialise (they have no territory, or belonging as such: their 'belongings' are always carried with them, decentred and deracinated) and intensify the schizophrenic tendency of capitalism, partially forming deterritorialised flows that are no longer subject to the constraints of commodity exchange. *Partially* . . . but then narratives are only good to think with, goods to think with – cultural modellings, not programmes of social action. At the end of the narrative, Jasmine still only knows what she does not want to become.

The space of dangerous memories

One of the pioneering examples of the kind of formative narrative that I am describing was Maxine Hong Kingston's controversial *The Woman Warrior*, first published in 1975. Ostensibly a work of autobiography, its narrative method worked against, and broke down, some of the prevailing currencies and conventions of such writings. It is not my purpose here to rehearse the controversies that the book has aroused, as these have been dealt with most effectively by Sau-ling Cynthia Wong (1992).

The major objection has been to its generic status. Is it an autobiography or a work of fiction seeking to validate itself, or be validated by Euro-American publishers, as 'ethnic' autobiography? Much of the debate has been stimulated by the book's formal and stylistic characteristics — its formative nature, its unfinalisability, and its speculative (playful, even) fictionalisation. To some critics, an autobiography has to be referential, a document shaped by a *bildungsroman* model. This is what has been called epireading by Krause 'a reading which proceeds under the privileging of "action" and "speech", transposing the written words on the page into a somehow corresponding human situation of human persons, voices, characters, conflicts, conciliations' (1984: 226). *The Woman Warrior* treats the irreducible and the irreconcilable; it refuses anything other than an arbitrary closure. The writing itself is constitutive and makes possible a 'graphireading' that 'deals with writing as such and does not think of it as transcribing an event properly construed as vocal and audible' (ibid.). This is, essentially, what I mean by formative writing and it is a condition that is shared by all of the texts I am referring to in this chapter. These are discourses with manifold and complex horizons, and with forms that remind us we are in the world of narrative, not the phenomenologically constituted 'real' world. In this sense, *The Woman Warrior* can be read as an extended series of cultural reflections and speculations on the specifics of the gendered experience of an Asian-American woman.

In the opening chapter, 'No Name Woman', we can see how the writer is excavating the sites of old, silent narratives to make new, articulate ones. Memory, timing and the writing itself have been manipulated to produce metaphor out of loss, absence and the suicide of her aunt, the no name woman. The aunt had belonged to her village in China by virtue of birth, family and residence; but her death, and that of her newborn child, at the bottom of the family well mark the depth (in all senses of the word) of her not belonging. The writing images and imagines the life, the birth and the death, and names them through the evolving narrative, but does not literally name the aunt whose presence and absence are mourned by her American-born, ethnically Chinese niece: 'The Chinese are always very frightened of the drowned one, whose weeping ghost, wet hair hanging and skin bloated, waits silently by the water to pull down a substitute' (22). The 'substitute' is metaphor – that distance or separation from referential identity, a figure of usurpation and transgression. The writing itself is the reparation, the substitute, pulled down, so to speak, so that the aunt can belong.

The book is subtitled 'Memoirs of a Girlhood Among Ghosts', and the opening chapter begins in this way: 'In China your father had a sister who killed herself. She jumped into the family well. We say that your father has all brothers because it is as if she had never been born' (11). She can only be manifested (ghostlike) through the process of writing, itself a form of birthing ('she had never been born') that erases the 'as if' of the mother's statement. It is through a tropological structure, a figure of writing and reading, of substitution, that the complex mutuality of aunt and niece belonging can be achieved: a consuming of biases that produces a fluid identity that is neither Chinese nor European, but a shifting and sliding Chinese-American compound. The compound itself denotes the bi-cultural focality and the double tracking of the perspective and the writing itself: a discourse of agency, possibility and self-creation in the face of death, ghosts, loss and negative belonging. (Non-Chinese are referred to as 'ghosts'.)

This opening chapter, 'No Name Woman', uses the figure of *prosopopeia*, a term from rhetoric in which an imaginary or absent person (the aunt is both, in a sense) is represented as speaking or acting (de Man 1984). The chapter takes the form of an address or apostrophe to an absent, deceased, passive and voiceless entity. The writing speculates upon and invents the aunt's reply, and confers upon her the power of speech and action (' "you must not tell anyone", my mother said, "what I am about to tell you" ') – it creates a mask or face. Autobiography is a means by which one's name is made as intelligible and memorable as a face, and the opening chapter generates this naming, facing process for both the 'no name woman' and the belonging/not belonging Chinese-American, American-Chinese writer, Maxine Hong Kingston. It is a chapter about nomination and transition, the giving and taking away of faces, figuration coming through disfiguration – 'wet hair hanging and skin bloated'. It is also an epitaph. When the aunt became pregnant by an unknown man, not her husband, the villagers destroyed her family house, ritually wearing masks. The writing becomes the inscription of the 'never said', a phrase which is also used in the chapter as a reference to desire.

The literal figure of the dead aunt may be an image gathered from suppressed family memory, from traces of the real person herself, the 'drowned-in-the-well-sister' (the text reproduces it as an indissoluble compound word), but she is also a 'Spirit', nothing less than infinity, hence the metaphorical use of her as a continuous being. The figure is given a new belonging: homelessness-as-home, in Abdul JanMohamed's phrase (1992). The literal aunt and the figural aunt become one: the fiction of the voice-beyond-the-grave, in de Man's formulation; she is a chiasmic figure, empowered to cross the conditions of death and life with the attributes of speech and of silence, transitional and transitory.

The survivor (the woman warrior) speaks in the person of the dead and in her own person contrapuntally, because identity is cultural, never simply individual: 'Unless I see her life branching into mine, she gives me no ancestral help' (16). The writing is the branching: a meditation upon transgression and rupture, a mourning that gives rise to the discovery of writing. Belonging is a figuration that conflates the experience of disappearance, loss and bereavement (by focusing upon the death of another, as substitute for oneself) with the experience of finding a space through writing and speaking: a coming to speech in, and through, narrative. The adversarial figure – a rival almost – of family experience is turned into a threshold of creativity and of belonging.

De Man refers to a section of Wordsworth's essays upon epitaphs in which he speaks against metaphor:

If words be not . . . an incarnation of the thought but only a clothing for it, then surely they will prove an ill gift; such a one as those poisoned vestments, read of in the stories of superstitious times, which had power to consume and alienate from his right mind the victim who put them on. (1984: 79)

By analogy, the writing of autobiography may not, after all, simply be the expression of a life but a disfiguring (and refiguring), a consuming and alienating process in which the reading and writing constructs a varifocal effect: a displacement/defacement through metaphor, *against* absolute and essentialist belongings, and for a complex, multi-layered, and dynamic pattern of syncretism – out of the past, out of death, out of the adversarial. Each narrative studied here is a 'poisoned vestment' (investment) with the power to consume and alienate; the power of the chiasm and the borderland.

In autobiography, the use of *prosopopoeia* to posit the voice or the face of the other means that what is lost is not 'life' but that belonging which can only be accessible in the privative way of understanding, characterised by the taking away or removal of something, and the loss or absence of some quality normally (literally) presumed to be present: self-identity as a given or fixed identity. The restoration of mortality, through the dialogue with the dead in 'No Name Woman', deprives and disfigures to the precise extent that it restores and creates (or it restores by creating) the other, the absolute stranger: the dead aunt. The writing is a way of creating a relationship with severance and separation; a discourse of mutuality in which both remembering self and other are dislocated, unhinged. A narrative has emerged, out of emergency (what does it mean to be a Chinese-American female, is it a hyphen of inequality?) and out of denial and erasure. As always, the writing is not a transcription but a rewriting, a descripting of prescriptions. The aunt is commemorated and given birth to. It is 'a story to grow up on' (13), a way of thinking the future, of survival and possibility, by trying to name the unspeakable past. The writing engenders – in all senses of that word – 'a prodigal aunt', a figure of excess in the sense that the speculative vestment-narrative enables her to exceed, go beyond, the subject identities in which she is invested. This includes the investments and appropriations of the niece's doubly articulated narrative. In one version, she is engendered as the obedient and passive raped woman: 'Women in the old China did not choose' (14). In another, '[the] aunt crossed boundaries not delineated in space' (15) and she is given the power of agency and choice, figuring (and figuring in) her own desire – 'the enormities of the forbidden' (15). 'She' becomes, for a hypothetical moment, the active subject of her own verbs or actions – 'she looked'; 'she liked'. In another narrative incarnation she is imaged as 'a wild woman' free with sex, but this is rapidly erased as a possibility (then and now: for aunt or for herself) by the narrator.

In the spaces of not knowing, in the interstices of distance, forgetting, and desire, the writing combs 'individuality' and 'eccentricity' into the narrative, delinking and deterritorialising both Chinese woman and Chinese-American woman from any transhistorical subjectivities or irreducible absolutes of identity. The narrator's mother had told her 'once and for all, the useful parts' (13) of the aunt's story: the instrumental and moralising parts. The narrative has to recover the discarded and the suppressed. The recovery can never be archival, since those traces have been erased, but must be imaginary – the entry, the breath and the mutual spaces: the secret voice and separate attentiveness of the aunt:

And one day he [the grandfather] brought home a baby girl, wrapped up inside his brown western-style greatcoat. He had traded one of his sons, probably my father, the youngest for her. My grand-mother made him trade back. When he finally got a daughter of his own, he doted on her. They must all have loved her, except perhaps my father, the only brother who never went back to China having once been traded for a girl. (17)

There are a number of complex substitutions in this extract, and out of the 'probably' and the 'perhaps' the writing process produces its own echo through its vagrant and extravagant forms; analogically rehearsing the break the aunt had made in the 'roundness' of the village, its homogeneous space. The narrative is linked with, but constructed against, the 'personal, physical representation of the break she had made in the roundness' (19) by bringing the aunt into the future (the time of writing, the niece's recall) and disengaging her from her overdetermined present/presence: 'homelessness-as-home'. The writing re-presents the extreme pain of the aunt's labour in a style that is 'unhinged', obliterative, spatial: out of time. She gives birth in a pigsty, a place of dirt, glad to have a fence enclosing her because the language has become a form of splitting and opening – she is 'a tribal person alone'. The writing is seeking to find analogues for the experience of the woman being taken out of her body as, finally, the child is expelled out of her body. The child, like the mother, has no marker, no name; she is joined to the mother only in separation: ghostlike. The narrative speaks both mother and child; names, marks, and memorialises as the text labours and gives birth in an act of substitution and propitiation. The aunt and child are rescued from the 'ghosts massed at crossroads', that site of transgression, magic and female power: the space of dangerous memories.

The writing is similar to shamanistic practice as defined by Taussig in *Shamanism, Colonialism and the Wild Man*: '[T]he power of shamanism lies not with the shaman but with the differences created by the coming together of shaman and patient . . . the joint construction of the healer and the sick in the semantically generative space of annulment that is the colonial death space' (1987: 460). 'No Name Woman' is a joint exploration of the semantically generative space in which the aunt is treated as if she had never been born; both niece and aunt are healed by the mutuality of the writing process. In the words of Joy Harjo's poem 'Anchorage':

Everyone laughed at the impossibility of it, but also the truth. Because who would believe the fantastic and terrible story of all of our Survival those who were never meant to survive? (1983: 15)

LIVING IN THE BORDERLANDS

Gloria Anzaldúa is a Chicana *tejana* lesbian-feminist poet and fiction writer who has also been active in the migrant farmworkers' movement. Her poem 'To live in the Borderlands means you' ends in the following way: 'To survive the Borderlands you must live *sin fronteras*, be a crossroads' (1987: 195), which links both with the crossroads and survival themes and with the forms of the writings discussed so far. Anzaldúa's book *Borderlands/La Frontera* (1987) is a complex, multi-layered text that refigures questions of language, class, ethnicity, gender and sexuality in ways which demonstrate how each is, in Stuart Hall's words, something 'constructed, told, spoken, not simply found' (1987: 45), a product of social and historical contingency. The work is a major contribution to the revisions of notions of identity politics currently being explored in those ' marginal locations as spaces where we can best become whatever we want to be while remaining committed to liberatory black liberation struggle' (hooks 1989: 54).

Borderlands can be places that defy the closure of frontier/border/ boundary and spaces similar to what Trinh T. Minh-ha calls the interval: 'a space in which meaning remains fascinated by what escapes and exceeds it . . . displacing and emptying out the establishment of totality' (1990: 96). They are also points of confluence, analogous to what Paula Gunn Allen, another writer of complex ethnicities, describes:

My life is the pause. The space between. The not this, not that, not the other. The place that the others go around. Or around about. It's more a Mobius strip than a line. (1987: 151)

The geographical borderland of Gloria Anzaldúa's book is the US–Mexican border, but this is simply the site for the 'local' narrative that extends into psychological, sexual and spiritual borderlands and the unique positionings consciousness takes at these confluent streams. She also crosses the borders and opens up the margins of other discourses – historical, mythological, political, linguistic and literary – traditionally enclosed by disciplines, subjects and genres. The writer becomes the 'officiating priestess at the crossroads' (80), a figure of continual creative motion engaging in the shamanistic practice described above. The new *mestiza*, like the writing process itself, is a 'morphogenesis', a term that Anzaldúa takes from Ilya Prigogine's theory of 'dissipative structures' and relates to a kind of birth that created unpredictable innovations (97). The text generates endless examples of rupture, transgression and nepantilism – of people torn between ways in the language of the Borderlands, the space of *los atravesados*: 'the squint-eyed, the perverse, the queer, the troublesome, the mongrel, the mulatto, the half-breed, the half dead; in short, those who cross over, or go through the confines of the "normal"' (3).

Borderlands interrogates and unsettles notions of the homeland, cultural constructions of women, gender, the 'other', power and normative sexuality. Anzaldúa sees in her chosen sexuality 'a strange doubling', conventionally deviant and inverted but with a potentially magic aspect: 'having an entry into both worlds', an evolving, unfolding, and sliding signifier of agency and new possibility. From her background as a lesbian, as a woman of colour, and as, originally, a poor *tejana*, Anzaldúa in her writing articulates the semantically generative spaces between the different worlds she inhabits in a multiple discourse of category breaking, genre crossing, and constitutive forms – a new *mestiza* at the level of style and structure: *una cultura mestiza*.

The work is poem, polemic, history and post-Christian spiritual thesis – episodic, eccentric, unfinalisable, transgressive, code/mode switching and excessive; she writes against white rationality by acknowledging the 'forbiddens' of body and soul, so often consigned to the margins as 'dangerous memories'. Anzaldúa sees a generative/germinative source in what she calls the Coatlicue state – 'a rupture in our everyday world' figuring in contradictions, as a *travesia*, a crossing that she is best able to represent in passages of prose which focus on a third person 'she', lost in textual spaces which open and contract:

She has this fear that if she digs into herself she won't find anyone that when she gets "there" she won't find her notches on the trees birds will have eaten all the crumbs She has this fear that she won't find the way back. (43)

The 'she' is distanced, severed from the writing 'I', eye, and 'they slit her from head to belly. *Rajada*' (43). As so often, the dialect usage does not act as a supplement or a repetition, but – in its phonetic emphasis and precision – has an explosive presence, the force of an irruption. It is this figure of the 'slit' that Anzaldúa uses to construct her *caracter multiplice* – split between 'the tongueless magical eye and the loquacious rational eye', *la rajdura*, the abyss, that only this new kind of multiple writing can bridge and span.

I have referred throughout this chapter to the ways in which narratives work with birth imagery, and sections of *Borderlands* break up the temporal shapes of conventional syntax and generate a fractured, dizzying, spatial language as, again and again, the writing tries to make 'sense', and approaches reconciliation (of magical eye and rational eye), only to:

'cross over,' kicking a hole out of the old boundaries of the self and slipping under or over, dragging the old skin along, stumbling over it. It hampers her movement in the new territory, dragging the ghost of the past with her. It is a dry birth, a breech birth, a screaming birth, one that fights her every inch of the way. (49)

Borderlands is divided into two main sections –'*Atravesando Fronteras/* Crossing Borders' (pp. 1–91) and '*Un Agitado Viento*/Ehecatl, the Wind' (pp. 102–203). The first section is arranged in seven parts, principally written in prose but constantly switching codes, references and registers as a way of signalling, structurally, the unsettled and unsettling nature of anxiety, unrest, boundaried and boundless, which enables the creative process, the shamanistic, shape-changing performance to take place. The cultural shifts that are recorded throughout the text, which *are* the text, constitute the new *mestiza* who/which will 'survive the crossroads'.

Surviving the crossroads is the dream, the energy, the new belonging of all of the narratives in this chapter: 'the green shoot that cracks the rock' (82), the progeny of a struggle of borders:

> Because I, a *mestiza*,
> continually walk out of one culture
> and into another,
> because I am in all cultures at the same time,
> *alma entre dos mundos, tres, cuatro,*
> *me zumba a cabeza con lo contradictorio.*
> *Estoy norteado por todas las voces me hablan*
> *simultaneamente.* (77)

Each of the narratives analysed has been concerned with undocumented women and women without documents. The gaps in documentation, the 'illegal' status of women, have been extended beyond the literal sense to produce a work of breaks, passages and bridges at a metaphorical level. Written against homogeneity, each text in its irregular and interstitial form is an irruption, a threshold crossing, a renewal of valorisation. There is a certain regression to amorphousness, prior to creativity and empowerment.

In a cultural landscape overfreighted with negative signs and flat horizons, each writer has produced a virtual structure, striving to find an analogical vocabulary, an analogical form of discourse that is appropriate for the opening up of a potentially different order. Nature, mythology, religion and history are all raided and quarried for borrowings to express the new *mestiza* in an irreducible language, sacral but not mystifying. The writings become modalities of orientation, means of founding possibility; constructions of space for thinking a new belonging, a settlement for new creativity, new symbols and rituals: a reclaiming.

The narratives in this chapter, and throughout this book, address lives filled with, or emptied by, consumerism; they seek to establish vocabularies, codes and 'improbable' discourses that embody new ideals and struggle against flat, and flattened, horizons. In a way, they start history by becoming first peoples (original and originating people) who are engaged in their own bloody, besieged battles for meaning, space, and recognition as human beings of a new belonging founded in sacrifice and struggle. Cultural politics have become increasingly important in our contemporary situation together with other levels of social and political action, and new narratives *(storia)* have a crucial role to play:

Stories are important. They keep us alive. In the ships, in the camps, in the quarters, field, prisons, on the road, on the run, underground, under siege, in the throes, on the verge – the storyteller snatches us back from the edge to hear the next chapter. In which we are the subjects. We, the hero of the tales. Our lives preserved. How it was, how it be. Passing it along in the relay. That is what I work to do: to produce stories that save our lives. (Bambara 1985: 41)

Throughout the rest of this book I shall continue to explore transgressions, excesses, and extremes as ways of searching for new communions/ communities and new subjectivities, means of linking the self with the collective.

2

Notes of a Native Speaker:
Becoming Asian-American –
The Joy Luck Club, Typical American,
Bone and *The Wedding Banquet*

The Asian-American presence in the United States goes back 150 years, but laws passed in the 1920s prohibited Asian nationals from entry to the country until the liberalisation of the US immigration law in 1965. Since that time the Asian-American population has increased from 1.5 million (in 1970) to about 7.3 million in 1990, and Asian immigrants have constituted 45 per cent of the total immigrants to the US over the past two decades. With the exception of the Japanese, the majority of the Asian ethnic groups are not American born, although at the beginning of a new century a significant second-generation population now exists (in the 1990 census 37 per cent were shown as American born). At present (according to the 1990 census) Asian-Americans constitute 3 per cent of the US population, but by the year 2050 the US Bureau of the Census projections indicate that this population will quadruple – a faster growth rate than any other sector of the population. All of the writers examined in this chapter were born in the US to parents of Chinese origin; the film director, Ang Lee, was born in Taiwan and went to the United States as a student.

Writing from outside the US I am very conscious that Asian-American culture is extremely complex and heterogeneous, and often sharply divided. Behind and beyond the stereotypes of the 'model minority' thesis – hard working, passive, close-knit families, success at school – lie a number of distinct, if overlapping, ethnic groups differently inflected in respect of the dominant culture but sharing in common histories of exclusion, exploitation, racialisation and marginalisation. The most sustained and sophisticated analysis of this cultural terrain is Lisa Lowe's *Immigrant Acts* (1996) which has deeply informed the writing

of this chapter. The Asian immigrant, Lowe argues, is 'at odds with the
cultural, racial, and linguistic forms of the nation' and 'displaces the
temporality of assimilation' (1996: 6). The use of the word 'Acts' in her
title stresses the ways in which, despite racism, institutional and
legislative barriers and discrimination, some Asian-Americans have
sought to actively produce alternative cultural images and forms which
challenge, and confront, hegemonic models of national identity designed
to absorb and 'tolerate' the passive and the complicit. What Lowe
explores throughout is the contradictory and ambivalent relationship
between the logics of identity and the politics of difference.

Not all of the texts examined here uniformly challenge dominant
hegemonic models nor do they work evenly against a closing, or enclosing, identity. Some operate fairly conventionally within what Lowe and
others have called the formative narrative based upon authenticity,
development and lineage. All of them are written in, what Amy Tan
calls 'Englishes' which interrupt and puncture not just the authority of
the sentence – 'Through me passed words, tiny syntagms, bits of
formulae and *no sentence formed*' (Barthes 1976: 49) – but also hierarchies of value, identity and meaning. I will attempt below to contextualise the writings in terms of their specific 'ethnic' configurations, but
they will not be reduced simply to examples of the so-called ethnic genre
novel or film, nor will claims be made for their representativeness.

Since the 1965 Immigration Act which produced the influx of new
Asian immigrants, some changes have taken place which have modified
this legislation. The Act was revised in 1976 to restrict the entry of
occupational immigrants with the result that 90 per cent of non-refugee
immigrant visas were given to those with relatives in the United States,
so-called 'family reunification' immigrants. Most of the Asian immigrants
of the past thirty years are economic migrants, although coming from
different political–cultural configurations, some with an already well
developed US cultural and ideological dependency – the Philippines,
South Korea or South Vietnam, for example. The largest number of
immigrants from a single country came from the Philippines, but mainland and diasporic Chinese form the most extensive Asian ethnic group.
Most recent Asian immigrants are from urban areas, are generally highly
educated and have had white-collar and professional employment. This
is in marked contrast to the profiles of most previous US immigrants from
Asia and Europe. It is also very different from British migration patterns
in a similar period.

California is the most popular destination for most of the Asian
immigrant groups (39.1 per cent in 1993), followed by New York state,
Hawaii and Texas. Unlike earlier European migrant patterns of settlement in the United States, Asian-Americans have, by and large, remained
in residentially segregated ethnic spaces, although there has been some

dispersal along class lines. Twenty per cent of Chinese-Americans in New York City live in Chinatown, while 35 per cent of the Koreans in Los Angeles live in Koreatown, for example.

Those ethnic groups with the least cultural homogeneity, like the Filipinos and Indians, have settled across a wide number of suburban areas. Having said this, however, it is also true that Asian-Americans from all ethnic groups are, compared to the general population, over-represented in suburban areas.

Reference has been made earlier to the conflicts and controversies generated by Asian-American cultural politics, and these may be partly a result of the tendency of the dominant 'national culture' to generalise, stereotype and homogenise what are extremely diverse ethnic groups with widely varying linguistic, cultural and religious traditions and practices. It may also be to do with divisions within, and across, groups in respect of ethnic 'nationalisms', integration or assimilation (including disputes over hyphenation), and pan-Asian politics. Differentiated colonial and neo-colonial experience, class, generation and gender locations also contribute. There are far more polarisations and splits than the coverall category of Asian-American acknowledges. As well as lifestyles, this also applies to socioeconomic status, occupational profiles and educational achievement. The 'model minority' thesis, therefore, has an increasingly limited application. Even though 'Asian ethnic groups individually and as a whole fare well in terms of median family income when compared to white Americans' (Min 1995: 27), this tends to conceal the proportion of Asian and Pacific Islander Americans, Vietnamese, Korean and Chinese families living at the poverty level.

This outline has attempted to provide a brief demographic context in which to situate the texts to be analysed but care should be taken not to conflate empirical and aesthetic categories. The texts do not reflect the demographic profile, but many of them do feature generational conflict, the loss of family languages and traditional practices, and the tensions caused by acculturation, inter-racial relationships and social and geographical mobility.

AMERICAN TRANSLATION

In the so-called culture wars among Asian-Americans, the works of Maxine Hong Kingston and Amy Tan are frequently cited in a negative context as pandering to the tastes of the dominant white culture, stereotyping and exoticising Asian women, and 'selling out' by becoming commercial and popular, and therefore 'inauthentic'. There is no space here to rehearse the details of these culture wars, nor is there need as they have been critically examined by Elaine Kim (1990), Garrett Hongo (1995) and Lisa Lowe (1996), all of whom suggest that what is really being

addressed are issues of gender and generation, tensions between nationalist and feminist concerns, and arguments about identity and
difference. Some, if not all, of these conflicts are embodied in the
distinctions which Lowe makes between a fixed symbolic identity
(masculinist/nationalist in origin) and her concepts of heterogeneity,
hybridity, and multiplicity.

Amy Tan was born in California in 1952 and her first novel *The Joy
Luck Club* was published in 1989, with a film version directed by Wayne
Wang in 1993. The book has sixteen inter-connecting narratives based
around four mothers and four daughters, all of whom know each other.
The mothers were born in China, the daughters in the US.

The novel opens in folk mode with the story of a woman and a swan
crossing an ocean heading towards America. In one brief paragraph the
phrase, 'over there' is ritually repeated, always with a positive inflection.
The woman imagines that she will have a daughter who will be just like
her to whom she will give the swan, symbol not only of hope and
expectation but also of 'exceeding': 'a creature that became more than
what was hoped for' (17). She also dreams that the daughter will speak
'perfect American English'. On arrival, the swan is taken from the woman
leaving her with a single feather, and she has so many forms to fill in that
'she forgot why she had come and what she had left behind' (17). This
brief synoptic fable, only a page in length, embodies much of the
narrative that is to follow, as well as many of the themes in several
other Asian-American narratives. Separation between the ageing woman
and her monolingual and Americanised daughter prevents the woman
from ever making a gift of the feather to the daughter, a spatial and
temporal alienation emphasised by the fact that 'she waited, year after
year, for the day she could tell her daughter this in perfect American
English' (17). The repetition of this last phrase, with its now negative
inflection, and separated from the original speculative utterance by the
intervening paragraph of actual arrival, stresses how much *translation*
functions as a metaphor of time, distance, and loss, the journey travelled
from identity – 'I will have a daughter just like me' – to difference. She is
not able simply to reproduce herself or to own/determine meaning or its
reception ('she will know my meaning').

The trope of 'forgetting' is also introduced in this prefatory setting and
the narratives which follow establish a complex archive of what Freud
called 'screen memories', combined with 'verbal bridges' which connect
past with present. While appearing to be autobiographical transcriptions
of past events, the mothers' 'China' narratives operate in the following
way:

Our childhood memories show us our earliest years not as they were but as they
appeared at the later periods when the memories were aroused. In these periods

of arousal, the childhood memories did not, as people are accustomed to say, *emerge*; they were *formed* at that time. And a number of motives, with no concern for historical accuracy, had a part in forming them, as well as in the selection of the memories themselves. (Freud 1899: 322)

There is, in other words, a certain fit between the event narrated and the time of narrating – the 'period of arousal'. The stories in *The Joy Luck Club* are also, in Foucault's wonderful phrase, hardened 'in the long baking process of history' (1977: 144). Migration is itself a crucial part of this 'baking process', the mental and physical journey of displacement and relocation. The narratives are also constituted by what Rushdie calls 'memory's truth': 'It selects, eliminates, alters, exaggerates, minimises, glorifies, and vilifies also; but in the end it creates its own reality, its heterogeneous but usually coherent version of events' (1982: 211). The telling is also a form of secondary revision constructed often in antagonism to an unspoken or rejected 'truth'. Rather than being seen as simply the record of the migrating generation, the 'mother narratives' need to be considered in the terms described by Marie-Claude Taranger:

There is thus imposed the necessity of bringing to light the multiple and changing relations which ceaselessly produce interference, in an infinite play of repetitions and variations, between the voices and the images of the individual and the group, of a past and of its futures. (1991: 57)

The concept of 'interference' is helpful in emphasising the ways in which the 'mother narratives' not only intercross and intersect with each other, but also with the 'daughter narratives'. There is more 'horizontal' interference in the China stories than perhaps seems at first apparent. There is an element of the performative in all the narratives, of working through, or inventing even, appropriately gendered forms dialogically engaged in a polemic with the absent, but hegemonic, masculine cultural traditions. One of the strengths of the text as a whole is the way in which Tan articulates 'that which is refused from construction, the domains of the repressed, forgotten, and the irrecoverably foreclosed' (Butler 1993: 245).

It seems that more is going on in this text than the simple production of a formative narrative, authentic and developmental. 'Authentication' is a claim staked out by each narrator and not the automatic property of the contents of that which is narrated. It is partial, fallible, agonistic even, and certainly polemical: 'She will know my meaning'. But, of course, migration and acculturation mean precisely that something is irretrievably lost in the *trans*, both the act and narrative of crossing: mediation itself, 'a continua of transformation'. Control is at stake, the intractability of signification: polysemic, the producer of difference and not identity; repetition, but with a difference. It is not a case simply of two sets of generational narratives in antagonism, but of eight 'doubled' narratives producing repetitions with the deterritorialising power of becoming-other. That 'becoming-other', arguably, is that very complexity which constitutes Asian-Americanness itself, without the hyphenation which only makes it a 'territorialising' representation, a given of the dominant, homogeneous, patterned and sedimented. The narratives supply the conditions of temporality to what commonly passes for a post-synchro-nised identity as 'other' or strangers. In a sense, the strangers are writing a letter from, and – in complex ways – to a motherland, against displacement and double marginalisation. The contents of these letters are not only private and familial; they also have a cultural and public discursive status. They are not evidential memories but cultural con-structions. The mothers narrate in order to make their memories become the property of their daughters (and of themselves by reiteration) through identification: a 'birthing' is going on, a suturing of the daughters into the narratives even if they are only indirectly, or implicitly, the object or addressee of the telling. In a complex way, it is the very existence of the mothers which gives these 'perfect American English' daughters their stake in Asianness. In the transitive sense, identifying the mothers as mothers is a fairly straightforward biological/genealogical process (although notice how often lost parents and siblings figure in the mother narratives). The reflexive sense of 'identification with' is much more complicated and involves a process described by Freud which is parti-cularly salient for this text:

The assimilation of one ego to another one, as a result of which the first ego behaves like the second in certain respects, imitates it and in a certain sense takes it up into itself. (1899: 63)

The phrase 'takes it up into itself' is precisely what the translational functions of The Joy Luck Club narratives are designed to do, but it is not an obvious or simple task as the woman's experience of loss at the immigration office shows. In a different context, Theresa Hak Kyung Cha wrote in Dictée: 'Somewhere someone has taken my identity and replaced it with their photograph' (1982: 56). This conflict between 'original' and 'image' ('what transplant to dispel upon?' asks Cha) marks much of diasporic writing. Identity becomes, in many ways, an 'idealised lost object', its recovery always deferred; its deferral may well be a condition of survival, the always to be completed vision, never finally settled. Although, at a realist level, The Joy Luck Club constructs a series of narratives which articulate singular subject positions, the textual strategies deployed also help to create a sense of shifting, fluid and actively negotiated differences – multiple object positions:

Over the years, she told me the same, except for the ending, which grew darker, casting long shadows into her life, and eventually into mine. (23)

As the Joy Luck Club itself was a strategy for constructing a future, so it in turn generated stories which always 'grew and grew'. It is, literally and metaphorically, an investment in an *American* future by means of the stock market. The mothers and daughters speak different languages, both in the cultural sense and also in so far as the mothers 'speak in their special language, half in broken English, half in their own Chinese dialect' (34):

My mother and I never really understood one another. We translated each other's meanings and I seemed to hear less than what was said, while my mother heard more. (37)

The families all belong to the pre-1965 migration period, part of what has been called the 'transitional Chinese Family' (Wong 1995: 70) in which 'The parent-child relationship was somewhere between the strict formality of the traditional Chinese family and the high degree of permissiveness of the white American family' (ibid.). So, although the novel may well have its basis in autobiography, and cannot be read as sociologically 'evidential', the inter-generational and transitional nature of the different narratives can be located in a quite specific historical moment, between 1943 and 1965. It is also a time when the majority of the Chinese population was native born unlike the post 1965 period. Given that each of the four families featured in the text is structured as a nuclear unit, the Joy Luck Club functions as a 'semi-extended' kinship group based upon traditional Chinese practices. It is not a group as such but one of the many instances in the texts of 'translation', of structural adjustment and adaptation, a synthesis. The families are all 'uptown': middle class, white collar or professional, in contrast with the ghetto or 'downtown' type of family, and they all reside at a distance from Chinatown in the surrounding urban areas and suburbs. The daughters are modern and cosmopolitan in their lifestyles and 'live' American more than Chinese. Although this may be a cause of tension in the families, it is also a source of pride.

By inviting Ling-Mei Woo (June) to replace her dead mother at the mah jong table, the epicentre of the Joy Luck Club, and to sit at the East position, the mothers structurally open up 'all the truths and hopes they have brought to America' (40) using Ling-Mei as a broker between the generations, a way of mediating their relationship with their own American daughters. The fact that Ling-Mei's mother has surviving daughters of her first marriage living in Shanghai also binds someone of the second-generation to their past horizontally. In this way, issues of both identity and difference are negotiated, similar to the means by which the multiply voiced narratives articulate a complex mix of singularity and plurality, memory and fantasy. Most of the mothers' stories have an allegorical and polemical element designed to produce a 'relay' function: 'This is how a daughter honors her mother' (48); or 'I once sacrificed my life to keep my parents' promise. This means nothing to you, because to you promises mean nothing' (49). In the second quotation the addressee 'you' is not specified (the speaker is Lindo Jong, Waverly's mother), but it is, in a sense, both second person singular and plural: daughter in particular, daughters in general. The narratives, therefore, almost always exceed their instrumentality; they are telling stories with a 'hidden' polemic. This is not history, or autobiography, but fable/fabulae: cultural 'truths' produced by women who, in America, find a voice, after having been socialised into thinking, in a patriarchal society, that they 'belonged to somebody else' (51). It is important to point out that it is not America *per se*, also a patriarchal society, that has liberated or loosened their tongues but their very position of dislocation and transition. It is still a fractured voice, a partial repositioning, a way of 'washing their thinking out of their skin', of restoring value. Other stories tell of invisibility, erasure and silence, not only in the past but continuing into the present and conditioning inter-generational relationships.

Each mother came to America in her thirties and, at the time of narration, each daughter is of a similar age; this is another textual strategy for articulating sameness and difference, replication and yet also the impossibility of repetition. In attempting to reterritorialise both their daughters and themselves, the mother narratives in fact deterritorialise, transform their relationship (filial and narratological) from within, produce 'repetition with a difference'. Micrologically, this strategy creates one of the characteristic features of migrant fictions. The shadows, dark sides, and restless natures which the narratives reveal of the mothers, are also analogues of the possibilities opened up for the daughters, but repressed in the earlier generations. The occasional mother–daughter 'stand-off' in the immigrants' stories also has a homiletic function. These are parables of loss as well as gain. It may be a cause of resentment and of conflict, but it is also seen as an advance that it is no longer socially and culturally necessary that 'a girl should stand still' (72). The stories of loss, separation, puberty, forced marriages, sibling and parental death are also simultaneously narratives of unbecoming and becoming, of transience and emergence: they are border crossings. A whole range of diverse moments of (Japanese) colonialism and patriarchy are conflated into an extended synchronised and simultaneous experience. Ying-Ying St Clair's 'Moon Lady' narrative (pp. 67–82), a story of the lost and found girl, opens out into a metaphorical search which exceeds its empirical base and its apparently transparent expression, and becomes agonistic, a site of struggle over identity and against fixity: 'I never believed my family found the same girl'.

The 'daughter narratives' set out to speak the unspoken of their mothers' imaginaries, as well as to articulate their own 'horizontal' peer relationships and conflicts, gendered and racist. Lena St Clair, the daughter of a Chinese mother and an Irish father, passes for white, and narrates in order to 'open her mother's eyes', to see with the eyes, even, of the woman who was a 'Displaced Person, lost in a sea of immigration categories' (104). Her mother was held at Angel Island Immigration Station until her category of 'otherness' could be determined. Living in paranoid space, the mother 'looks as if she were neither coming from nor going to someplace' (105), a figure of stasis. Lena often lies when she translates for her, and is also caught in a situation whereby, 'I could understand the words perfectly, but not the meanings. One thought led to another without connection' (106). This words/meaning disjunction precisely locates the way in which, throughout the text, the linguistic in its widest cultural sense is the site of conflict over meaning – the imperfect 'crossing'. It is not just a struggle over meaning in a limited semantic sense but is also a matter of ontology. In 'Half and Half' Rose Hsu Jordan comes to realise through the death of her little brother when she is fourteen and, later, through her marital separation, that her existence is conditioned by undecidability and that identiy is fluid and erasable; it is a narrative of *rift*. Even Ling-Mei Woo's affirmative declaration of identity is predicated on negatives: 'I won't be what I am not' (134). Lena's mother 'raised a daughter, watching her from another shore' (251).

One of the features which separates the generations is the issue of choice. For the most part, emigration has been 'unchosen', and for the first generation choices in America have been confined by language, housing, employment, gender legacies and racism. At best they could only ever be hyphenated, Chinese-American by naturalisation (an interesting phrase in itself), living for the next generation. The second generation has extended choice, although 'there was a serious flaw with the American version. There were too many choices, so it was easy to get confused and pick the wrong thing' (191). The daughters lead multi-directional lives, but not all meanings are as available to them as they might think. If the daughters can go in many directions, their mothers came from many different directions. It is one of the strengths of the text that it particularises and differentiates, specifies and locates, writing against homogenisation, stereotype and generalisation. It is acknowledged that there is a 'China of the mind' – the idealised lost object – also a China of the past: 'That was China . . . They had no choice. They could not speak up. They could not run away. That was their fate' (241), as well as a China of the present: 'But now they can do something else'. So even the China of the mothers' narratives is not uniformly fixed or simply a reflection of migrant 'misrecognition'. Not only are they watching America 'from another shore', the same is now true of China; they are split, dwellers in an 'intervening space', in-between, seeing from an interstitial space. The boundary between mother and daughter is that place 'from which something begins its presencing' (Bhabha 1994: 1).

Ironically, at a point when the daughters are beginning to use their Chinese names again, and it is fashionable to be Chinese, Waverly Long is mortified when her mother reminds her that in China, 'They know you do not belong' (253), that 'she didn't look Chinese', only in America! Her mother is thinking in essences and specifics, as she is when she speaks of 'Chinese character' and 'American circumstances' as though these are readily calculable and not fluid. But at the hairdressers, at a moment of sharp generational and lifestyle conflict, she reveals how much she is aware that identity is stage-management:

I smile. I use my American face. That's the face Americans think is Chinese, the one they cannot understand. But inside I am becoming ashamed. I am ashamed she is ashamed. Because she is my daughter and I am proud of her, and I am her mother but she is not proud of me. (255)

Waverly has not only been translating for her mother (who does not need it), she is effectively translating her mother into her new class codes. However, even if her mother's eyes did begin to 'follow the American way', she always retained her 'double face', despite paying an American-raised Chinese girl in Peking to coach her how to hide her true self and prepare to live 'American'. There is a strong sense of the performative in how she has lived in America, as well as of pragmatism, and she criticises her daughter for 'mythologising' her parents in terms of 'Chinese non-sense' when she effectively had lost her 'Chinese face'.

In the latter stages of the novel, the apparently clear nativist/assimila-tionist binary – as Lowe calls it – breaks down and the mothers are revealed as negotiating a different paradigm of networking and becoming, and less 'essentialist' Chinese than their daughters have represented them. The relationship between the mothers and daughters in respect of China and America are more fluid and transformable than they at first seem, and identities are more complex and fractured than nativist/assimilationist suggests. More splitting and decentring has taken place, something which is confirmed by the last two narratives: 'Double Face' and 'A Pair of Tickets'. The words 'double' and 'pair' indicate repetition and combination, but these narratives are more transgressive and deconstructive than the earlier sections of the novel. Identity is seen much more reflexively and as far less categorical, more scattered and hybridised. Lindo Jong's second narrative reveals how when she and her husband first met in San Francisco, they could not speak to each other in their Chinese dialects, only in broken English, and that she was horrified that as a Mandarin she could even think of marrying a Cantonese. In

America such rigid boundaries can be crossed and their marriage is the first stage of an assimilationist trajectory. In addition to this her sons are given American names, and her daughter, Waverly, is named in such a way as to not only ground her spatially, but her mother also. The process is an interesting space–time compression, locational and future oriented:

And that's why I named you Waverly. It was the name of the street we lived on. And I wanted you to think, This is where I belong. But I also knew if I named you after this street, soon you would grow up, leave this place, and take a piece of me with you. (265)

This is an example of identity as 'relay' mentioned above, and an act of trans-hyphenation. The signifiers 'Chinese' and 'American' are both placed in doubt, open to question, under erasure. This can be linked to what Stuart Hall says about identity and identification:

I use 'identity' to refer to the meeting point, the point of *suture*, between on the one hand the discourses and practices which attempt to 'interpellate', speak to us or hail us into place as the social subjects and particular discourses, and on the other hand, the processes which produce subjectivities, which construct us as subjects which can be 'spoken'. (1996b: 5–6)

The naming of Waverly can be seen as such a 'point of suture', a meeting point and stitching together, a recognition of those *American* discourses and practices embodied in the street name (perhaps symbolic of change, variation and fluctuation) which will 'hail' her into place (in all senses of the word) as social being, and also of those future processes (grow up, leave this place) which will produce her subjectivity. A similar notion of *suture* can be applied to Lindo Jong's fractured identity of which she becomes aware when she visits China after an interval of almost forty years:

I had taken off my fancy jewelry. I did not wear loud colors. I spoke their language. I used their local money. But still, they knew. The knew my face was not one hundred per cent Chinese. They still charged me high foreign prices. (266)

The use of the pronoun 'I' four times (and 'my' and 'me' three times) to refer to herself, indicates that she is 'entering into a conscious, communally shared system of signification' (Childers and Hentzi 1995: 298), she is at a 'meeting point', suturing part of herself to something outside of her. However, as Childers and Hentzi point out, 'That: I . . . is a mere substitute for myself; using it represents a fundamental alienation from the unconscious drives and desires that can never be articulated within language' (ibid.). By removing her jewelry, wearing 'quiet' colours, and speaking Mandarin, Lindo has sought to place her 'I' within a communally shared system of signification – Chinese. But the repeated succession of 'theys' intrude and block out that 'I' and suggest a fundamental alienation, an unstitching; she is now constructed as a subject which cannot be spoken as 'Chinese', but 'Chinese-American'. The conscious 'I' is revealed as an inadequate substitute for 'herself', a fluid and trans-formable subjectivity; there is no 'nativist' essence that can be recovered or returned to.

On the contrary, Ling-Mei Woo (the only figure whose stories appear in both mother and daughter narratives, again suggesting a breakdown in the nativist/assimilationist binary at a structural level) in the concluding narrative, 'A Pair of Tickets', feels that she is 'becoming Chinese' when the train leaves the Hong Kong border and enters Shenzhen, China. Her mother had described this genetically: 'Once you are born Chinese, you cannot help but feel and think Chinese' (267), but for the daughter it is more at the level of the imaginary, a matter of identification. She is fully aware, even if there is a contrast between her passport photo – with its styled hair, false eyelashes, eyeshadow, lip liner and blusher – and her present limp hair, plain, unadorned, make-up-less face and melted mascara, that 'she could never pass for true Chinese'. She stands five feet six and 'I am eye level with other tourists' (272). Empirically true or not, the point is made metaphorically – she is a Chinese-American 'tourist'. This is compounded by the use of various dialects, so that she feels as if she were in the United Nations 'and the translators had run amok' (275).

What 'Chinese' means to Ling-Wei is de-essentialised when her father tells her that their relatives, rather than opting for the traditional banquet that she has envisaged, want to order room service, 'sharing hamburgers, french fries, and apple pie à la mode' (278). Whether the relatives choose this in deference to their guests is not clear, but it is evident that it is *their* choice. Another 'identity' is under erasure! Yet her father tells her her dead mother's story in Chinese, although he has begun it in English: ' "No, tell me in Chinese", I interrupt, "Really, I can understand" ' (281). What is happening in this final section is that we are presented with a series of crossovers, 'translations', relays. It includes the only 'father narrative', which is designed to speak for the absences and silences of the dead mother: 'Finding my mother in my father's story . . .' (286).

It is also a narrative which provides a meeting point for Ling-Mei with her lost Chinese sisters, the daughters of her mother's first marriage. She is the bond between them and their dead mother, the bearer of memory. The sisters remind her of her mother and yet she also sees no traces of the mother in them when she looks a second time. The whole of this final narrative works within the dimension of images, and the meeting with the sisters is mediated, in a sense, by the relationship of Ling-Mei's body to the image of her mother, refracted/reflected by the sisters. Metaphorically, it is a prototype for all of the dual relationships that characterise the novel as a whole – identification and disidentification:

> Yet they still look familiar. And now I also see what part of me is Chinese. It is so obvious. It is my family. It is in our blood. After all these years, it can finally be let go. (288)

It is a moment of recognition, of identification and of 'letting go'. It also may be the awareness of connection to the maternal body, an extension of self in what Kristeva has called the semiotic chora: 'Together we look like our mother' (288).

The design of *The Joy Luck Club* is constructed around the signification of identity and the tensions produced by the demands for sameness. What the narratives produce is a complex sense of difference with continuities, an ongoing process of becoming Chinese-American and of a diasporic (or travelling) identity, despite the polarities which are presented and are used in inter-generational antagonisms. The last two narratives make this most apparent: inter-changeability, not fixity, is a characteristic of identity, even though certain features are 'etched into the very fabric of the body, into gestures, lineaments and markers of who we are' (Andermahr et al. 1997: 125). This works both ways as we have seen with these 'lineaments' disclosing both what Ling-Mei has been and what Lindo Jong has become: old and new affinities and configurations etched into the body and its languages.

The series of heterogeneous events of narration which constitute *The Joy Luck Club* can be considered in the terms of what Lyotard called the immemorial: 'That which can neither be remembered (represented to consciousness) nor forgotten (consigned to oblivion)' (Readings 1991: xxxii). As is evident from the very last narrative, it is also a work of mourning, of anamnesis: 'the search for that which remains unthought although it already has been thought' (Lyotard 1986: 158). In a sense, those who have criticised Maxine Hong Kingston and Amy Tan could be said to represent that model of Asian America which 'already has been thought', while their texts produce a *pagan* account of this, designed to work through an 'initial forgetting' and 'to search for that which remains unthought' in gendered terms, another temporality, against cultural programming and for singularity. In the terms used by Lyotard, what Tan is attempting to do is to produce a narrative of an event in the sense which this disrupts 'any pre-existing referential frame within which it might be represented or understood' (Readings 1991: xxxi). Writing within, against, and outside the referential frame, 'Asian-American', the text produces singularity, 'the radical specificity of *events*, their radical, once and for all "happening" or eventhood, and hence their heterogeneity or sheer difference from all other events' (ibid.: xxxiv). In a very telling phrase, Readings expresses precisely what is at the root of *The Joy Luck Club*: 'singularity is what is lost in translation'.

THE PROMISED LAND

Gish Jen grew up in Scarsdale, New York and is the author of two novels, *Typical American* (1991) and *Mona in the Promised Land* (1997), together with a collection of short stories, *Who's Irish?* (1999). In the title story of this collection, a first generation Chinese-American grandmother is the narrative voice which describes her battle with her three-year-old Chinese-Irish American granddaughter, Sophie. Widowed, at a tangent from her daughter's busy, professional life, she reflects upon a number of presumptions of 90s American lifestyle and some of the contradictions of ethnicity and colour – white, brown, Chinese, Irish – and inter-marriage. Her stereotyping of the Irish is compared by her daughter with the stereotyping of Chinese in America. As unpaid babysitter to Sophie, the grandmother dedicates herself to rescuing the 'Chinese' side of the child from her 'wild' Irish nature: 'It is inside that she is like not any Chinese girl I ever see' (*Who's Irish?*: 8). The child's behaviour – characteristically middle-class 1990s American – affronts the grandmother's traditional beliefs about children, especially girls. There is a generational and gendered conflict: Sophie's demonstrative, creative and 'permissive' behaviour is attributed to her 'wild inside', her Irish blood, while at the same time several references are made to her 'Chinese side', being 'a nice Chinese girl', and 'millions of children in China, not one act like this' (12).

The narrator is not named – she has been stripped down to the role of grandmother – nor is the addressee specified, but the tone takes for granted complicity, peer agreement and understanding, and endorsement of the values encoded. A family dispute arises over the issue of smacking. The parents are diametrically opposed, the grandmother thinks she can spank the Irish out of her and the Chinese into her. There is an ironic distance between the narrative voice and the broader narrative perspective. The grandmother's 'categorical ethnicity', the misrecognition of her *American* granddaughter, and her pre- (or is it post-, now?) feminist views are all subject to criticism, but the 'nucleated' 90s liberated family lifestyle is not treated uncritically.

The grandmother, no longer asked to babysit, leaves her daughter's home and, ironically, moves in with Sophie's other grandmother, Bess Shea, and begins to shift some of her views under the influence of the voice of Bess, even neglecting Chinese satellite television programmes in favour of American ones. Echoing earlier white ethnic prejudices, Bess's sons keep on asking when the narrator will go home. Their mother's response, reaches across the generations to encompass their shared granddaughter: 'She's a permanent resident, say Bess. She isn't going anywhere' (15). Sophie, neither Chinese nor Irish, but Chinese and Irish and American, occupies a third space: an alternative belonging. Even the narrator enjoys her new status as 'honorary Irish'. The point of the story is that Gish Jen emphatically *does not* 'beautifully translate what it is to see the world through Chinese eyes' (*The Independent*), as this is to misread the aesthetic for the sociological, but presents it through a more complex lens, a different scopic regime, in which she restores a dynamic to processes of ethnicity in which peoples of the diaspora can come to inhabit 'an autonomous space in which they can determine their own trajectories for constructing cultural identity' (Ang 1994: 11). Against the grain of the narrating voice, we reread, reinvent and reinterpret the questions: 'who's Irish?', 'who's Chinese?', 'who's American?'

Mona in the Promised Land focuses on the post-1968 second genera-tion of Sophie's mother and her peers, or, more precisely, on Mona and Callie, the daughters of Helen and Ralph Chang, the first-generation immigrants of *Typical American* which is based mainly in the 1950s.

As Michael Fischer has argued in his seminal essay 'Ethnicity and the post-modern arts of memory':

To be Chinese-American is not the same thing as being Chinese in America. In this sense there is no role model for becoming Chinese-American. It is a matter of finding a voice or style that does not violate one's several components of identity. (1986: 196)

The exotic or essentialist approach to ethnicity sees it as entirely synonymous with a limited idea of identity; the reverse is also true. *Typical American* traces the development of a small number of people from a point of being Chinese in America to becoming Chinese-American through the putting on and the taking off of a number of voices and styles. Their role model, in a sense, exists only in negative terms – typical American – as something to be avoided. For all this, they do align themselves in many ways with 'the melting pot rhetoric of assimilation to the bland, neutral style of the conformist 1950s' (ibid.). While not writing a fictional social history, Jen's three books to date do trace the shifting parameters of ethnicity across conflicting generational self-definitions. More than transmission it is seen as a complex process of transformation. In Fischer's terms, it is both 'ethical and future-oriented' (ibid.); in my terms, they are narratives attempting to shape and ground a new belonging. Like the grandmother in 'Who's Irish?', many of the figures in the texts come to see 'others against a background of ourselves, and ourselves against a background of others' (ibid.: 199). Elsewhere, I have called this varifocality; Fischer also uses the phrase 'multiple tracking'. Both forward looking and backward looking, the narratives use memories as a resource for the new and the future, a setting in motion again of what has become static or inert: crossing borders and opening up frontiers.

The three principal characters in *Typical American* – Ralph (Yifeng) Chang, his wife, Helen, and his sister, Theresa – are not economic migrants or refugees, but each one comes to America as a student. Initially, they fit the 'sojourner' category of temporariness, figures with expectations of return. This is particularly true of Ralph, the scholar/ outsider, the figure of fun, the comic *naif* foreigner, determined to study and not be distracted by the American landscape, only as an occasional tourist. His mission is to achieve a doctorate to hand to his father. Initially, everything is figured in terms of paternal imagery. Ralph sets out with return uppermost in his mind, but when his good intentions prove short-lived he sees his infractions, including the romantic fantasy woven around the departmental secretary, Cammy, as having an Oedipal edge. He dreams extensively of China, of a displaced and ultimately slain father. In his immediate American space he converts every term and image into Chinese currency, a familiar trope of migrant experience.

Unlike many of the fictions described in this book, *Typical American* does not use a first-person narrator nor is it manifestly semi-autobiographical. Jen uses a third-person narrative with, initially, a strong and directive voice addressing the reader, commanding movements in time and space, ranging backwards and forwards. The narrating time is never specified; it is an unstated, or absent, present. The voice is that of an insider, sometimes distant, sometimes close, speaking of outsiders. In the first instance, the narrative voice is a powerful, omniscient presence, overseeing and staging events and responses to events: 'picture him', 'years later when he told this story', etc. The voiceover is a translator, guide, gently mocking 'friend'. Stylistically, it is 'old culture talking'. As the narrative develops and the outsiders enter the language and culture, appropriate it and adapt it, the telling gives way to showing – the characters do not need prompts or stage directions, they are no longer marionettes, but visible and voiced, embodied and mobile – and the voiceover is stilled. The use of analepsis and prolepsis technically is also a metaphor of the ethnicity process itself – emergent from a dialogue between past, present, and future.

At one point, Ralph refers to a colleague at Graduate School: 'You know, someone at school was talking the other day about a person who took his house apart, and moved it, and then rebuilt it, just the way it was' (*Typical American*: 64). In many ways this resembles the first-generation migrant's 'ethnic anxiety' and the longing for equivalence and continuity, the nostalgia that fantasises that nothing is lost in translation. Interestingly enough, Ralph continues with the story and says: 'The odd thing was that that house had a leak. So why did the man move it, if it had a leak? That's the question' (64). Metaphorically, the leak is the process of ethnicity itself, both that which is lost and that which seeps through: the narrative of emergence. Nothing is ever 'the way it was', even the 'way it was'. As soon as we use the past tense, we admit another temporality, the continua of transformation.

The five-part structure of the novel has an architectural, constructionist design: Sweet Rebellion; The House Holds; This New Life; Structural Weakening; A Man to Sit at Supper and Never Eat. This is not a narrative of formative development, there is no simple linear progression. Initially, being Chinese in America is a matter of tactics, staking out a territory in which you are always at the borders, linguistically, culturally, racially. Passive, reactive, unreflexive, Ralph unwittingly becomes an 'illegal', a fugitive, by forgetting to renew his immigration papers. The Chinese Revolution and American support for the Nationalists, prevents him from returning to China and he becomes a displaced person, in several senses. Surviving as a Chinese in America gradually becomes a strategy, the trying on of different voices and styles in an era when the Cold War and 'unAmerican' meant homogenisation, co-option, and the suppression of interest in difference and ethnicity. 'Typical American' may be a family joke in the Chang household, but outside it the phrase had an uglier resonance. Underground, invisible and alienated, Ralph is 'brought back to life' by the presence of his sister Theresa.

Theresa is also a graduate student in the process of breaking the mould of Chinese women in America: 'the Asian-American woman thing – we're reliable, loyal, smart but non-threatening' (*My Year of Meat*: 157). She becomes a doctor, dominates the household, and also has an adulterous affair with an academic colleague of Ralph's, Old Chao. Old Chao, his wife Janis, and the long-time Chinese-American, Grover Ding – 'A short, American-born, English-speaking businessman with no degree' (86) – combine with Theresa, Ralph and his wife Helen, to constitute the core of the narrative. The presence of Grover, and Ralph and Helen's children, Mona and Callie, helps shift the three original migrant Chinese in America towards becoming Chinese-American, as English increasingly takes over as the principal medium of exchange. The little girls speak 'broken Chinese' as their parents had once spoken 'broken English'. Grover does not even know which province in China his original family came from. Having lost contact with their families after the 1949 Revolution, the Changs increasingly realise the need to 'enter' America. Accordingly, 'they discovered stories everywhere' and, in the midst of household tensions and splits, they found their own 'bit of story-making [that] allowed the family to go on' (113). Immediately after the Revolution, Ralph had both refused to be made an American citizen and declined help from the relief act, 'as though to claim his home was China was to make China indeed his home' (23). This undecidability marks a key stage in enabling identity as a matter of agency, the opening up of ethnicity as a negotiation, not a given, a process of transformation.

Grover Ding is the catalyst of change in the narrative, both a positive and a negative force. Self-made millionaire, confidence man, trickster and philanderer, he is a totally assimilated figure to the point of being the eponym of the novel. Only his surname bears the traces of his Chinese ancestry, and even that could also be construed as onomatopoeic – the sound of a 1950s cash register! He epitomises the conspicuous consumption, cash-nexus values and individualist rhetoric of the American 'dream'. Ralph becomes utterly absorbed by him and in a process of transference, aided by Carnegie's *The Power of Positive Thinking*, becomes a mimic man, an 'imageener', a post-emotional clone, Riesman's 'other directed' citizen. All three Changs also progress from the status of Permanent Residents to full citizenship, and jokingly style themselves as the 'Chang-kees', both naming and creating themselves in the process. The chapter entitled 'Chang-Kees' (123–8) marks this 'entry' into America: Radio City music hall, Christmas, popular musicals, a Davy Crockett hat, baseball games. Their 'wide-eyed' acceptance of all things American – the language of outside the house had seeped well inside – is checked by a comment at a baseball game when they were told to go back to their laundry, a reminder that assimilation is always provisional, conditional, Anglo-centred. Nevertheless, they begin to co-habit both the spaces of Chinese and English – 'slipped from tongue to tongue like turtles taking to land, taking to sea; though one remained their more natural element, both had become essential' (124). In time, it is uncertain which is 'more natural' and the amphibian metaphor is peculiarly apt. They all had 'English thoughts' and things they did not know how to say in Chinese: 'Was this finally the New World? They all noticed that there seemed to be no boundaries any more' (126). As they discover, this is an illusory perception but it is a measure of the distance they had travelled.

Up to this point in the narrative, the family is self-contained, assuming naively that they could pick and choose their levels of Americanisation. Each member of the family is conventionally role-bound to a certain extent. Ralph, tenured professor in an engineering faculty, Theresa, a trainee doctor, and Helen, the dutiful housewife, all occupy positions acceptable to and tolerated by the dominant ideology, culturally appropriate (engineer, doctor) for the model minority. They move to suburban Connecticut – 'almost as nice as China' – which they see as a point of arrival, a 'hometown'. Their mobility – marked by the house purchase and Ralph's acquiring a car – is also the beginning of their structural weakening, their implosion as a secure Chinese family in America.

'Helen is Home' is the title of one chapter and, initially, she *is* in all senses of the word – domestic, passive, secondary and supplementary – and living with her learned circumspection as though still in China: 'like

a skating rink, a finite space, walled' (85). Helen lives in China in America
in terms of the food she cooks (when she could not have Chinese food, she
did not eat), the clothes she wears, writing home every day, and visiting
Chinatown three times a week, as though it were a foreign quarter of
Shanghai. She lives on the edge of a strange world, holding her breath,
but gradually tries 'to make herself as at home in her exile as she could'
(63). Ralph even controls the way she breathes. As she develops muscles
(literally and metaphorically), fantasises about a magazine-style romance,
has an adulterous relationship with Grover Ding, befriends the real
estate agent Janis Chao (socially beneath her had they remained in
China), she and the rest of the family become ungrounded, floating in
space.

   Ralph, increasingly Babbitt-like, gives up his academic post, buys into
a fast food chicken outlet (prompted by Grover Ding) which Helen enters
into as 'in a new country', becomes preoccupied with his cash register to
the neglect of all else, and ends up semi-bankrupt, without a business or
property. The unwalled and the infinite become treacherous spaces. As
Grover Ding, the totally Americanised crook who cheats Ralph, puts it:
'You are either somebody or a Chinaman'. Ding is a somebody, Ralph a
Chinaman, a 1950s Lemuel Pitkin, the picaro and fool. He becomes the
'absurd man as picaro':

A picaro is a metaphysical outsider dangling between commitments and value
systems. An author who transmits through this form is acutely aware of the
profound dislocation in his [sic] social and political universe. (Galloway 1980: 87)

Ralph is the outsider, the dangling man, who deludes himself into
thinking he is an insider. He is gullible and vulnerable, unaware of
the profound dislocation between America's Horatio Alger ideology of
openness and the dream of success, and the realities of a highly stratified,
conformist and 'finite' society. Assuming that society is simply a vehicle,
or medium, for the individual, Ralph alienates his wife and family,
becomes increasingly violent, and almost kills his sister in a car crash.
   Theresa, initially also circumspect:

Now, though, she tried to box herself up. She had always been nice about her
morals; she grew nicer still. How dangerous a place, this country! A wilderness of
freedoms. She shuddered, kept scrupulously to paths . . . Now she stiffened and
turned away. (142–3)

becomes involved in an affair with Old Chao, Janis's husband, leaves her
brother and sister-in-law's house, and almost dies after being hit by a car
driven by her brother. This, among many other things, brings all of the
characters back to the mortal, the finite, and the contingent: 'the meaning
had worn off of things like so much gilt' (287). Where they had seen order,

pattern and design all shaped by their own power of choice, they become aware of the role of accident, the loss of agency, and structures of power outside their control: 'Was death possible in this bright country?' (286), that meaning is never a transparent and one-way transmission.

Much earlier in the narrative, Ralph had clearly articulated the myth of opportunity: 'Anything could happen, this was America. He gave himself up to the country, and dreamt' (42). What follows, in a sense, is the substance of that dream, culminating in the nightmare I have described. The phrase 'gave himself up to the country' is revealing because it suggests the action of a fugitive, a man on the run, who surrenders and becomes a captive of the country. As a prisoner of his, and the American, dream he is only released by his awareness of the enormity of what he had done as Theresa lies in a coma. This use of a 'surrender' metaphor is echoed in the final chapter focused solely on Ralph, forced into reflexivity, standing alone, hailing cabs in a wild snowstorm – beyond the land of perpetual sunshine and smiles. He remembers a time in their childhood when he had caused Theresa to fall off a seesaw, but: 'This time, an adult, he would have to say something. He would have to find words. But what words?' (295). The blandness and platitudes of 'imagineering' are no longer adequate; the child of the American dream has to re-enter the world and the word. The imagery is significant: 'Cold masked his face'; 'His coat stiffened around him, a prison'; 'trapped in his coat'; 'What escape was possible?' (295), all images of enclosure and foreshortening:

He could not always see, could not always hear. He was not what he made up his mind to be. A man was the sum of his limits; freedom only made him see how much so. America was no America. (296)

The seeing and the hearing are metaphorical, signifiers of a failure in decoding, a breakdown in cultural transmission. Imprisoned, he is in thrall to an individualist rhetoric, the log cabin to White House mythology, a Dale Carnegie fantasy; free, he is able to see the bars and the walls. In a sense, he has entered a second exile, first from China, then from an America 'of the mind' ('America is no America'), white suburban America of the 1950s, a soap opera and a soap bubble. Winter, nevertheless, has brought progress, insight, and survival, if not assimilation: 'And yet Ralph held his arm up in the snow all the same' (296).

Typical American is a novel about misreading, the search for an imaginative space outside of the 'always already known' of being 'American'. It is also about misrecognition in so far as the 'child-like' characters fantasise their integrity as an entity or 'self' and misrecognise themselves as a unified being. This observation is, obviously, based upon a Lacanian understanding, but the concept can also be more fruitfully explored in Bourdieu's use of misrecognition, especially in terms of its appropriateness to the novel. Bourdieu sees misrecognition in the form of what he calls symbolic domination, 'in which the hierarchies of domination validated by a "sacralised" culture are embodied in the very bodily hexis or habitus or dispositions of the dominated' (Andermahr et al. 1997: 169). The three principal characters embody this symbolic domination, as they open up their house and their bodies (literally in the case of Helen and Theresa), their language and their lifestyle, to the everyday life of America, not realising that they were not only purchasing goods but values and a hierarchy of domination – typical American. This arbitrary category is mistaken as authentic, fixed and natural: an identity that comes with the (suburban) territory.

In some ways, a novel which critiques the 'immigration and assimilation' ethnic genre, *Typical American* is a satire both on 'American values' and those of unreflexive 'ethnicity' – Chinese in America: 'his [Ralph's] fortune was to live in the other America, the legendary America that was every wish come true' (237). The narrative gradually translates the family to that other 'other America', a place with another set of legends/legible spaces. In the words of the title of the chapter from which this quotation is taken, the narrative opens up America as a set of 'constructions', a play between cultures. In a narrative of displacement and emergence, sameness ('typical American') is replaced by difference. Chinese-American, or Chinese American, like all other ethnicities, is something which has to be particularised, worked out and worked through, constructed and (re)-located:

The term ethnicity acknowledges the place of history, language and culture in the construction of subjectivity and identity as well as the fact that all discourse is placed, positioned, situated, and all knowledge is contextual. (Hall 1992: 25)

A textualised, contextualised, and 'textured sense of being American' (Fischer 1986: 230) emerges in the course of the narrative.

AN AWKWARD FLIGHT

The most profitable film of 1993 (based on the budget-to-box office ratio) was *The Wedding Banquet*, directed by Ang Lee, which received a whole raft of awards and nominations and was distributed on a worldwide basis. Very much a film of the 'intersection', gay-themed and transethnic, its 'sparkling comedy' raises a number of questions about the symbolic domination of normative values. Given that the film uses both English and Chinese languages, and that part of the narrative depends upon apparent linguistic misunderstanding, one of the producers' comments on the writing process is of interest:

Writing screenplays in such a cultural stew is no easy feat . . . First drafts were
written in Chinese, then translated into English, re-written in English, translated
back into Chinese, and eventually sub-titled in Chinese and English and a dozen
other languages. (Schamus 1994: xi)

The film is concerned equally with issues of cultural translation, ideologies of masculinity and fathering, sexualities and gender appropriate
behaviour. The narrative is focused on five principal figures: Wai Tung is
a young, professional ostensibly 'model minority' man from Taiwan who
has been in the US for ten years and has citizen status; he also owns some
real estate, bought by his father. His partner, of a similar age, is Simon; he
is a physical therapist and their seemingly equal relationship has lasted
five years. Wei Wei is an art student from mainland China, living in one
of Wai Tung's properties, initially rebellious and demanding, and in
trouble with immigration; Mr and Mrs Gao are Wai Tung's parents,
resident in Taiwan; Mr Gao is a retired general who fought with Chiang
Kai Shek.

Wai Tung's parents have conventional expectations of their son: that
he will marry and produce grandchildren for them, a son in particular. Mr
Gao's role as 'Commander' (the term used by Old Chen, one of his former
soldiers, now running a restaurant in Chinatown, New York) is both
literal and metaphorical. It signifies his paternal and patriarchal authority, his identification with warrior masculinity, and the privileging of
inheritance in terms of the male. Illegal in Taiwan, Wai Tung's homo-
sexuality has to be closeted from his parents and he goes along with their
plans to arrange a marriage through a computer dating agency in Taipei.
Class and gender expectations, normative sexuality, and generational
and cultural 'misrecognitions' form the staple of the ensuing comic
narrative.

As the woman who is sent from Taiwan by the computer dating
agency, Mao, discovers that Wai Tung is gay and is also in potential
conflict with her parents over her secret white boyfriend, any possible
'arrangement' between them is terminated. Her singing of an extract from
an aria in Madame Butterfly is prefigurative of a fantasy which the film
partly displaces. In thrall to his parents, blackmailed by his father's ill-
health, Wai Tung reluctantly agrees with Simon's plan that he should
'marry' Wei Wei to keep his parents happy and secure her Green Card; in
the process, he is also blackmailing her. Wei Wei moves into their
apartment and prepares for the immigration exam, coached by Simon
in Wai Tung's habits, lifestyle and bodily characteristics. Simon's 'command' and choreographing has paternal traces, something which is
developed later in his collusion with Mr Gao. The plot misfires when
the Gaos announce their intention of visiting New York, and a 'real'
marriage ceremony has to be arranged. The apartment is transformed by

the removal of all signs of gay culture and their replacement by Chinese calligraphy and family photographs.

According to James Schamus, producer and screenplay collaborator, the script was modelled on the Hollywood 'remarriage' farces of the 1930s and 1940s, transmuting the white heterosexual, twin-bed ideal into a gay and mixed race 1990s couple. During the wedding ceremony and in the subsequent banquet, Simon shifts from command to periphery as he is located in a number of isolated, single shots, silent and unsmiling. In a sense, a 'transferred' oedipal struggle takes place between Simon and Mr Gao over the body of his son. At the Marriage Bureau, Wai Tung has to be switched into the groom's role by the registrar. At a number of levels, gender, sexuality and ethnicity are seen to be matters of performativity. Wei Wei's 'cooking' is stage-managed by Simon who is proficient in the kitchen, where she is not. The formality of the parents is not just a cultural cliché, but also an indicator of their strategic role-playing in the whole charade. By giving Mr Gao a blood pressure monitor and Mrs Gao protein facial cream, Simon signals his desire to distance them from their son, to remind them of their mortality, while – in his broken Chinese – coming over as a model of courtesy. There is irony, obviously, as the whole charade is about not 'losing face'.

Mr Gao silently observes certain tell-tale signs, like the two garden chairs close together, the fact that Simon is presented as Wai Tung's landlord when he himself owns property, and the moment when, meeting Old Chen at the restaurant, Wai Tung introduces Simon to him and does not mention 'our new daughter-in-law' as Mrs Gao styles her. Chen's exaggerated respect and sycophancy towards Mr Gao refer back to army days and evoke a homosocial bonding.

In what is, superficially, a transgressive text, there is considerable play with essences and fixities. After the wedding banquet, Wai-Tung and Wei-Wei are 'compulsorily' bedded by the throng of guests in their hotel room, and have penetrative sex. It is significant that the only reference to a penis in the film is in a heterosexual context. If, as Richard Fung suggests (Eng 1997), in Western society 'the Asian man is defined by a striking absence down there', it is of interest that it takes an Asian woman to give it presence. In gay communities, there is also a stereo-typing of the passive Asian male as feminised. Hence Wai-Tung's assumption of the bride position at the Marriage Bureau. This marriage, and Wei-Wei's resulting pregnancy, split Simon and Wai-Tung apart, even though an abortion is arranged. At this stage, the Hollywood 'remarriage' model has almost completely receded, and the mood is nearer to tragedy with a number of irreconcilable rifts. The fact that Mrs Gao has responded to Wai-Tung's 'coming out' with relative equa-nimity suggests that this is not the full story, as does Mr Gao's 'broken English' conversation with Simon which indicates he may have caught the gist of the furious argument between the two young men earlier. As Gao says, 'If I didn't let everyone lie to me, I'd never have gotten my grandchild' (Wedding Banquet: 205).

There is a sense that the parents' formality, their 'Chinese' conservatism, and belief in fate and superstition ('quick son soup'), are all part of a strategic performance to secure their own ends, an heir to secure the family name (Wei-Wei decides to keep the child). The transgressive sexuality is set aside as the Gaos leave New York for Taipei coyly and calculatingly, pleased that they have a second 'son' (Simon) and a putative grandchild. Mrs Gao still hopes that her son might 'revert back to normal' – as he has, of course, in the hotel room. Wei Wei asks Simon to be one of the fathers of her child, and the circle is cosily renewed, except that when Simon puts his arm round the two of them, 'Wei-Wei breaks from the circle' (207). (At the airport, for the sake of the parents, all three stand with their arms around each other.) On departure, Mr Gao is frisked by an attendant with a metal detector, and 'He lifts his arms, as if in awkward flight', but the gesture is also triumphant and celebratory. For all the transgressive sexuality, inter-ethnicity, and gender shifts (Wei-Wei says 'a tough guy has to take responsibility for his actions', and 'not really' when Mrs Gao suggests that 'husband and children are still the most important thing to us right?'), conservative, normative values have fundamentally been sustained, at a deep structural level. Marriage, even sexuality, are 'negotiable', but perpetuating the family name is not. Gay-themed it may be, but gay values, gay partnerships, are still marginalised, and women, in the person of Wei-Wei, are tamed, secondary and disposable, bearers of sons for male families, foregrounded only for her reproductive, labour value, and no longer rebellious or demanding. Wei-Wei will have her own apartment and a semblance of independence, but she will do the parenting; for Simon and Wei-Wei 'fathering' will be a pastime.

No significant movement has taken place in racial and sexual formation, Asian-American or American; a neat domestic compromise has been effected which leaves both heterosexuality and Asian 'values' intact; a transfusion has taken place in which the transnational flow of 'capital' (symbolic and cultural) has resumed the US–Taiwan inter-dependency, with Taiwan as America's Chinese outpost; and Wai-Tung a 'Chinese in America' still, even after ten years. Mr Gao speaks of being pleased with the return on his investment. The vertical hierarchy, domestic and heterosexual, supplants the horizontal 'democracy'. Claims by both the Asian-American and the homosexual 'to the domestic space of the nation-state as home and as citizen-subjects' (Eng 1997: 36) are still seen as very much conditional and subject to the symbolic domination of national, and transnational, models of race and sexuality. Consent is withheld as a legitimate model of negotiation. We are still within a narrative of an old belonging, a dominant ideal subject, normatively masculine. The conditions for a transgressive and dialogical relationship are put in place (and, in a sense, can be read against the grain of the film's conclusions) but only provide a secondary, marginal and unthreatening dynamic, what Eng calls its 'queer and diasporic formation'.

Innovative in many respects, and working against Hollywood stereotypes of Asian-American males and of gay partnerships, the 'queer and diasporic status' (Eng) of Wai-Tung is code-breaking at a number of levels. Nevertheless, the fact that the film travelled so well within and beyond the United States suggests that audiences were responding to a classic dilemma which is foregrounded as 'universal' and 'crosses all racial and sexual divisions' (*Virgin Film Guide* 1996: 785). In the process, arguably, they were perhaps able to translate, or convert, it into terms which emphasised the generational and ethnic conservatism at the expense of the 'queer and diasporic'. Wei-Wei's pregnancy was the result of 'safe sex' after all.

NOT EVERYTHING CAN BE TRANSLATED

Concepts such as the melting pot or the mosaic presume coherence, resolution, completeness, and, in Edward Said's phrase, 'the symmetry of redemption' (Said 1986: 150). They arise out of hegemonic projects of assimilation and propose a model of identity as static and finally formed. Some of the fictions explored in this book come close, at times, to this 'symmetry of redemption' and verge on the apolitical and sentimental, but, for the most part, they challenge and resist homogenisation, and present narratives in which identity is partial and incomplete, always in a process of becoming, of emergence. They are dialogical and transactional, not just concerned with telling stories, but preoccupied with 'storying' itself, the structures and processes by which a narrative is shaped from fragments, memories, and erasures, and the absence of continuities. *Bone* (1993) by Fae Myenne Ng (who was born in San Francisco) is a structurally complex example of this storying; an illustration of what James Clifford calls 'presents-becoming-futures' (Clifford 1992: 15), a record of 'broken bodies'.

The novel has fourteen chapters and, instead of moving forwards in linear fashion, it has a recessive structure in which the present (Chapter 1) becomes a future by way of an excavation of, not just a densely layered past, but by looking at a 'now' with its own striations. This striature is not only the basis of the narrative structure, but is also related to the identities of the Leong family – mother, father, and three daughters – in San Francisco's Chinatown. The opening chapter starts with a closure: 'In Chinatown, everyone knew our story' (*Bone*: 3), which the narrative proceeds to undermine as 'our story' becomes increasingly fractured and elusive, impossible to render in terms of causality and coherence. Like identities in Paul Gilroy's comment about 'inescapable hybridity', the narrative moves relentlessly backwards and forwards, 'always unfinished, always being made' (Gilroy 1993: xi). Its core feature is improvisation, a narrative of mutability and instability, never readily yielding to the settled or forensic. *Bone* opens up spaces and opens up times, both Chinatown and migrant 'consciousness' with its doublings and *bricolage*. Certain stories are returned to again and again – in particular, the middle daughter's suicide – but instead of layers being stripped away each time to reveal a core meaning, new perspectives are introduced, fresh layers added.

In Chapter 1, the family is split, with Leila, the narrator and eldest daughter just married while on vacation in New York, but still partly living with her mother in Chinatown; Nina, the youngest daughter lives in New York; Ona, the middle daughter, jumped to her death off the Nam Ping Yuen housing project in Chinatown; the mother, Mah, and father, Leon, (Leila's stepfather) live in separate parts of Chinatown. From this split condition, the 'shreds and echoes' of an immediate and distant past are shaped from what Peter Marin called, 'the generational legacy of every family, a certain residue, a kind of ash, what I would call "ghost values"' (Singh et al. 1994: 8). It is these 'ghost values', shared, individual and historical, which the narrative sets out to trace in its concentric way.

In many ways, Leon is the most alienated and disoriented figure in the narrative, the most profoundly disconnected. A 'paper son', who paid $5,000 dollars for his passage from China to an 'American' identity, and preoccupied with his failure to return the bones of his sponsor to China, Leon is caught between American time and China time; 'always pushing through another time zone' (25). Trying to fashion a life from the odds and ends of newspapers, official documents, containers, cans and other detritus that he collects, Leon sets up a number of unfinished projects, incomplete inventions between his voyages as a laundryman on numerous Pacific journeys. His is a narrative of loss and incompleteness, symbolised in his 'Going-Back-to-China' fund, a marker of transience, trapped between spaces and times, a creature of endless travelling, living in 'diasporic time'. He never really goes beyond his 'paper history', the counterfeit identity of his moment of arrival; his 'gangster suit' is his only American signifier – outmoded and inappropriate. Suspended between the point of arrival and the point of departure, Leon inhabits Chinatown as a 'transit camp', a way station, and uses his voyages to 'time travel', to move through different zones in order to travel as far as possible from a self he is never able to confront. He is the sum of a history of rejections in America, a life of incompletion both personal and also generational, and collects everything in the vain hope that somewhere, in the sheer volume of material, meaning or identity will reside.

Leon lives, in a sense, the illusion that Leila would like to sustain: 'as if time broke down' (15) when she learns of her sister's death. She knows, however, that then and now cannot be easily severed and, if they all snapped apart, as narrator she has to try to achieve some measure of reparation, to voice the silence left by Ona's death. As translator, forced to deal 'with death in two languages', the only daughter left in San Francisco, she has to navigate, to visit (with its root sense also of 'to see') the spaces of Chinatown and of her family's lives, not in order to find the cause of Ona's death, but to discover the traces and histories of displacement and dispossession of which her suicide is one of many possible consequences. In de Certeau's terms, Leila's narrative is not an unfolding, or an act of recovery, but a practice that 'invents the spaces' she travels through, a makeshift process, composed from the 'fragments of scattered semantic places' (de Certeau in During 1993: 160). Rather than everyone knowing their story, no one, including themselves, actually does; and Leila has to start at a point 'below the thresholds at which visibility begins' (ibid.: 153). She has to both make legible and 'writeable' the 'thicks and thins' of Chinatown, as a reappropriated text. As narrator her task is to weave times and places together, to conjure out of the known spaces, unknown times and histories: texts and textures. In her job, Leila also has to act as a bridge between classroom teacher and parents, to deal with 'life' in two languages, to make time (in several senses of the word) for the recent immigrants, the latest in a history of expropriation and exploitation, for whom 'one job bleeds into another' (16).

At home, at work and in the narrative, Leila has to constantly work with 'the whole translation number', and it is not simply linguistic, but also cultural and emotional. Aware that not everything can be translated, and that some currencies remain inconvertible, Leila is 'broker' but also lost in a world of words that were beyond her. This realisation causes her at times to readily hand over the narrative to her mother's sweatshop 'sewing-lady friends', saying 'Let them make it up', tell 'their long-stitched version of the story' (23). Being of the second generation, Leila does not have access to this 'long-stitched' version but has to 'seam' the 'ellipses, drifts, and leaks of meaning' (de Certeau: 160). Both family and story have been punctured and torn open – the narrative is, on one level, a suturing – but there is always something just outside the frame, beyond narrat- ability. When Mah learns of Nina's abortion, she says to her, 'I have no eyes for you' (25) and there are points in the story where it has 'no eyes', where no 'master narrative' is available.

Mah and Leon, bound in some respects by custom, represent their situation in the terms of a fatalistic or superstitious narrative, but Leila opens up another perspective, interstitial, on what might be called the circumstances of the family's choices in which history, politics and inscriptions of race and gender displace fate, guilt and luck as modes of explanation. Deprived by language and confined by their labour to Chinatown or 'Chinese' functions, Mah and Leon cannot open up meanings and directions, take a long view or transform 'action into legibility' (de Certeau: 158), but are locked into 'functionalist', time-bound identities which cause the condition of their own possibility – the space itself which they inhabit – to be forgotten or never recognised. 'Leon picked up his English from his shipmates . . . the cursing was a replay of how those guys cursed him out' (56). Leaving Chinatown (for two of the daughters, and, periodically, for Leon) or entering its 'deep space' by jumping from the thirteenth floor (lucky in their Chinese dialect, unlucky in American) of a local building, 'a *migrational*, or metaphorical, city thus slips into the clear text of the planned and readable city' (de Certeau: 154).

For Mah and Leon Chinatown is their only planned and readable space, a place of surfaces, static representations, and functions. *Bone* is a 'rereading', not just of Chinatown, but of all that constitutes the migrational in the sense that, for the first generation, Chinatown is a point of arrival, the end of a journey for the immigrant. *Bone* opens up spaces of departure, provides a new momentum which enables the migrant to continue travelling beyond the 'beginning', the point of arrival, and to enter 'America'. It does not do this in any romantic or sentimental way, it does not prescribe or propose a future, but makes accessible 'another spatiality', another form of mobility which turns *inland*, unlike Leon's voyages of 'incomplete return', crossing and recrossing the Pacific. It is, in terms discussed at several points elsewhere, a deterritorialisation of becoming in which the constant repetitions in the text are 'repetitions with a difference' (Nealon 1998: 119), opening up 'alterity' and 'heterogeneity' (at a banal level, rice on a plate and with a fork, chopsticks to hold your hair up). In all senses of the word, it is a mapping process and also an excavation of how 'much memory there was in one word' (30).

As Leila says at one point, family exists only because somebody has a story. *Bone* stories the family into existence, against the grain of realist and formative conventions, and goes beyond the localised instance to connect up with a wider history of humiliation, suffering and dispossession. Leila is anxious for her mother to leave the sweatshops as, 'I'd watched the years of working in the sweatshops change her body . . . Work was her whole life, and every forward stitch marked time passing' (163). By 'walking' Chinatown's spaces, with time sometimes slowed down, sometimes speeded up, Leila comes to know *its* story and develops an understanding of the original migrant experience which makes it more than a compelling or affecting tale: it becomes a *lived* history.

Looking out, I thought, So this is what Chinatown looks like from inside those dark Greyhound buses; this slow view, these strange color combinations, these narrow streets, this is what tourists come to see. I felt a small lightening up inside, because I knew no matter how close they looked, our inside story is something entirely different. (145)

Unlike some of the more 'sociological' migrant narratives which 'tell' histories as background or context, *Bone* 'shows' history by endlessly traversing the spaces of its 'events', the radical singularity of happening. It is a narrative made up of, and by, complex and multiply layered 'inside stories': not always accessible, sometimes refractory and untranslatable. *Bone* is distinguished by this 'thick description', a narrative of singularity yet one also in which 'fields of synecdoche are created' (Clifford 1992: 38); it is not just another migrant narrative, but is in itself, in its very structure, a migrant and disaporic narrative, fluid and wandering, organic and ongoing – a close-up discourse, although Leila is 'too close to see the whole picture' (*Bone*: 135). By analogy, what Ng has produced is a model of textualisation, what Clifford calls a prerequisite to interpretation:

It is the process through which unwritten behaviour, speech, beliefs, oral tradition, and ritual come to be marked as a corpus, a potentially meaningful ensemble separated out from an immediate discursive or performative situation. (Clifford 1992: 38)

In *Bone*, Chinatown is brought into textualisation, is marked as a corpus, potentially meaningful and capable of interpretation. The narrative does not try to close off this interpretative potential but opens it out, even if the characters try to reduce or simplify explanation to a single cause; the right answer is not written anywhere: not everything can be translated. The whole family inhabits the 'immediate' and 'performative' situation; what the narrative 'realises' is that this world cannot be accessed directly (nor can the complexities of the migrant experience), but can only be presumed or inferred from the 'local' instances, so that these have to be 'conceptually and perceptually cut out of the flux of experience' (ibid.). This is why the text deploys a recessive structure, a spiralling process which visits and revisits the same event or episode in flux. By using this form, 'textualisation generates sense through a circular movement that isolates and then contextualises a fact or event in its englobing reality' (ibid.), and, in this way, a dialogical local-global narrative is produced. Chinatown becomes finally a place with both entrances and exits: a space of remembering and forgetting, a site 'to keep them from becoming strangers' (89).

3

This Body is Your Only Real Home: Migrancy and Identity – *Dreaming in Cuban, Native Speaker, Wild Meat and the Bully Burgers* and *My Year of Meat*

This chapter focuses on what John Berger has called the quintessential experience of the twentieth century: migration (1984). It will address both the material reality of migration as well as its extensive cultural use as metaphor in certain contemporary literary forms. The principal texts concentrated upon will be those which resist genre boundaries as well as geopolitical borders, and which involve fundamental changes in modes of narration. All of the narratives have been produced by writers resident in the United States, three of whom were born outside the country.

Since 1945, American imperialism and its associated Cold War activities have led to the deconstruction of existing geopolitical boundaries, to internal crises of coherence and stability, and to the construction of a new social space, at once globalised and local, predicated upon 'migrant identity': a fluid becoming in which there is the possibility of developing citizens of a borderless world in which national boundaries are anomalous. So far, this tendency is mainly evident in the realm of the cultural where border crossing as a concept is not confined to the literal migrant but has also come to refer to the borderline consciousness of already existing inhabitants of a country. In very different ways, American hegemony has been exercised in respect of Korea, Haiti, Cuba (in the form of sanctions), Hawaii (a state since 1959) and, in less obvious ways, Japan. Each of these societies has a presence in the narratives which are examined in this chapter.

It is crucial that the migrant should be able to find space to construct an identity that can accommodate what he or she once was and is now supposed to be: an identity that is somewhere in-between. This is true also for those who now find themselves actively marginalised/minoritised in societies where they have long been settled. A spatialised aesthetic is a characteristic of the narratives which this chapter will address. They are 'borderline' narratives, texts of 'incomplete significa- tion' and hybridity, constituted by in-between spaces in which indistinct and indefinite diasporic identities are negotiated.

Is it possible for identity to be conceived of as a point of arrival or, more hopefully, as a point of departure? Are we prepared to acknowledge that the in-betweenness of migrant identities, in the literal and meta- phorical sense, both calls up, and calls into question, existing referential notions of cultural authenticity and traditional, stable identity? Can the deeply sedimented and codified social definitions of common sense be fractured, opened to their arbitrary nature and a new viewpoint adopted which offers scope to people moving in and out of borders constructed around co-ordinates of difference and power? These cultural fictions help us to reflect on the answers to these questions.

More than here

Cristina Garcia was born in Havana in 1958 and grew up in New York. Her novel *Dreaming in Cuban* was published in 1992. Set in Havana, Brooklyn and Santa Teresa del Mar, time rearranges the borders. The narrative is organised around different times, ranging from 1934 to 1980, and very different temporalities. Describing one of the characters, the narrative says: 'She charts sequences and events with colored pencils, shuffling her diagrams until they start to make sense, a possible narrative' (*Dreaming in Cuban*: 154). The novel as a whole is structured along similar lines, except that it constructs a number of possible narratives in which sequences and events lose their conventional locality and surface in fragments, bits and pieces.

In the last section of the book, 'Lost in Languages', one of the women says to her granddaughter: 'Your grandfather took me to an asylum after your mother was born. I told him all about you. He said it was impossible for me to remember the future' (222). She also says: 'Women who outlive their daughters are orphans, Abuela tells me. Only their granddaughters can save them, guard their knowledge like the first fire' (222). The fractured referential, spatial and temporal structure of the text unprivi- leges the sovereignty of the present, setting up a continua of transforma- tion which enables the 'future to be remembered'. The final page of the text is unnumbered: it is of, but not in, the narrative, and is entitled 'Celia's Letter: 1959'.

January 1, 1959

My dearest Gustavo
The revolution is eleven days old. My granddaughter Pilar Puente del Pino, was

born today. It is also my birthday. I am fifty years old. I will no longer write to you, mi amor. She will remember everything.

My love always,
Celia

Celia's letters to Gustavo Sierra de Armas (a married Spanish lawyer from Granada with whom Celia has a brief, passionate relationship in the early 1930s when he visits Cuba) from 1934 to 1959 are reproduced at various intervals throughout the text. It is the only narrative voice Celia has. She writes him a letter on the eleventh day of each month for twenty-five years, then stores it in a satin-covered chest beneath her bed. Even this voice then is silent, as the letters are written but unsent and, therefore, unread – symptomatic of her gendered repression and of the hidden and secret recesses and interstices of the text. Pilar, her granddaughter, is the narrative epicentre (the ongoing narrative time is 1972 to 1980) and only she, and her generation, have a first person narrative. None of the daughters of the second generation has an 'I' space in the text.

Throughout the text Pilar is in constant conflict with her boundary-loving, simplifying mother, Lourdes, and she shares a communication with her grandmother in dreams and a common disregard for boundaries. Pilar says of her mother:

Mom's embellishments and half-truths usually equip her to tell a good story, though. And her English, her immigrant English, has a touch of otherness that makes it unintentionally precise. Maybe in the end the facts are not as important as the underlying truth she wants to convey. Telling her own truth is the truth to her, even if it's at the expense of chipping away our past. (177–8)

Lourdes systematically rewrites history to suit her views of the world.

The narrative does not rewrite history or restore the past, but engages with gender marginality, exile and memory in the context of pre- and post-revolutionary Cuba, and American constructions of Cuba. Pilar, an anarchic punk artist, remembers her grandmother through the medium of painting on her return to Cuba. She uses the colour blue as a metaphor of the endlessly complex shades, edges and curves of narrativity with which the text works – a series of becomings and emergences which never settle, ceaselessly storying and producing difference in ways which take each figure beyond her/himself, in a process of revising, reconstructing and exceeding:

Mostly, though, I paint her in blue. Until I returned to Cuba, I never realised how many blues exist. The aquamarines near the shoreline, the azures of deeper waters, the eggshell blues beneath my grandmother's eyes, the fragile indigos tracking her hands. There's a blue, too, in the curves of the palms, and the edges of the words we speak, a blue tinge to the sand and the seashells and the plump

gulls on the beach. The mole by Abuela's mouth is also blue, a vanishing blue.
(233)

Blue becomes the colour of the secret, the hidden, and the unspoken/
unspeaking, but, above all, the under-represented and the unrepresented.
The characters share the same spaces differentially – Pilar's mother lives
the exile's American dream, while she dreams in Cuban (a cultural
experience rendered as a language) and eventually in Spanish. The
family's Catholicism is punctuated with other, forbidden spiritualities,
especially West African practices hybridised/creolised in their translation to, and beyond, slavery. Ellegua, god of the crossroads, is one of
many chiasmic, borderline figures which exist in the text; denizens of the
in-between spaces. Pilar's grandmother and her aunt, Felicia, both
experience periods of 'madness', and are asylumed. Felicia, violently
abused, syphilitic and subject to delusions is a 'social misfit' (she is
placed in a training camp to reconstruct her for the revolution, but in a
bizarre parody of desire ends up by masturbating to an image of Fidel
Castro). She is a dislocated figure in every sense; for her, colours escape
their objects, sounds distort and 'something is wrong with her tongue. It
forms broken trails of words, words sealed and resistant as stones' (83).

Of the first generation in the narrative, Pilar's grandfather dies in
America, separated from his wife and hostile to the revolution; Celia, her
grandmother, writes her letters, dreams her dreams, and equipped with
binoculars, a member of the People's Court, guards the Cuban revolution
throughout. Finally, she chooses suicide and enters the tides which
rearrange the borders throughout the narrative – a tidal figure throughout. Her children 'Lourdes and Felicia and Javier are middle-aged now
and desolate, deaf and blind to the world, to each other, to her. There is
no solace among them, only a past infected with disillusion' (117). Pilar's
mother, Lourdes, is a keeper of the binaries; she has no patience for
dreams or for people who live between black and white (the condition of
many Cubans, of course). For her, everything is either black or white,
America or Cuba, fat or thin (she gains and then loses more than a
hundred pounds in weight), over-sexed or celibate. She even becomes an
auxiliary cop, thus policing her 'dreams' in her hyphenated, hybridised
exile neighbourhood; she is also indirectly responsible for the death of
one mulatto child. She abhors ambiguity.

Her disoriented sister Felicia, clinging to her son and the repeated
playing of old sentimental music, alienated from her husband and twin
daughters, is close to the experience of the narrative as a whole: 'Felicia's
mind floods with thoughts, thoughts from the past, thoughts from the
future, other people's thoughts. Things came back as symbols, bits of
conversation, a snatch of an old church hymn' (76). As her syphilis
worsens and her delusions increase, she converts to the Cubanised

African religion and finds some meanings, before dying in her mother's arms.

Pilar shuttles across frontiers – literal and metaphorical – defies her mother's simplifications, and experiences America and Cuba in a relationship of fluidity: 'I think migration scrambles the appetite', Pilar says, helping herself to a candied yam. 'I may move back to Cuba someday and decide to eat nothing but codfish and chocolate' (173). She has the flexibility and mobility denied to the first-generation migrants who are localised and bounded, neither Cuban nor American, only broken versions of both.

This brings to mind two other hyphenated artists. Tomas Ybarra Frausto (Chicano) uses the term *rasquachismo*: 'the utilisation of available resources for syncretism, juxtaposition, and integration. *Rasquachismo* is a sensibility attuned to mixtures and confluence . . . the manipulation of *rasquache* artefacts, code and sensibilities from both sides of the border' (Bhabha 1994: 7).

This code-switching is also a feature of Gloria Anzaldúa's writing and can be linked to the kind of cultural translation and in-betweenness described by another Chicano writer, Guillermo Gómez-Peña:

The new society is characterised by mass migrations and bizarre inter-racial relations. As a result, new hybrid and transitional identities are emerging . . . The bankrupt notion of the melting pot has been replaced by a model that is more germane to the times, that of the *menudo chowder*. According to this model, most of the ingredients do melt, but some stubborn chunks are condemned merely to float. (quoted in Bhabha 1994: 218)

In the melting pot, nothing is incommensurable. In our contemporary situation, the 'stubborn chunks' are the basis of cultural identifications, trans- and post-national as well as hybrid.

At one point in *Dreaming in Cuban*, Pilar says: 'Cuba is a peculiar exile, I think, an island-colony. We can reach it by a thirty-minute charter flight from Miami, yet may never reach it at all' (219). Speaking of her mother, she says: ' The language she speaks is lost to them [the Cubans she is hectoring on her return to Havana]. It's another idiom' (221). She is not speaking of language literally – it *is* Spanish, but of the untranslatable cultural–ideological idiom; one of many lost languages in the text. We read Celia's letters to Don Gustavo in English, but they were written in Spanish, and remain unread in that language, or any other.

Back in Cuba on a visit, Pilar says:

I've started dreaming in Spanish, which has never happened before. I wake up feeling different, like something inside me is changing, something chemical and irreversible. There's a magic here working its way through my veins . . . And I love Havana, its noise and decay and painted ladyness. I could happily sit on one

of those wrought iron balconies for days, or keep my grandmother company on
her porch, with its ringside view of the sea. (235–6)

Thus far, we have a narrative of return and discovery, the finding of the
originary roots in 'authenticity'; a trope of nostalgia. However, the text
moves from a myth of return to a discourse of borderline and emergence –
a hybridised trope, a hyphenated becoming:

I'm afraid to lose all this, to lose Abuela Celia again. But sooner or later I'd have
to return to New York. I know now it's where I belong [and in a telling statement]
– not *instead* of here, but *more* than here. How can I tell my grandmother this?
(236)

It is this moment which is also part of the remembered future of
grandmother and granddaughter: 'For many years, Celia spoke to Pilar
during the darkest part of the night, but then their connection
suddenly died. Celia understands now that a cycle between them
had ended, and a new one had not yet begun' (119). It begins again
with the painting.

This 'not instead of, but more than' sums up much of what I have been
trying to articulate throughout this book. It is the insider/outsider
perspective, the hyphenated/hybridised voice, reflecting nostalgically
on a permanent return, but recognising that 'translation passes through
continua of transformation, not abstract ideas of identity and similarity'.
It is in the terms of these abstract ideas that, initially in the text, the
teenage artist-punk rebel in New York claims an 'other' identity.

In her cultural passage, here and there, as daughter of migrant, self-
chosen exiled workers, part of the economic and political diaspora of the
contemporary world, she embodies the complex, fractured present; what
Benjamin called that moment blasted out of the continuum of history. The
only continuum in the text – Celia's letters, 1935 to 1959 (even here there
is a one-year lacuna in 1941) – are hidden, secret, unsent, traversed by the
continua of transformation. Hence the use of episodic, dislocating time in
the narrative; the formlessness of transformation. Pilar negotiates the
powers of cultural difference across transcultural and transhistorical
sites – she is a figure of the boundary.

The narrative is an extended process of remembering of the nomadic
and diasporic – the literal and the mental travellers: 'Pilar writes in a
Spanish that is no longer hers. She speaks the hard edged lexicon of
bygone tourists itchy to throw dice on green felt or asphalt' (7). It is the
language of her parents, an alien, pre-revolutionary, capitalist playground Spanish. Her cousin Ivanito, living in Cuba, starts to learn
English from a 1919 grammar book belonging to his grandfather, but
he soon moves on to a 'new' culturally different English of American
radio broadcasts and advertising. Pilar, however, keeps a diary in the

lining of her winter coat, hidden from her mother's scouring eyes. In it, she records everything. Grandmother and granddaughter, as we have seen, communicate with each other in their imaginations (neither sees the other for years). Celia lives in a synchrony of memory, dream and daydream, writing her unsent letters, reading and reciting the gypsy ballad poems of Lorca. She is forced to live her desire at a distance. After her breakdown, she overhears the doctors telling her husband to 'keep her away from Debussy'. They feared that the Frenchman's restless style might compel to rashness, but Celia hid her music to '*La Soirée dans Granade*' and played it incessantly while Jorge travelled. She remains an exemplary revolutionary cadre, seeing pre-revolutionary Cuba as a parody of a country, but lives affectively through a Spanish filter of passion and romance. Every one of her children breaks down or breaks up. Felicia I have discussed; Lourdes miscarries after being raped and brutalised by a revolutionary soldier, and lives out in Brooklyn a caricature of 'the new world order'. Javier, Celia's son, moved to Czechoslovakia, marries a Czech, and has a baby girl; Celia wonders how she will speak to this granddaughter, how she will be able to show her ways to catch crickets and avoid the beak of the tortoise. She wants to teach the child the morphology of survival, but Javier's wife leaves him, taking her daughter, and he returns to Cuba broken and silenced.

For Celia, her past is eclipsing her present, which is why Pilar's remembering is so critical: 'That night Celia sleeps restlessly. Voices call to her in ragged words stitched together from many languages, like dissonant scraps of quilt' (95). In one of her letters she says: 'I've made a friend here, [in the asylum] Felicia Gutierrez. She killed her husband. Doused him with gasoline. Lit a match. She is unrepentant. We're planning to escape' (51).

She does not escape – none of the women of the first two generations do. However, no figuration in the narrative is finally stable or settled – even Lourdes breaks with the Cuban woman's designated role; she adapts to the US and works for a living: 'Immigration has re-defined her, and she is grateful. Unlike her husband, [who could not be transplanted] she welcomes her adopted language, its possibilities for re-invention' (73). What is textualised is the interstitial lives of women who, publicly for the most part, remain passive and subordinated, at the side of their own lives: caught in between but in different ways (Celia's cadre role; Felicia's 'African' religion; Lourdes's ownership of the bakery) finding possibilities for reinvention.

Celia's epistolary discourse is, mostly, plaintive, limpid, rhythmically 'interior'. Pilar's 'I' narrative is Americanised, with a very different register and rhythm, lexis and reference. She says, however: 'Painting is its own language, I wanted to tell him [a psychiatrist she is referred to by her school]. Translations just confuse it, dilute it, like words going

from Spanish to English. I envy my mother her Spanish curses sometimes. They make my English collapse in a heap.'

In one of her letters (11 May 1945) Celia says:

If I was born to live on an island, then I'm grateful for one thing: that the tides
rearrange the borders. At least I have the illusion of change, of possibility. To be
locked within boundaries plotted by priests and politicians would be the only
thing more intolerable. Don't you see how they are carving up the world,
Gustavo? How they're stealing our geography? Our fates? The arbitrary is no
longer in our hands. To survive is an act of hope. (99)

The transcultural and transnational narratives, texts of cultural translation, do not so much restore geography and the arbitrary, but, rather,
open up again their conditions of possibility, a release, especially through
women's writing, from the 'locked within boundaries' of patriarchal
hegemony – not by simple reversals, but through the emergence texts
of the third scenario; the indeterminacy of diasporic identities, the
production of difference as the political and social definition of the
historical present, the contemporary. *Dreaming in Cuban* charts the time
of cultural and historical displacement and the space of the, ultimately,
untranslatable – the borderline negotiations I have referred to throughout.

Pilar says: 'I feel like a new me sprouts and dies every day' which leads
me to conclude this section with a quotation from Fanon whose writings
made the post-colonial perspective possible: 'In the world through which
I travel, I am endlessly creating myself . . . And it is by going beyond the
historical, instrumental hypothesis that I will initiate my cycle of freedom' (1986: 229–31).

REAL AND PERMANENT NAME

The negotiation of complex spaces and multiple codes and languages is a
staple condition of much migrant experience, and all three women in
Edwidge Danticat's 'Caroline's Wedding' (of Haitian origin but resident
in Brooklyn, New York) daily encounter the conflicting structures of
exilic living. Although the youngest woman, Caroline, was born in New
York, she, her sister Grace/Gracina, and their mother, all inhabit the
boundaries of split identities in differing ways. This is most evident at
the level of what Lotman calls: 'self-description [which] implies a first
person pronoun' (1991: 131). Lotman argues that one of the primary
mechanisms of 'semiotic individuation' is the boundary which he defines
as the outer limit of a first-person form. For the mother, her first-person
form is marked by everything Haitian, even though she has lived in the
US for twenty-five years, or, more accurately perhaps, a 'Haiti of the
mind' which she has carried with her in increasingly rigidified form.

Grace, the narrator, recovers her 'real and permanent name', Gracina Azile, when she finally qualifies for an American passport after being 'naturalised'. Both passport and naturalisation certificate have metaphorical value, both a confirmation of, and interference with, 'semiotic individuation'. Caroline's wedding has a similar function. As the narrator says, 'I couldn't help but feel as though she was divorcing us, trading in her old allegiances for a new one' ('Caroline's Wedding': 680).

Trading, negotiating, divorcing all involve a form of dialogue at the boundary, and they are the organising characteristics of the story. Lotman, in the work cited above, describes the way in which every culture divides the world into 'its own' internal space and 'their ' external space. The mother in 'Caroline's Wedding' does not speak for a culture as such, but represents a first-generation migrant tendency to set such a binary division which the daughters, and ultimately she, have to negotiate in the context of their conflicting 'takes' on difference. Initially, the mother can be seen to be shaping the narrative, although not the narrator, in the sense that the boundaries of 'our' internal space are secure, organised and logical, whereas 'their' external space is enemy territory. Gracina uses this binary discourse on a number of occasions. When she emerges from the courthouse with her naturalisation certificate, she wanted to wave 'the paper like the head of an enemy rightfully conquered in battle' (651); when she receives her passport, for the first time in her life she felt truly secure living in America: 'It was like being in a war zone and finally receiving a weapon of my own, like standing on the firing line and finally getting a bullet-proof vest' (685).

This martial imagery is not gratuitous, nor is it necessarily the currency of all migrant experience, but stems from the material and symbolic domination of white America which marginalises its poor, black, immigrant labour. Gracina may think she has the 'head of the enemy' conquered in battle, but gaining a passport does not mean that she has become 'the enemy' (a condition of colour); she has simply shifted her position in the war zone and on the firing line of American racialised politics. Becoming American is more than a courthouse process. 'Their space' remains hostile – witness her mother's years of sweated labour, arrests by immigration authorities and loss of spirit. Even Caroline, 'our child of the promised land', 'our New York child', who has never known Haiti, is limited to teaching English as a Second Language to Haitian students in an Intermediate School (named after Jackie Robinson, another victim of American racism). Both Caroline and Gracina, who also teaches in the same school, are enclosed in an essentialist 'ethnic' circle, enabling though their role may be within this boundary. They are both American, but without access to the ethnocentric hegemony of the dominant culture or economy.

Caroline's wedding takes place in the same courthouse from which

Gracina emerged with her naturalisation certificate, and as a space of legitimation it operates in the story as a site both of transition and transformation, but not of simple transcendence as the Brooklyn Haitian district remains a conflicted hybrid area. The wedding is the catalyst which brings into focus many of the family's unspoken tensions and anxieties. The fact that Caroline is marrying a Bahamian-American is a source of discontent for her mother as 'No one in our family has ever married outside' (654), and she sees the marriage as yet another stage in the erosion of her secure, Haitian internal space, and an act of transgression. She serves up bone soup on a daily basis to try to 'magic' Caroline away from her fiancé, Eric Abrahams. The narrative does not simply represent Caroline's decision as a progressive action and her mother's response as first-generation reactionary. The mother had spent three days in an immigration jail when she was pregnant with Caroline and had been given an injection to quieten her down. She attributed the fact that Caroline was born without a left forearm to this shot, so she has surrounded herself with the protective armoury of her creole language and cuisine, customs and culture, and even the old suitcases brought from Haiti so many years ago. All of these constitute her 'first-person form', the ballast of semiotic individuation against 'invasion'. They have a prosthetic function (like the arm Caroline fits for her wedding) as she feels her life in America is an amputation. Her 'lost' belonging is compounded by the Mass which she and Gracina attend for a drowned refugee woman and her infant child. This incident, together with the priest's recital of the names of 129 Haitian refugees drowned at sea that week, helps to contextualise the mother's anxiety and insecurity. The promised land has been a place of pain, loss and exploitation: 'In New York, women give their eight hours to the white man' (656). Ethnicity becomes more than a reactionary essentialism; it is a strategy for survival, managing to live the present, with its roots in slave memory (the drownings at sea also bear traces of this). 'Ma says all Haitians know each other', Gracina responds when Caroline wonders why her mother is so upset by the Mass as she doesn't know the people concerned. For the mother (whose first name we never know) refugeeness is a permanent condition, as her internal space is also and always a refuge which is why 'she wanted Eric to be Haitian' (658); she is unable to leave any space for the other.

Separated in some ways from the mother's experience – a kind of prolonged mourning – the sisters are able to create space for the other, including the 'other' that is their mother and her 'country of memory'. The narrative itself becomes an act of reparation, a set of founding metaphors in the sense developed by Hélène Cixous when she speaks of writing as discovery:

Originally, the gesture of writing is linked to the experience of disappearance, to the feeling of having lost the key to the world, of having been thrown outside. Of now having to acquire the precious sense of the rare, of the mortal. Of having to find again, urgently, the entry, the breath, to keep the trace. (Cixous 1988: 131)

The mother embodies this feeling of being thrown outside (of her self), a feeling heightened by the fact that, in order to escape the misery of their shantytown existence in Port-au-Prince, her husband had to take vows in a false marriage with a widow leaving for the United States. Later he divorced and sent for his wife and the child, Gracina, but the pain suffered weakened the marriage. Gracina is the bridging narrator between her mother, her father (dead for more than ten years but a constant, almost sexual presence in both daughters' dreams) and Caroline. She is the keeper of the family stories, and it is her role to 'story' the present, to find again 'the entry', 'the breath', 'the trace', to enable the family to achieve a forward, future-oriented momentum, a new dynamic. 'Caroline's Wedding' is very much an entry, a becoming, narrative, in which Caroline breaks the 'spell' of both mother and father but does not entirely 'forget herself', despite her 'chemically straightened and streaked bright copper ' hair; nor does the mother remain intransigent, buying Caroline a black and gold silk teddy with a plunging neckline as a shower present, a very un-Haitian gift.

Eric, with his learning disability, and Caroline, with her missing fore-arm, come together as the embodiment, ethnically and physically, of a new set of possibilities. Caroline's decision to wear a false arm (which the mother says does not look very real) just for the day is perhaps symbolic of a need to signify 'completeness', to overcome the 'phantom limb pain' which could be associated with her severance from her mother's 'Haiti', a form of amputation. Like the chemically straightened and streaked bright copper hair it is artificial but it enables her to reach out, literally and metaphori-cally, to an American future while welcoming her mother as a guest in her house. Ceasing to be just daughter, ceasing to be just sister, she is taking another step on the journey begun by her parents (the wedding lunch is at a Haitian bistro). As in the Haitian song, 'Beloved Haiti, there is no place like you, I had to leave you before I could understand you' (684), Caroline has to embark on a process of departure in order to understand. Gracina is still in thrall to both her mother and her father, 'owned' by both of them, one in the everyday, one in dreams. Caroline's wedding gives Gracina a new per-spective, helped by the new passport, and she has a dream in which, rather than desiring, she comes to fear her father. A visit to his burial place in Queens confirms this point of departure; symbolically, she reinters him and is able to answer the question asked by him, and her mother:

Why is it that when you lose something, it is always in the last place that you look for it? she asked finally.

Because, of course, once you remember, you always stop looking. (686)

'Caroline's Wedding' is a narrative of loss, search, memory, and discovery. It is simultaneously a narrative of arrival and departure, a tracing of the migrant trajectory, ways of 'managing to live the present' (Cixous 1988: 131), of living in America. The complexity of the narrative voice means that the characters 'can become the place of the other's inscription' (ibid.: 133), split, disrupted, figures of 'interference' (bearing across, or bearing between). From a position of initial stasis, shifts and slidings have taken place, and the text has helped the women to remember, to chart their radical singularity against the threat of obliteration and erasure, of simply 'being Haitian' or 'being American' with their respective generalisations. In Cixous' terms, the narrative is an act of translation, of transferring or carrying across, a bridgehead, making a 'journey through the other's imaginary' (ibid.: 146), rather than trying to reduce it to sameness. Plural selves are created.

Cixous speaks of this act of translation in a way which helps to situate 'Caroline's Wedding' as precisely this journey, a migration even, into the other's imaginary:

For you are strange to me. In the effort to understand, I bring you back to me, compare you to me. I translate you in me. And what I note is your difference, your strangeness. At that moment, perhaps, through recognition of my own differences, I might perceive something of you. (ibid.: 146)

Caroline takes her mother for granted, Gracina takes herself for granted, and the mother sees them both in terms of ownership: 'In Haiti, you own your children and they find it natural' (686). As the narrative develops, each one translates the other in themselves, and in the process note their difference, their strangeness, inscribes in them a second-person pronoun belonging, a voyage beyond the boundary of self to that other's space, their singularity. It is a ritual crossing, an act of recognition. At the wedding, there is no best man and no one gives Caroline away; it is a moment of choice, both of semiotic individuation and of 'coupling', identity and alterity, a 'graduation' ceremony: reconfiguration and transformation. At a number of levels, the narrative explores displacement and re-creation, reinvention. It would be simplistic and sentimental to conclude by suggesting that Caroline and Eric occupy that 'third space', of which Bhabha, Hall and others speak, but the whole narrative, in a sense, inhabits that space, as a space of *possibility*, not something achieved, an opening up of the ' "deterritorialising" power of becoming' (Nealon 1998: 119). The unnamed mother, Grace becoming Gracina, and Caroline Azile taking her husband's name, Abrahams, all point to those

fluid practices by which identity moves across certain positions and manouvres around given borders ... in order to draw attention to productivity that is

generated by the existence of a third space between a name and its alternate.
(Papastergiadis 1995: 17)

BUILDING HOMEMADE SIGHT

The ethnic and cultural composition of Hawaii consists of Caucasians
(*haoles*) who make up 24 per cent of the population, Japanese (22 per
cent) and Filipinos (15 per cent). Chinese, Koreans, Blacks, Samoans,
Vietnamese, Laotians and indigenous Hawaiians (less than 1 per cent)
comprise the rest. Many of the population are bi-racial – part-Hawaiian –
and Kathleen Tyau's *A Little Too Much is Enough* (1995) takes its
bearings from the symbolic domination of *haole* values, and the split
between the Chinese and Hawaiian cultures experienced by her central
character, Mahealani Suzanne Wong (Mahi): 'We were Chinese, but
Hawaiian – and now Americans, able to vote – and many of us could
not read or speak Chinese of any dialect' (Tyau 1996: 49).

   The novel uses a number of interwoven narrative voices, but mostly
those of Mahi and her mother. From the very outset, the mother projects
her daughter towards *haole* culture and the mainland. She wanted her to
have an American first name – Suzanne – as *haoles* 'can't say Mahealani'.
She also sees her daughter as 'mostly Chinese' living in a place which is
not just Hawaii any more: 'This is America' (4). Physiologically the child,
Mahi, is 'mixed' (with her 'daddy's Hawaiian lips') but none of her
movements rhyme with the local demands of story, dance or song.
Her brother, Benjie, tries to develop a 'pointy *haole* nose' while she
exercises to reduce the size of her lips. Food is a constant source of ethnic
and cultural crossover, as well as also being a marker of the 'pure' at
times – Hawaiian *poi* or Chinese rice. One of the early chapters, 'Poi
Knuckles, Rice Feet' characterises Mahi entirely in terms of her rice
mouth, poi knuckles, rice hands and feet, and poi brain.

   Mahi's paternal grandmother is Hawaiian, her grandfather Chinese.
Her father was 'shanghaied' to China as a child. The narrative does not
develop in a linear, forward-moving fashion but shapes a layered set of
'histories' from a source in the present, with Mahi's family a repository of
complex intersections and movement, spatial and temporal. Through
ceremony and story, the adult Mahi pieces together memories, not simply
in order to retrieve the past but also to establish her own identity: 'new
blood, not the kind we had before we were born but the kind that belongs
to only us' (22).

   Identity is a confluence, not a simple matter of subjectivity. This is why
the subject of each chapter changes, and sometimes within a chapter
there are shifts of voice. This multi-accentuality is heightened by the
narrative strategy of including apparently 'subjectless' chapters, for

example, 'Still the Same Saimin', where a series of imperatives and instructions shape the direction of the second person as she moves through a range of social and cultural spaces – fair, movies, restaurant, beach. This shows how belonging is not just individual but communal and cross-cultural, something which is emphasised by the range of 'uncles' who work for the military (one of the largest employers of labour in Hawaii) and are 'whole or part Chinese, Japanese, Portuguese, Hawaiian' (30).

The main frame of the narrative is constructed from the mainland, where Mahi is at college in Oregon, and the addressee of each narrative voice is the distanced young woman, a series of set pieces: events, recipes, manuals. Through these cameos a whole range of social and cultural snapshots emerge, markers of ethnic and class stratification –the family's relief that a cousin is marrying a Chinese girl who is also wealthy; not using pidgin (the narrative uses a double language); the scale of a wedding banquet; having mainland relatives and friends. Each event exceeds its function in order to signify status, ethnic 'purity' and difference. There is a defensiveness, a feeling of secondariness, about an island belonging: 'A cousin and his wife from LA on their honeymoon. Nobody could figure out why they came here when they lived next door to Disneyland, where Beetle and Tesna were going for their honeymoon' (48).

At several points in the narrative, reference is made to the ethnic and cultural mix of Hawaii, in particular the chapter 'Hapa Haole Girl' which focuses on Annabel – half Chinese, half Irish. Despite being hapa haole (half Caucasian), Annabel is fated by her illegitimacy to perpetual 'in betweenness', and not only in the ethnic sense. Her mother will never get to live in her Chinese lover's house at Diamond Head, nor will she inherit the family restaurant at Kaimuki. Mahi has a haole boy friend at one time, Tommy: 'pure haole, the American kind, all mixed up' (60). Often the term pure is used ironically, as on this occasion, and ethnicity is a mask for what are really power relationships based upon the material and symbolic domination of European values. One of the uncles, Wing, raised as Chinese, is actually Japanese. Annabel may be cute but her mother's status – as mistress – and gender invalidate her haole ethnicity and marginalise both her and her daughter in a heavily stratified society. Tellingly, Mahi sees Tommy, in keeping with the primary metaphors of the narrative, as 'just part of a recipe I'm cooking. I want to be hapa haole, like Annabel. I want her lips, her hair, her eyes. I want to be Annabel but not her mother' (63). An adolescent fantasy, logically and biologically impossible, but culturally understandable given the normative presence in the islands of white bodies, white power. The Hawaii that emerges is a long way from the tourist fantasy of the exotic and the paradisal. For Lucy, Mahi's aunt, the ties of family, obligation, and island living left her anostalgic, embarking on a 'long journey away from home'.

The chapter 'Pouring Tea' (immediately following the sentence 'a long journey away from home') reroutes and reroots Mahi, as she watches her newly married female cousin embody, in all senses, gendered custom and obedience – 'Chinese style' – as she pours tea, kneels and bows in accordance with her mother's silent instructions. Coaching from the sidelines, so to speak, Mahi's mother guides and comments on the custom, the fragile body of the china designed to be passed from daughter to daughter in a relay of patriarchal obligations. There are frequent references in the text to the secondary status of women – 'Chinese style'.

While on leave from college in Oregon Mahi starts to date a local *haole*, Roger (Rascal) Lang, but her parents confine their meetings to one night a week. She is jealous of the *haole* and *hapa haole* women she imagines he could have, and longs for more 'exotic' blood, Portuguese perhaps, and not just Chinese-Hawaiian. Her aunt, Nona, is rumoured to have 'Pohtagee' blood and Mahi wants to be different like her – 'I wanted her to belong', so that all the family might claim a similar heritage. In Oregon, Chinese-Hawaiian was exotic but not in Hawaii – this is her dilemma. The family resist him, not because he is *haole*, but because he is not Chinese and not born in the islands. The family attitude helps to crystallise a whole set of feelings:

What amazed me most about the mainland was the realization that I could go for so many miles in one direction before arriving back at home. My choices seemed infinite. Yet my parents kept pulling me back to the finite, back to their narrow, island way of thinking. (208)

It is in the latter stages of the narrative that this contradiction takes its strongest hold, although it is there throughout. It is almost a commonplace of hybrid cultural fictions: locational, generational and gender conflicts partly produced by education, partly generated by displacement. The 'narrow, island way of thinking' is, in some ways, a generation's defence against change – Pearl Harbor, statehood, Americanisation – and also a means of surviving in a profoundly unequal society, manifested at one level by Rascal's house. Mahi's mother had been to Business School in San Francisco but had returned home to Hawaii, the response of a dutiful Chinese daughter to her father's bidding. From the very beginning, however, she had wanted an American name for her daughter and had planned on her going to the mainland. Her mother tells Mahi that it is just as well that there are not so many island people in Oregon, as it is:

Better if you can get away from so many people telling you what to do. Then you can hear yourself talk. You can hear yourself think. (224)

It is this independence lost to her (she longs for a place 'where all I have to do is what Anna wants') that Anna wants for her daughter, advising her not to 'shack up with a man' and that, for her generation, it's acceptable for a girl to be smart. Deeply aware of the limitations of home, she is setting her daughter free: 'you can come home anytime'. Her grandparents, of a migrant generation, left home never to return, never seeing family again. For the 'global' generation this is no longer necessarily true, although many political migrants may never return home, of course. For Mahi, leaving Hawaii is not because it is, in itself, negative or inferior but because she needs to journey away from the confined gender spaces of a particular cultural tradition, in order to make a new beginning.

Mahi and Rascal consult a couple of 'expert' newspaper columnists about inter-racial dating and inter-racial marriage, and resist her parents' prejudice and double standards. There is a sense in which Mahi's relationship with Rascal is less to do with him than with marking out a territory not dominated by her parents. Inspired by her Aunt Nona, who 'needed space . . . and had a way of making things hers', she comes to realise this and, by refusing to go to Maui with Rascal, effectively ends their relationship. The penultimate chapter, 'Makai', extends the territorial metaphor and summarises the ways in which the whole narrative has been about finding out 'where you wanted to go and how to come back home' (218). Mahi learns how to go *mauka*, towards the mountains in the middle of the island, and how to go *makai*, toward the ocean lying all around. The narrative is a mapping of the various geographies of home, the dialectic of island *mauka* and ocean *makai*. As a child Mahi has an old and torn map on which, as she grows, she metaphorically fills in the gaps, repairing the torn sections, until eventually *mauka* is not enough; she needs both island and ocean, whereas for most of her mother's generation (the females at least) the island marks their limits. Mahi is freed to choose her own *mauka*, another becoming, having emerged into awareness of the cultural ties that no longer bind but bond.

In some ways, Kathleen Tyau, in company with a range of other island- or mainland- based Hawaiian writers, has sought to redefine a complex set of cultures against the grain of 100 years of colonisation by the United States in which, according to Mindy Pennybacker, 'we locals bought the processed vision of ourselves imported from the mainland' (1997: 33). As with many other writers discussed elsewhere in this book, comedy is often used as a means of articulating conflict, contradiction and intercultural, cross-generational difference. The Honolulu-based, Japanese-Hawaiian writer Lois-Ann Yamanaka uses Hawaii's pidgin dialect extensively in her novel *Wild Meat and The Bully Burgers* (1996), a loosely connected series of stories held together by the figure of Lovey Nariyoshi, on the threshold of adolescence. Irreverent and outrageous, yet poor and

marginalised, Lovey's experiences throw into relief the tensions, prejudices and insecurities of her family and of her peers. Yamanaka uses
stereotypes and caricatures in order to reflect the narrow, sectional and
sometimes racist ways of seeing of her characters. Above all, the
narrative places critically the 'processed vision' of non-*haole* Hawaiians
mentioned above. Lovey's schooling is shaped by Standard English and
she is shamed by her own and her parents' use of 'pidgin' English, as well
as by their food, ramshackle car and impoverished housing. Very much a
'coming of age' novel, a rite of passage, it is about more than the
'becoming' of a single figure, as it is also concerned with giving shape
to ways of seeing which decolonise local culture. For most of the
narrative, Lovey draws her values from, and secretly wishes to be, *haole*
– to look, eat, and talk 'white'. Nevertheless she and her peers value
above all a *hapa* boyfriend, part Hawaiian, part Japanese; perhaps
because there are no *haole* boys in the school. Overweight, unpopular
and bullied at school, Lovey fantasises about the white world but 'my
words will always come out like home' (Yamanaka 1996: 13).

Valuing, and revaluing, home in all the complex senses of the word
motivates the narrative and shapes its concern with rendering symbolically central what is economically and socially marginal. That the
symbolic value of home exceeds its 'empirical' function is shown in
the latter stages of the novel when Lovey runs away from home and takes
a plane to Kaua'i where she visits the plantation estate at Kipu where her
father, now blinded, lived. Her intention is to collect dirt and stones from
this place to take to her father, as he had said to her that he wanted soil
from Kipu to be poured over him when he dies. Refused access to the
plantation, she snatches dirt from the side of the road and, returning
home, mixes it with soil from their own home, so that he can be in two
places at the same time: 'He tells me across the night, "I be home"' (278).

This simultaneity, or bi-location, extends beyond home to the uses of
language (pidgin and Standard English), as well as to values and beliefs.
As well as 'colonising' her language, the school also has another teacher
who, in missionary fashion, tries to convert Lovey and her friend Jerome
to the Jehovah's Witnesses. In micro form, the linguistic and religious
conversions, and the father's plantation childhood, echo the larger
history of Hawaii – the exploitation of indentured labour, the symbolic
domination of white hegemony which banned Hawaiian languages, and
missionary activity which suppressed all manifestations of local culture.
At a metaphorical level, Lovey's journey to Kipu is designed to provide
her father with surrogate, second-hand eyes and, in a telling phrase
which resonates throughout this narrative and also links with Tyau's, to
build 'homemade sight' (271). It is this homemade sight which is at the
root of the novel's decolonising project, taking apart the 'processed
vision' which has also contributed to the suicide of the sixteen-year-

old Crystal, Lovey's 'idol', who is taken by her mother to Japan for an abortion, away from local gossip and local shame.

The chapter called 'The Crossing' marks a turning point in the novel and converts it from a loosely structured and episodic series of anecdotes and stories, into a narrative which locates and focuses Lovey's poverty and marginal island status, giving it a context and a history which takes it beyond the immediate family or issues of individual pathology. It is a ritual crossing in which father hands to daughter through 'talking story' a memory linking her with her grandfather who came from Japan as an indentured labourer in the sugar fields in 1907, worked all his life on the plantation for meagre wages, was severely disabled by an industrial accident, and died of a heart attack in the fields. He never returned to Japan, nor even spoke of it, but carried with him a package of Japanese soil to be buried in: 'That was his way of going home' (176). The chapter, like the soil, is a model of anamnesis, 'a *figure* for consciousness and its attempts at representing itself historically' (Readings 1991: xxxii), a symbol of singularity, or 'a caesura in space-time'. After the crossing nothing will ever be the same again, and the referential frame up to this point in the narrative is disrupted and relocated/redirected. Lovey gains perspective and sets up a distance from the 'hassles' of her immediate school and peer culture. For all their looks, clothing, style and pretensions, most of the children in her school, she comes to realise, share the same history, although, when she is mocked by the others, her responses all come too late and when she is on her own, except for a lame 'Oh yeah?'

Yamanaka's work has been a subject of controversy in the last three years, but her work is textured with the once outlawed, silenced Hawaiian Creole English (pidgin; her 'first language'), and she finds voices which enable 'the local . . . to be worried into existence' (Wilson 1994: 38) and, like Tyau, creates identities which 'bond to place' (hence the soil metaphors), but are not simply place-bound. For Yamanaka, the mainland is not even a presence in *Wild Meat*, and the localised uses of language, custom and land can be read symptomatically, as metaphors of a wider cultural struggle for space, image and identity. Like the son in Juliet Kono Lee's 'Yonsei', her figures are 'mired into this locality'.

THE FAINTEST ECHO OF OUR LANGUAGE

What is lost in translation, unrepresentability or 'the resistant or irreconcilable trace of a space or a time that is radically incommensurable with that of discursive meaning' (Readings 1991: xxxi), is also at the heart of Chang-Rae Lee's *Native Speaker* (1995). Unlike many of the fictions of the so-called ethnic genre, *Native Speaker* is not autobiographical, in an explicit sense, but it does use a first-person narrator. It has been called, quite aptly, 'a cross-cultural spy story' (*Vanity Fair*), and it also draws upon certain features of the detective genre. If it is a spy story – and as Henry Park the narrator works undercover in New York it obviously is at one level – then the ultimate object of surveillance is the narrator himself.

Chang-Rae Lee was born in South Korea in 1965 and emigrated to the United States at the age of three. In an essay, 'The faintest echo of our language', published in *Under Western Eyes* (Hongo 1995), he writes of the death of his mother. His mother was of the generation in Korea that carried the traces of Japanese colonialism (her name was Japanese in style and origin), saw their language and history erased and criminalised, and slave labour introduced. The essay simultaneously addresses the loss of his mother and also of his losing his Korean language, a process unconsciously helped by his mother urging him to learn English and be 'a true American'. It is a common migrant experience where the home language is not the culturally dominant one. Lee speaks of one moment when his mother had endured the two tongues of her shame, one past, one present: profoundly broken English, and the shreds and remnants of Japanese. He contrasts the strong, private figure with the mute and uncertain public woman, alien in a 'land of always-talking strangers and other Americans' (Hongo: 217). The son is forced into the role of doing 'the work of voice', having to 'negotiate *us*, with this here, now', with the parental absent in their present tense.

This grammar of migration marks the essay and the novel, with communication being at the core of both. Reflecting on his mother's dying, Lee recalls his early short stories with narrators or chief characters 'of unidentified race and ethnicity', meaning that everything was 'some kind of white' and designed to belong to the 'authentic' canon of non-ethnic (because white) writing. Only in one story, where the character was unidentified but his mother was Asian 'that a cleaving happened', 'That the land broke open at my feet' (ibid.: 220). The essay itself is also, of course, such a 'cleaving', a 'breaking open', and its purpose is to provide a medium through which the writer can enunciate: 'I am here to speak. Say the words'. Although the use of first- and second-person pronouns suggests separate identities, the 'you' becomes 'I' in so far as the speaker acknowledges that he 'might finally speak the words turning inward, for the first time, *in my own beginning and lonely language* ' (ibid.: 223; my italics). Ostensibly addressing the mother, he says, 'You may die, but you will have been heard. Keep speaking – it is real – you have a voice' (ibid.).

The 'you' who has a voice is also the writer/speaker and the theme of voice and 'the beginning and lonely language' form one of the principal concerns of *Native Speaker*, as well as interrogating the native/assimilationist binary.

Henry Park's marriage to Lelia is under pressure throughout the narrative, with neither able to come to terms with the death of their son. Lelia is a speech therapist, working with children who have articulation problems, some physiological, others cultural – 'non-native speakers'. She is American born and in a list which she made of who Henry was, she accuses him of being a 'false speaker of language'. The very listing is itself an act of essentialising, but in his role as undercover operative Henry is similarly involved in posing in 'essences' even if they are always simulations, the basic equipment of a confidence-man who can make 'you feel good about yourself when you are with me' (6).

In the early stage of their relationship, language is a central issue. Lelia 'executes' the language – 'she went word by word. Every letter had a border' (9), whereas Henry, conscious of his accent, even in a city where people speak 'mix up' and everywhere you heard different versions, looks like 'someone listening to himself' (11), according to Lelia, 'taking in the sound of the syllables'. Lelia says that, if she had to guess, 'you're not a native speaker'; native in this sense always means white – it is not just a question of language. Lelia 'was very white, the skin of her shoulder almost blue, opalescent' (8). The contrast runs like a refrain throughout the text, reaching well beyond the specific persons of Henry and Lelia, the splitting and decentring functioning at all levels, empirical and metaphorical.

The nature of Henry's work is never fully specified, except that his company seems to have been set up in the 1970s to track migrants to the United States in the wake of the liberalisation of immigration legislation. The firm specialises in 'ethnic coverage' and engages staff according to their 'ethnic belonging' to trace incomers from anywhere except Western Europe, primarily non-whites. Their clientele are multi-national corporations and the bureaux of foreign governments, the targets those people working against their vested interests, immigrants of a radical or dissenting persuasion in any way questioning capitalist hegemony. The role of Henry and his colleagues is to specialise in 'emotional conspiracies', producing simulacra of the personal and private, thereby authorised to write their 'unauthorised biographies' and to spy on the 'transplanted'.

Living in the wrong scale, at moments running short of his story, his chosen narrative, Henry's task is to construct and sustain a plausible 'legend', a readable, speakable, 'identity' as if he were 'native' to it. On the Kwang assignment he employed his own life for his alter identity. His professional role – the 'cover' story – resonates throughout all the other levels of the narrative: his work is a string of serial identities. His immediate quarry is John Kwang, self-made Korean millionaire and potential mayoral candidate. Advocate of bi-lingual education, mediator in Black/Korean disputes, 'ethnic challenger', Kwang crosses the ghetto boundaries which help keep 'Anglo' America dominant. In a sense, he is also putting together 'a string of serial identities', an ironic counterpart to

Henry's company, but with a firm base in the Korean business and church community, a highly visible presence of middle-class immigrants (12 per cent of all Korean-Americans live in New York State and 80,000 in New York City).

The novel oscillates between the public and private domains, linked always by different inflections of immigrant experience. Henry's father embodies many of the characteristics of the first-generation Korean migrant – self-employed, long hours of work, economic (but not social) mobility, family centred, high level of ethnic attachment, and sustaining the role of the 'middleman minority' (Min: 212) 'through twenty-five years of green-grocering in a famous ghetto of America' (45). Henry is unusual in that very few young Korean males inter-marry, and where they do it is with Asian women.

In the initial stages, Henry's family lived in a Korean enclave, sub-scribed to a 'money club' (a *ggeh*), and maintained a high level of ethnic solidarity and relatively low level of assimilation. As their business prospered they moved away from the enclave, in common with other flourishing Koreans, and began to develop 'extra ethnic' contacts: 'In America, he [Henry's father] said, it's even hard to stay Korean' (47). Henry becomes embarrassed by, and impatient with, what he sees as his parents' deference to anything WASP American, their 'sham of propri-ety'. In the family store, he refuses to perform his 'Shakespeare' English, grunts in Korean, and tries to keep in the shadows, a 'near native' American. He experiences shame and anxiety as an adolescent and tries to distance himself from his 'sacrificing' parents, seeking the company of his white peers at tennis or pool clubs. As he grows, his profile of his family becomes more subtle and complex, and he begins to understand their humiliations and experience of racist violence. For his part, Henry's father liked the fact that Lelia was white and thought she and her family might help his son 'make my way in the land' (53). This view is a mixture of deference and hard-headed pragmatism; not necessarily self-contempt but an attitude shaped by social marginalisation and uncertainty.

The 'public' narrative – part of the diegetic present – is focused on the charismatic, iconic John Kwang, representative of the huddled masses, the 'countless unheard nobodies' who constituted his multi-ethnic mi-grant base or constituency. Populist, media friendly, and marketable, Kwang is the cynosure of a transcultural, potential community counter to those who 'tell difference' which is, presumably, why Henry is placed under cover in his organisation. Ethnic politicians are supposed to speak for, and out of, their ethnic belonging; Kwang transgresses the essenti-alist categories, in particular the black boycotts of Korean businesses where he acts as mediator. Unlike The *Joy Luck Club* or *Typical American*, *Native Speaker* consistently maintains a perspective on the wider social, cultural and political issues of being 'Asian' in America, and the black boycott movement against Korean merchants (five since 1981) is present as an important context.

Much of the 'private' realm of the narrative is diegetically past, perhaps because the split marriage has left a void which the 'public' role is covering, in several senses of the word. The need for Henry to invent a cover story – a legend – for professional purposes is a metaphor sustained throughout the text for his interstitial American presence, the doubly articulated narrative of the 'in between'.

I had always thought that I could be anyone, perhaps several anyones at once. Dennis Hoagland and his private firm had conveniently appeared at the right time, offering the perfect vocation for the person I was, someone who could reside in his one place and take half-steps out whenever he wished . . . I found a sanction from our work, for I thought I had finally found my truest place in the culture. (118)

What he fails to realise is that he cannot be anyone, or several anyones, but that, in his vocation as spy, he could only ever be ethnic Asian, however many legends he creates. It is a ghetto vocation, spatially fixed, essentialised – his 'half steps out' are an illusion of voluntarism. His 'truest place in the culture' is as a permanent 'other' employed to simulate other 'others' in an ethnic enclosure.

Unlike the Anglophone formative novel in which the bi-racial son of Lelia and Henry would develop, reconcile and assimilate, their son Mitt dies at the age of seven, one sign among many of 'incomplete translation' – the 'mutt, mongrel, half-breed, banana, twinkie' (96) of white suburban racist discourse. Lelia's parents, also separated, practise a tolerant racism, seeing Henry as exotic, an emblem of the Oriental culture and mind – homogenised and essentialised – and his father as part of the 'model minority', mimicking the self-made American. Mitt's death sepa-rates and decentres his parents, splits their 'inter', 'trans', 'cross' relation-ship. Lelia even wonders if his death occurred because 'he wasn't all white or all yellow' (120). This is an emotional and despairing response, but culturally 'logical' in so far as a racist society makes it even discursively sayable.

Kwang is particularly vulnerable to Henry's 'assignment' because, like him, his persona is a series of borrowings, resistant to 'ethnic' dilution or reduction. He has become 'part of the vernacular', a figure 'willing to speak and act outside the tight sphere of his family' (129), a native, and therefore dangerous, speaker in many ways. Kwang is also vulnerable in so far as, in Henry's eyes at least, theirs is 'a kind of romance', with Henry as 'someone we Koreans were becoming, the latest brand of an American. That I was from the future' (129). The irony is that what Kwang sees is a simulation, a cover story, an illusion; the ambiguity resides in deciding whether the 'becoming', 'the latest brand of an American', and 'the future' are also fantasies of adjustment/assimilation – 'false speakers of language'.

Henry sees Kwang one-dimensionally, as raw material for a role he might be playing in a theatre. He assumes that there is a simple correlation between intention and outcome, and that all he has to do is set up a narrative, authorise and choreograph it. Kwang becomes Henry's invention/creation, he believes he has a grasp of his identity, as though this were something fixed, conscious and accessible. Working with surfaces, the 'grit of an ethnicity', he comes to realise that identity thus conceived is a sham and that it is something slippery and fluid, a series of faces and masks. What he is unable to penetrate, and had not thought to seek, was 'the last mask', a 'final level that would not strip off' (131).

Kwang's message to his constituents is simple: 'Kwang is like you. You will be an American' (133), the promise to newer immigrants not only of citizenship, but of subjectivity and identity, transformed into 'Americans' as if 'white ethnic old New York' would not exercise its perpetual power to exclude. This inclusion/exclusion dialectic motivates Kwang's political bid. Henry misreads, misrecognises the message for the figure behind it. Kwang, in turn, sometimes calls upon Henry, in critical terms, to speak for 'Koreans everywhere', to put the Korean-American position, lingering on the hyphenation as a way of underscoring the negative effects of enclosed, and inward-looking, ethnicity. Both men see each other reductively, as necessarily representative, although Henry begins to perceive the gap between his 'realist' narrative with its transparency and a more elusive, complex and opaque subject. Not only does his assignment become narratively more difficult, but emotionally and morally also. The text itself begins to address the impossibility of writing, with shifting angles and perspectives on Kwang all coming up against the limits of a dominant, but increasingly inappropriate, scopic regime. In trying to read Kwang as a Korean, Henry also confronts the American, a man breaking away from his background and seeking to create a broader foreground away from the '600 square feet of ghetto retail space' of Henry's father.

So much thinking about ethnicity is in terms of background, or place of origin, rather than of foreground, the present location. This conflict between residual and emergent identities (not always clearly demarcated) is at the centre of the whole text. Without dissolving the particularities of specific ethnic backgrounds, Black or Asian for example, Kwang's 'threat' is that he tries to open up common, boundary crossing histories and memories of exploitation, colonialism and oppression. Henry, the virtuoso newcomer with a face to please all and ten years of an unassailable body of cover, and a covering of body, is hired to break this transgressor, this creature of excess, the man whose perfect English he couldn't abide, suspecting a kind of 'dubbing going on' (the model is always 'Anglo', its use by the non-white ethnic always seen as stylised).

There is a subtle interaction between the construction and modelling of Kwang by his image makers, that of the media, and Henry's 'legend'/his reading. All converge around the idea of the representational, of an original Asian referent. It is a process of exposure simultaneously working with closure, designed to produce him within the terms of the prevailing currencies of meaning, doxic practices. Everything Kwang says is converted into a matter of colour, a statement of race. It is the deconstructive, heterodox and contradictory possibility of Kwang that has to be foreclosed in the interests of the 'old syntax' (183). Henry is complicit with this syntax, his cover enabling him to create his own 'live burial', invisibility and disappearance – the model minority.

As noted earlier, Henry's assignment is to produce a realist 'migrant politician' narrative built around character, action, time and place: a cognitive genre, empirical and transparent. The nearer he gets to his subject the more it fragments and disperses, disappears from sight. In the process, Henry's narrative begins to shape a different story, his own, 'through the crucible of a larger narrative' (192). His boss had told him at one time that 'to be a true spy of identity . . . you must be a spy of the culture' (192). The culture forms the larger narrative and Henry turns his lens on this culture and his positioning within it. The 'leap of identity' he traces in Kwang he covets for himself, 'to think of America as part of him' (196), the treasured conflation, the closing down of difference.

In compiling the register of the members of the 'money club', formed on *ggeh* lines but extended to a range of immigrants, Henry is creating another narrative, his own as culturally immigrant, even though he was born in the United States (the author was not). It is this same narrative which contributes to Kwang's downfall, as the list which Henry hands over to his boss contains the names of illegal immigrants. Kwang's public disgrace is compounded by being in a car crash with a sixteen-year-old 'hospitality girl', also an 'illegal', but the real damage has been done by another agent employed by Henry's firm, Eduardo, exposed as a traitor to Kwang and blown up by a local Korean gang. Encircled, broken, Kwang relinquishes the streets to white American power and to dispersed and sectionalised ethnic enclaves. As Henry says 'We eat our own, you know' (269). The illusion of openness has been punctured: 'The people had never imagined a man like him, an American like him' (283). This is why he has to be destroyed, because there is no room for him in the (white) American 'imaginary'. When he falls it is not as just another politician, or an American, but as an 'Asian', and ethnic other; he is restored to an essentialism which he had flouted by refusing to be a wealthy, minority model success story living privately in his family-centred mansion in a fashionable suburb, but had dared to go 'public' and transethnic, a 'natural' American and something other in between: 'effortlessly Korean, effortlessly American' (305).

Henry Park realises that what he has done with his life is the darkest version of what his father only dreamed of, 'to enter a place and tender the native language with body and tongue and have no one turn and point to the door' (310). This is his cover story throughout the whole narrative; his other cover has helped to undermine those newer immigrants who, unrepresented, are left to face guns and rapes and riots, beatings and murders, living eight or nine to a room, and working for a pittance. Kwang was symbolic of a radical 'other' menacing the dominant culture. To the realtor selling the Kwang house they are '"Foreigners", she says. "They went back to their country"' (322). Henry has helped to restore that ethnic otherness, to bring about the return of the foreigner. Racialised into usefulness by his employers, he has unwittingly secured the relations of power of a racialising hegemony.

Leaving the espionage company, Henry reflects on his deceptions and betrayals:

My ugly immigrant's truth, as was his [the father], is that I have exploited my own, and those others who can be exploited. This forever is my burden to bear. But I and my kind possess another dimension. We will learn every lesson of accent and idiom, we will dismantle every last pretense and practice you hold, noble as well as ruinous. You can keep nothing safe from our eyes and ears. This is your own history. We are your most perilous and dutiful brethren, the song of our hearts at once furious and sad. For only you could grant me these lyrical modes. I call them back to you. Here is the sole talent I ever dared nurture. Here is all of my American education. (297)

This is both a lament and a hymn of, and to, second-generation immigrants, entering into the language, history and rhythm of American culture, seeing, hearing and speaking as 'natives', forever transforming and becoming American, the repetition with a difference mentioned earlier: 'calling all the difficult names of who we are' (324). It is also the ambivalent 'song' of the mimic man.

The novel has worked with, and against, the traditional 'orientalist' narrative, taking up and dismantling the realist aesthetic, displacing the subject from its place at the point of intelligibility and opening up questions about 'categorical ethnicity', and also exploring the capitalist logic that orders, and disorders, the 'ethnic ghettos' for its own vested interests, not as subjects or citizens but as labour, disaffiliated horizontally, zoned and antagonistic to each other. In the old syntax 'we eat our own'.

UNAMERICAN GOTHIC

Ruth Ozeki's *My Year of Meat* (1998) is a hybrid text in several senses. It uses a range of different narrative registers – documentary, fax, television script, memoranda, first- and third-person narrative voices, journal, poem, inter-textual references – and a narrator who is Japanese-American. Additionally, the novel has a bibliography of research sources and scholarly footnotes. It also has a double setting, in the United States and in Japan. Ozeki herself was born in the US. At different times, Jane Tagaki-Little, the narrator and central figure says: 'Halved as I am, I was born doubled' (176) and: 'Halved, I am neither here nor there' (314); both of these characteristics shape her narrative. The use of a variety of discursive styles and forms is one level of hybridity. At another level the narrative focuses on the splitting of the subject of culture in the way described by Bhabha:

The margin of hybridity . . . becomes the moment of panic which reveals the borderline experience. It resists the binary opposition of racial and cultural groups . . . as homogenised political consciousness. (Bhabha 1994: 207)

The basic story is constructed around the year (1991) Jane Takagi-Little spent producing a Japanese television show sponsored by BEEF-EX (for a number of reasons it rhymes with defects), an organisation promoting US meat export. The programme she co-ordinates is called 'My American Wife!' and is designed to bring the 'heartland of America into the homes of Japan' (9). In the course of the narrative both 'American' and 'wife' as referents are interrogated, taken apart and destabilised as the text develops into a satire on ethnicity, race, family, identity, sexuality and gender as these are scripted in the doxa of middle America and middle-class Japan. The programme is designed to produce stereotypes to market to stereotypes; American images of Japan, and Japanese preconceptions of America: 'sufficiently exotic and reassuringly familiar' (13). In the process of detonating these stereotypes – embodied in the journey of the housebound battered wife, Akiko (wife of Joichi Ueno, or John Wayno, who works for the advertising agency handling the BEEF-EX account) from Tokyo to Northampton, Massachusetts, with its significant lesbian population – the novel raises questions about 'authenticity', not simply in terms of media representations but, more importantly, in respect of ethnicity, identity and national cultures. As the programmes script, stage, edit and narrate images of identity into being, always in relation to a presumed but absent other ('unAmerican'), sooner or later the images begin to liberate themselves from their prescriptive belongings, from the authority of a hegemonic discourse. Conflict, contradiction, multi-acccen-tuality and hybridity are narrated from the margin to the centre: 'And in a

voice that was low, but shivering with demented pride, I [Jane] told him,
"I . . . am . . . a . . . fucking . . . AMERICAN!' (11); this in reply to the
constantly asked, racialised question: 'Where are you from?'

Unlike Amy Tan or Gish Jen, Ruth Ozeki does not concentrate upon
Asian-American families, but, in a more political fashion, upon images of
the family as the embodiment of a particular conservative discourse
around American values; a discourse of homogenisation predicated upon
a model of white ethnicity. In marketing meat to Japan as an authentic,
pure product, dominant class, gender and ethnic codings have also to be
marketed. The sound-bite and the image-bite have to be synchronised in
terms of sameness (of American identity) but also of difference (from
Japanese identity). The programmes are works of cultural translation in
which nothing must be 'lost'.

As Jane begins to research the American family and the American wife,
both begin to come apart in her hands, and as she increasingly becomes
aware of how 'polymorphous and perverse' both are, she seeks to
produce programmes which interrupt and puncture the essences and
fixed images; metaphorically speaking, on the cutting room floor of
American culture she finds all those things 'lost in translation', the
unauthorised and unedited transcripts. In all senses of the word,
adulteration comes to occupy the core of the narrative. At the simplest
level this adulteration is Akiko, watching the programmes in Tokyo and
obliged to fill in a questionnaire by her husband on issues such as
wholesomeness and authenticity, who always adds Japanese ingredients
to adapt the American dishes.

Much of the comedy, and absurdity, of the novel comes from Jane's
attempts to sabotage John Ueno's demands for appropriate family images
and beef-centred recipes. She manages to produce films based on lamb,
pork and vegetarian menus, and with 'rainbow', adoptive, bi-racial and
lesbian couple families. Ueno censors the Southern Black family, the
others slip through his grasp. 'American' expands into the heterodox and
the heterogeneous, multi-ethnic, multiple and contradictory positionings.
'Wife' is extended to include unmarried mothers, 'battered' women and
lesbian partners. A national cultural and social order is represented from
another angle; an alternative set of memories and identities are developed. Those supplementary and secondary categories, wife and woman,
are deterritorialised, ironically through a representational regime (television) which is designed to transmit hegemonic values. The programmes, like the novel itself, become revisionist works, mediated re-
visionings. They were intended, however, to produce visual images and
linguistic signs designed to identify beef as embodying social and
cultural values: consumption as lifestyle, beef as a metaphor of monolithic America. The distance between the US and Japan was seen as
guaranteeing the effectiveness of the symbols and images used: the

unspecifying long shot. Jane's films, on the contrary, work with close-ups, particularising and differentiating. The subsequent value exchanged is other than the signifier 'beef' was designed to carry.

The final film in the series (before Jane's contract is terminated) is a double transference: packaged and 'depackaged', valorised and deconstructed. One film, the authorised one produced by Ueno, shows the Dunn family on their ranch in Colorado as the model desired by BEEF-EX. Jane's film shows the same family, not only in their dysfunctionality, but also as the perpetrators and victims of cattle adulteration produced by growth hormone and steroid injections.

It is this adulteration which takes up almost one-third of the book and which I want to tie in with the central role played by the body in the narrative. In his essay 'For a sociology of the body: an analytical review', Arthur Frank writes: 'Constituting the body involves the practical work of formulating an inside and an outside, and developing a bodily practice in which inside and outside reproduce each other' (1991: 46). Both Jane and Akiko have bodily problems, related to reproduction. Jane's fertility is affected by a drug her mother took in pregnancy (DES), which also makes her vulnerable to adenocarcinoma (she was diagnosed with a pre-cancerous condition while in Japan as a graduate student). She conceives a child but it dies in the womb. Akiko has an eating disorder and her periods have stopped. She is both unable, and unwilling, to conceive, but writes articles for a magazine on women's health issues. Raped by her husband, she becomes pregnant, leaves Tokyo for the US, and decides to have her baby alone, but close to the lesbian couple she has seen on 'My American Wife!' Jane and Akiko communicate with each other, and Jane urges her to leave her violent husband.

The body image of woman represented on 'My American Wife!' (property of the male possessive pronoun), airbrushed, sanitised and 'kitchened', and the body image which Akiko presents socially are at odds with the lived bodies of Jane, Akiko herself, Bunny Dunn and her daughter Rose (the family featured in the Colorado episode of the programme). This lack of equivalence between body image and body practices is analysed at length in Donald Lowe's important study *The Body in Late-Capitalist USA* (1995) and the following discussion draws extensively upon it.

Firstly, the body images projected in 'My American Wife!' can be linked to the representation of the family (with the woman as cynosure) as 'an ideological unit rather than merely a functional unit' (Lowe 1995: 93). It is the realm of the private, a form of nostalgia (given that in 1990 only 56 per cent of American households were married couples), perhaps closer to Japanese demographics than American. Lowe cites May's argument that the white middle-class family ideal had Cold War origins; the programme aims to produce a modern role model, perhaps for post-Cold War times.

At the level of image the programme still operates within this ideology, a private/public framework, but reconfigured so that 'the household has become instead a center of consumption' (ibid.). The programme is about marketing not just a product, but a model of consumption; the wife is 'meat made manifest' (*My Year of Meat*: 8).

The novel explores the ways in which the body consumes for more than functional purposes, but also how that body which consumes also reproduces, and the relationship of bodily reproduction to the reproduction of capital. The links between what the body consumes and its reproductive capacity are articulated in the drug, DES, given to Jane's mother and to cattle, poisoning both Benny Dunn and her daughter, disfiguring and distorting their bodies. It is a complex circle in which the needs of capital accumulation, the extraction of surplus value, and the opening up of global markets are all returned to the body of the female, split between the American 'imaginary' and diseased lived bodies. Tied in with this is the recurring figure of differing male agents manipulating these processes, 'hegemonic capitalist practices which construct our body' (Lowe 1995: 174). The visualised body, in all senses, is quite other. As Lowe argues:

The body has emerged as the sole, remaining other in the monologic of late-capitalist accumulation. Capital accumulation and the body constitute the new binary opposition: the body acts as the other to late-capitalist development . . . bodily needs change for the sake of capital accumulation. (ibid.)

In the case of the females in the Dunn family their bodies have been changed by the needs of capital accumulation, a micrological symptom of a much larger process.

My Year of Meat is centrally concerned with the exploitation of bodily needs on a global basis, but also localising and particularising it, bringing it back to the lived body, not commodified or visualised, but corporeal and reproductive. In this text, the female body is seen to have a history which is related to its embodiment in different social contexts. Hybrid, split, dispersed; in the end, the narrative comes close to the body of the teller (both Jane and Shonagon, the writer of *The Pillow Book*, who dared to write in 'men's language', and extracts from which preface each chapter) and it becomes a narrative 'spoken from the experience of the body' (Frank: 89). The book is based upon a twelve month structure, a menstrual narrative. In that year the narrator made documentaries about 'an exotic and vanishing America' (15), a year in which she learned something real about America:

All over the world, native species are migrating, if not disappearing, and in the next millennium the idea of an indigenous person or plant or culture will just seem quaint.

Being half, I am evidence that race, too, will become relic. Eventually we're all
going to be brown, sort of. Some days, when I'm feeling grand, I feel brand-new –
like a prototype. Back in the olden days, my dad's ancestors got stuck behind the
Alps and my mom's on the east side of the Urals. Now, oddly, I straddle this
blessed, ever-shrinking world. (15)

4

We Need to Speak Even with Our Mouths on the Ground: Becoming Asian-Canadian – *Disappearing Moon Café*, *Diamond Grill* and *Chorus of Mushrooms*

A number of critics have analysed 'the cross-breeding of cultures' (Todorov 1992) and hybridity has been used extensively as a term in much of recent post-colonial analysis (see Bhabha 1994). Attempts have been made to confine the use as a contemporary phenomenon (by deploying terms such as 'third space') but others have stressed the long-term historical interactivity of cultural transaction as a constant feature of diasporic experience. Todorov cites the example of Mexican Catholicism with its strong traces of syncretism, and Brazil has an extensive number of practices which combine Catholicism with Yoruba and other African religious traditions (Cantomblé, for example, which also incorporates nineteenth-century spiritualism). Rosaldo reminds us of the fact that hybridity 'goes all the way down', seeing it as the founding experience of the earliest cultural contacts and encounters: an interzone (1989). Aijaz Ahmad also reminds us that: 'the cross-fertilisation of cultures has been endemic to all movements of people . . . and all such movements in history have involved the travel, contact, transmutation, hybridisation of ideas, values, and behavioural norms' (1995: 1–20). In this chapter I feel there is a need to return to some of the concepts introduced earlier, partly to refine them in the context of a number of critical debates around the politics of diasporic cultures but mainly to develop the idea of thinking about 'hyphenated' cultural fictions in the terms of syncretism which, I would argue, has more value as a sociogeneric category which allows other, collective or communal, positions – possibilities for shared agency – to emerge than does the concept of hybridity with its more individualist inflections confined to the realm of the discursive and to textual strategies.

Syncretism is often used in a derogatory sense, or to refer simply to attempts to unify and reconcile diverse or conflicting philosophical or religious systems. Cross-culturality, or cultural syncretism, may however be more helpful than the concept of hybridity, with its roots in breeding and plant culture and nineteenth century racist discourse. In a sense, perhaps, the term hybridity tends to refer to an individual situation whereas syncretism acknowledges wider, ongoing and historical processes of a more social and collective nature. It also suggests appropriation, making over and customising in an eclectic and creative way. Cultural syncretism – which Pieterse (1995) refers to as montage and collage – is usefully described by Canevacci as: 'cross-cultural plots of music, clothing, behaviour, advertising, theatre, body language, or . . . visual communication, spreading multi-ethnic and multi-centric patterns' (Canevacci 1992). In this sense, syncretism suggests an active process, it stresses creativity arising out of possibly adversarial or antagonistic contexts – certainly sites of difference – a process in which each agency in the contact 'consumes its own biases' (Harris 1985). It is more than a mix or a meld, a passive transference – and definitely not a melting pot – but something dialogical. Syncretism is an instance of cross-cultural creativity; what Wilson Harris calls the miracle of a dialogue with eclipsed selves: a reterritorialisation of otherwise deterritorialised and diasporic identities in a globalised world. Diasporic cultural fictions produce an endless series of flexible cultural translations, arcs or bridges of new possibility, brought about by a creative fracturing of surface cultural representations. Identities are articulated across this fracturing, this hyphenation.

This recognises the dislocated and differentiated nature of the diasporic, analogous to what Stuart Hall calls, with reference to globalisation, the 'dialogical character of its alterity' (1996a); it is also ruptural in the sense that it makes impossible any return to ethnically closed and 'centred' original histories. Syncretism is an anti-essentialism, it erodes the originary and absolute, it works with fissure and deferral within/ against the apparently seamless textures. What I am wanting to emphasise is the ways in which what I am describing deconstructs the process of symbolic exchange as monodirectional or universal, and locates the phenomenon of hybridity in both metropolitan cities of different diasporas and Third World cities. A complexifying takes place: a doubling of vision occurs. Hybridity has, if anything, both localised the global (for example by the 'Japanification' of American fast foods, the halal-isation of foods in Singapore or the timing of Sumo wrestling) as well as globalised the local – for example, Thai cuisine in Nottingham. As Ella Shohat (an Iraq-Israeli Arab Jew, living in the US) reminds us, metrocentric thinking about hybridity needs to be shifted towards a recognition of the multi-culturalisms of India and Brazil, Iraq and Israel/Palestine, the Middle East and Latin America, with their own 'take' on globalisation: crossroads of hyphenated and hybridised identities (Shohat, cited in Hall 1996a). This third space has been described by numerous theorists and it is neatly summarised by Chambers in this way:

> This is to engage in a 'third space' . . . in which asymmetrical powers, dissonance and the unsaid are inscribed in a rendezvous in which the West and its others emerge modified. *Neither* term is guaranteed by presumptions of an autonomous history and identity; and neither term can simply be added to the other – Asian-American . . . to create a facile composite. Both . . . become part of a double and compounded condition that 'does not limit itself to a duality between these two cultural heritages'. (1996: 49)

Homi Bhabha puts it in this way:

> The theoretical recognition of the split-space of enunciation may open the way to conceptualising an *international* culture, based not on the exoticism of multi-culturalism or the *diversity* of cultures, but on the inscription and articulation of culture's *hybridity*. To that end we should remember that it is the 'inter' – the cutting edge of translation and negotiation, the *in-between* space – that carries the burden of the meaning of culture . . . And by exploring this *Third* Space we may elude the politics of polarity and emerge as others of ourselves.
> (1994: 38–9; italics in original)

Chambers's term 'double and compounded' describes the condition of most of the narratives examined in this book and can be linked with another sense of the syncretic, to use an idea from Canclini, as something which takes place 'precisely in the crossings', on frontiers, at the borders – both literally and metaphorically (Canclini 1995). Cultural forms move through time and space and interact with other cultural forms at the *crossings*.

   Originally, and for centuries, this interaction was a literal/physical encounter; globalisation and global diasporas have meant that this now takes place increasingly in an 'electronic' space and, as Martin-Barbero has argued, '[people] first filter and re-organise what comes from the hegemonic culture and then integrate and fuse this with what comes from their own historical memory' (1993: 74). As I have already argued, the reverse is also true. New, synthesised cultural genres emerge, but the notion of diasporic cultural communities is an attempt to unthink the model which sees cultural flow as necessarily hegemonic in a global process; or, possibly, the notion that the West is necessarily hegemonic even, nowadays, rather than economically and militarily powerful. For instance – to use an example cited by James Lull – is the global flow of rap music (from America's inner city ghettos to Latin America, China and elsewhere) hegemonic? (Lull 1995). Syncretism, then, is a mode of activity, of creativity, and cultural diasporisation is ruptural, adversarial and continually transformative – not simply a byproduct of economic globalisation, although, of course, articulated with it.

I am thinking about syncretism as a mutual transformation, a matter of con-centricity, which takes place out of initially adversarial contexts, or contexts of difference: 'the many-stranded possibilities of the borderlands' (Rosaldo 1989: 216). It is performative, not propositional. Cultural forms can no longer be assumed to exist in any settled territory or genre; even 'form' itself is a questionable term, as cultural phenomena are increasingly appropriated for the purposes of symbolic creativity, symbolic exchange, and as a resource in 'reterritorialisation'. Even, or particularly perhaps, a hegemonised commodity culture is capable of becoming an adversarial zone, a site of contestation. Reterritorialisation is like Nomad thought in Deleuze and Guattari: it synthesises a multiplicity of elements without effacing their heterogeneity or hindering their potential for future rearranging; it breaks constraints and opens new vistas. Nomad space is smooth or open-ended – one can rise up at any point and move to any other. Its mode of distribution is the nomos: arraying oneself in an open space (like holding the street; which is why there is so much aggressive policing of street cultures), as opposed to the logos of entrenching oneself in a closed space (like holding the fort) (Deleuze and Guattari 1988). Globalisation, which is arguably motivated by transnational capitalism is, for all its apparent movement, ultimately working within the logos of entrenching oneself in an enclosed space – in the sense that it is confined to a horizontal plane, and limited by the order of that plane to preset paths between fixed and identifiable points (such as stock exchanges or world markets): a homogenous space. Diasporic movement, on the contrary, is closer to the movement of the nomos.

What I have referred to has also been commented on by Chambers in what he calls 'the double movement of globalisation', both from the perspective of the powerful (he gives the examples of automobile and media cartels, finance and futures capital) and that of the 'weak' (he points to the shift from ship to plane, and mentions sound systems and audio and video cassettes). From this encounter, he argues, can emerge what he calls 'counter-memories, counter-histories and counter-communities' that can produce a non-linear and syncopated version of globalisation, articulated perhaps in, and by, diasporic cultural activity. All forms/processes become relational. Cultural diasporisation, which itself partakes of this double movement, offers in the form of 'nomad thought' to displace the closed equations of representation which analyse the world into discrete components and reduce their multiplicity to the one of identity (as well as ordering them into invariable ranks), by 'summing up' a set of disparate forms in a shattering blow (compare my earlier point about fissure and creativity). Nomad thought places the variables in cultural/symbolic exchange in a state of continuous variation and differentiation: it is a model of itineration. Each deterritorialisation (of people, of identity, of form or genre) constitutes and extends the territory itself; it is a way to keep on opening up meanings. We are talking about radical refiguration: against boundary, limit and demarcation. Castenada, as quoted by Deleuze and Guattari, may help us to focus these issues:

Go first to your old plant and watch carefully the watercourse made by the rain. By now the rain must have carried the seeds far away. Watch the crevices made by the run off and from them determine the direction of the flow. Then find the plant that is growing at the farthest point from your plant. All the devil's weed plants that are growing in between are yours. Later . . . you can extend the size of your territory. (Deleuze and Guattari 1988: 372)

As has been seen previously, both Homi Bhabha and Trinh Minh-ha have developed this notion of a 'space in-between', of intermediacy, to conceptualise hybridity in terms of the interstitial, or the interval, and of a translational cultural process. It is, as Bhabha has pointed out, also one of the main areas of discussion in debates around cosmopolitanism and questions of what it means to be a citizen. In a sense, the *locus classicus* of all of these controversies is the text, and the subsequent context, of Salman Rushdie's *Satanic Verses* (the very 'devil's weed plant growing in between').

There are two problems with many of the current versions of hybridisation (including the one presented here). One is that the concept tends to be used in an uncritical and celebratory way which overlooks the often negative experience of the person of 'mixed race', the impoverished and marginalised, for whom the so-called 'new ethnicities' are not a viable option (for example, the offspring of Turkish–German relationships; the 'mixed race' child in care). The second point, not unrelated to the previous one, is that the hybrid of ethnoracially defined identity is almost always foregrounded as the exemplar of hyphenation, and the exception, whereas – as Goldberg points out – the supposed norm remains the 'ethnoracially neutral, nonhyphenated, authentic American', or British, or the northern European white (1995).

Friedman, one of the main critics of what he calls cosmopolitan hybridity, argues the latter points very forcefully:

The urban poor, ethnically mixed ghetto is an arena that does not immediately cater to the construction of explicitly new hybrid identities. In periods of global stability and/or expansion, the problems of survival are more closely related to territory and to creating secure life spaces. Class identity, local ghetto identity, tend to prevail, just as the local arena itself may be divided in gang territories. The shift from the mid-1970s to today has been towards an increasing ethnification of such public social arenas, a generalised increase in identity politics that has affected urban ghettos as well as the middle and upper classes. In such a process there is little room for the hybrid identification discussed and pleaded for by cultural elites. Even hybridity tends to become ethnic, that is, bounded and oppositional. Ethnification entails the reinforcement of boundaries and of boundedness in a positive feedback process whereby increasing conflict leads to increasing closure, which in turn leads to increasing conflict. (Friedman 1997: 84)

Apart from Friedman's work, one of the most sustained criticisms of the current use of the concept of cultural hybridity has been made by Aijaz Ahmad (1995). His first argument is that the celebration of a 'post-colonial, transnational, electronically produced cultural hybridity' cannot be squared with the material conditions of countless millions living in decaying countries and continents without access to basic amenities for survival, and with no likelihood of schooling or even seeing a telephone. Like Friedman, Ahmad is deeply suspicious of the migrant, post-colonial intellectuals living in the metropolis and generalising from their particular, and privileged, experience of cultural hybridity as a way of accounting for the total bi-cultural migrant experience. He cites the example of Said, Bhabha and Rushdie who speak of the superiority of the 'migrant's double vision', and yet remain indifferent to the deeply structured inequalities of caste, class and gender (this is not true of Said, it must be said). For Bhabha, agency occurs in a moment of cultural displacement producing a politics of contingency, whereas Ahmad contends that for vast numbers of migrants, powerlessness, unbelonging and displacement deprive them of agency or forms of political action unless their cultural and material experience can be located in specific historical understanding and in the context of a carefully grounded analysis of conquest and colonialism.

What Ahmad does not acknowledge is that this very location in 'displacement' may also be (particularly for the second, and subsequent generations) a condition of the possibility of agency in a new 'historical' situation. In the dialectic of belonging and not belonging a new agency may be formed but not unless it is recognised that, as Ahmad argues, post-coloniality is seen as also 'a matter of class'. A politics of identity which stresses a third space, new ethnicities and the performative and transgressive but which denies the complex intersections of colonialism, 'race', class, ethnicity and generation runs the risk of over-emphasising the power of individual agency. Unless firmly grounded in the historical, political, economic and empirical, concepts of cultural hybridity – like those of border, diaspora and migrant – are susceptible to over-metaphorical usage. As Avtar Brah reminds us in *Cartographies of Diaspora* (1996), migration takes place in a world – globalised or not – riven by racism, ethnicism and nationalism. The bi-racial child in the inner city can be the subject of everyone's racism – white, Asian or black. Brah's subtitle – 'Contesting identities' – with its double meaning, indicates the conflictedness of cultural syncretism. The important point, as Ahmad and Brah argue in their different ways, is that identities need to be 'placed' – situated in all senses of the word.

The migrant's 'double vision' is the legacy of specific histories, collective and deeply contested. As Brah says, 'the individual "narrator" does not unfold but is produced in the process of narration' (10). In a similar fashion, it might be most helpful to see cultural syncretism as a production, ongoing and ever-changing, a complex process and not a new anti-essentialist 'essentialism'. The strength of Brah's book is that, although autobiographical in several respects, it does not privilege self-representation at the expense of other complex intersections of representation – a possible weakness in Bhabha's theorisation of hybridity.

Like Rosaldo (cited above), Ahmad argues that hybridity – the cross-fertilisation of cultures – has been a characteristic of all movements of peoples within and across national borders. Contact is, in itself, the first condition of hybridisation. Colonialism was only one phenomenal form in which hybridity has taken place; it is neither a necessary, nor an exclusive, form for the process to occur. It is not specifically post-modern nor even specifically post-colonial, although migration could be seen as one of the defining experiences of the twentieth century. Ahmad's final criticism is reserved for Bhabha: 'That frenzied and constant refashioning of the Self, through which one merely consumes oneself under the illusion of consuming the world, is a specific mode of post-modern alienation which Bhabha mistakenly calls "hybridity", "contingency", "post-coloniality"' (Ahmad 1995: 18).

What is at stake in the argument between Ahmad and Bhabha is, of course, not simply a conflict of ideas, but the much deeper issue of a dispute between the anti-colonial intellectuals who remain in the colonised space to engage in an ongoing internal struggle based on class, caste, gender and 'mentality', and the globalising, diasporic, post-colonial intellectuals who choose to move to the metropolis and, arguably, engage in a post hoc celebration of their situation as somehow symptomatic of the wider migrant experience. The key word is 'choose' as, for the vast majority of migrants and refugees, displacement has not taken place under circumstances of their own choosing. Beyond this level of disagreement there are also fundamental political and ideological differences.

Certain features of Ahmad's argument recur in the book *Debating Cultural Hybridity: Multi-Cultural Identities and the Politics of Anti-Racism* (Werbner and Modood 1997), particularly in the introduction by Pnina Werbner and the chapter already referred to by Jonathan Friedman. The book is distinguished by its explicitly political engagement with the issues, and the way in which it demonstrates how racism undermines the foundations of multi-culturalism. Like Ahmad, the contributors do not attempt to deny the existence of cultural hybridity as such, nor do they deny fluidity, ambivalence, fissure and reflexivity as characteristics of contemporary, post-modern identity. What they seek to establish is an understanding of ' "ethnicity" as a shifting, hybridised politics of identity or collective self-representation' (227) in the context of power, domination, structural inequality, racial violence and 'communities of suffering'. It is the uncritical celebration and dehistoricised, depoliticised concept of 'cultural hybridity' which is subjected to extensive analysis and critique. Negotiating differences across cultures – above all, perhaps, for the bi-racial, the hyphenated, and the hybridised – is seen as profoundly difficult and a deeply conflicted process.

If we shift the focus on cultural hybridity from celebratory metaphor to activist politics, from play to confrontation, then we need to remind ourselves of the material conditions of impoverishment, exile, xenophobia and racism for the majority of the world's 40 million migrant workers and 18 million refugees. Having said that, and remembering that for many the crossing of boundaries is an experience of pain and loss, the new situation for migrants is not only negative precisely because of the post-modern, globalising and fluid circumstances in which they are constituted, and of which they are also partly constitutive. Reconfigurations can, and do, constantly recur.

Hybridity is not, as has been argued already, simply a post-modern phenomenon, nor is it exclusively a site of possible resistance or the counter-cultural. Friedman gives an example, from Central America, when hybridity assumed a hegemonic and oppressive form through the alliance of *mestizos* and white elites against Mayan Indians (the majority of the population in Guatemala). This is a rare instance of the hybridised in a position of dominance; far more common are the examples cited by Friedman, and others, of people living on the margins of white society, fragmented and ghettoised by class, generation and racialised ethnicity, recognised, if at all, always and only as a minority. Certainly to be born to Moroccan parents in Brussels, to Algerian parents in Paris, or to Bangladeshi parents in Nottingham, or to be bi-racial in any of these cities, is to be racialised into disadvantage. Nevertheless, while class and gender exploitation, and racial oppression, must be factored in to any theorising of hybridity, it has to be recognised that a remaking of culture is taking place through music, dance and fashion, particularly for second- and third-generation migrants. People are increasingly able to play with their identities while still valorising them and putting into question the over-ethnification of public social arenas. Contrary to what Friedman argues, explicitly new hybrid identities are being constructed in ethnically mixed, poor inner-city areas in the UK and the US, even if only sometimes by default. This is not to claim that crossing over is easy or permanent, but there is evidence, as Henry Louis Gates argued in *The Guardian* (19 July 1997), that in certain cities in the UK black culture *is* youth culture as 'speaking with a Jamaican inflection has become hip among working-class white kids'. This may mean no more than that hybridity has become a matter of style, but, at least, it indicates that there are cultural spaces opened up by hybridity despite the still-prevalent racism and racialised ethnification in the UK.

As suggested earlier, some sociologists and anthropologists have argued that diasporic black and Third World intellectuals have had a disproportionate influence upon the debates around hybridity and they question how much impact they have upon the realities of ethnicity, racism or nationalism. They are thinking both of academic theories and of artistic works. In a sense this is an argument which it is impossible to refute as such an impact is hard to quantify. However, if an analogy is drawn with the autobiographical and fictional work of writers such as Maya Angelou, Alice Walker and Toni Morrison, and their influence upon women of colour, it should be possible to assume that Maxine Hong Kingston's *The Woman Warrior* and Amy Tan's *The Joy Luck Club* have had some effect upon developing a cultural consciousness of hyphena-tion, of the cultural politics of hybridity. It would otherwise be difficult to account for the 'explosion' in the publishing of fictions by Asian-Amer-ican women in the past decade, even allowing for the argument that this may be simply because they have become marketable, unthreatening and the 'acceptable' face of ethnicity.

In a collection of autobiographical essays, *Under Western Eyes* (Hongo 1995), a range of Asian-American writers address the material and emotional conditions of migration – immiseration, marginalisation, ra-cism, discrimination and violence – as well as the historical circum-stances, political, economic and social, which led to the Asian diaspora (often a double diaspora in the case of Hawaiians or other overseas Chinese) throughout North America. There is no simplified or elite celebration of play, but a reflexivity out of which comes a recognition that the bi-racial and bi-cultural experience of the second-generation migrant can produce, from communities of suffering, humiliation and exclusion (like the concentration camp experience of thousands of Japanese Americans – most of them US citizens – in California after Pearl Harbor in 1941) the possibility of new belongings, more fluid and less rigid identities, shaped by the politics and histories of imperial power and domination. The distinctiveness and boundedness of their parents' culture and experience is respected (a recurring trope is the 'origins' journey of so many second-generation narratives), but it is also acknowledged that 'hyphenated' living requires new currencies, new validities, of the kind described above in terms of syncretism. For most of the writers this experience is full of contradictions and ambivalences, split between home and school languages, physically and racially marked as other yet only knowing America, and tempted into accelerating the process of belonging by 'marrying white'. Historicised, gendered and politicised, these essays in cultural hybridity are full of deeply conflicted, tense and complex experiences of those forced by white hegemony into creating a 'third space', a new ethnicity both Asian and American, although some remain neither Asian nor American, but see their identity as syncretic/diasporic and not tied to a national culture. Against ethnic absolutism or simplified notions of authenticity, the writers realise that 'living in the hyphen' (Wah 1996) is a painful process of articulation: 'When you're not "pure" you just make it up' (Wah, from *Waiting for Saskatchewan*). 'Making it up', faking it even, is precisely what so much cultural hybridity is about; the inventions and innovations of those 'living in the borderlands'. *Under Western Eyes*, with its punning title, is about the making of new Americans.

Fred Wah's *Diamond Grill* is a clear example of the hyphenated cultural process I have been discussing. It is both autobiography and fiction (and autobiography as fiction), reflexive in style and structure – 'not true stories but, rather, poses and postures'. Fred Wah's father was a Canadian-born Chinese-Scots-Irishman raised in China; his mother a Swedish-born Canadian. Out of this complex and multiply resourced heritage Wah creates a syncretic text which explores Chinese-Canadian history, racialised politics and the third space of a neither/nor, both/and, identity. The book is rooted initially in the Diamond Grill Chinese restaurant owned by Wah's father, and the restaurant remains throughout as a site in which, and from which, the writer speculates on a range of issues relating to his immediate family and beyond them to the complex, contradictory and often brutal history and politics of diasporic communities since the beginnings of migration to Canada in the nineteenth century. Not only is the book about hybridity but it is itself a syncretic form – part essay, poem, memoir, recipe, menu, family album, documentary and meditation. There is a series of inner monologues, dialogues, shifting voices, genders and persons, fluid tenses and moving spaces which weave in and out of differential histories and temporalities. The certainties of place, person and memory – the stable/staple forms of empiricism – are all subject to confusion, conflation and reconfiguration as part of a search for metaphors appropriate to the complex intersections of a new cultural and ontological space of belonging. As the Chinese becomes separated from the Canadian, the Canadian from the Chinese, and then rehyphenated, new voices are tried out and discarded, poses are struck and dismantled, and fresh configurations are improvised. Language is mined for ways of articulating the unspoken and the unspeakable.

Hyphenation is not only a given, but a construction produced out of
struggle, linguistic, political, personal; it is part invention, part simulation (the cooks in the restaurant produce an improvised imitation of
Empire cuisine, but no imitation is an exact reproduction as something
happens in between the original and the copy). The 'in between' is the
space of growth, imagination and possibility. It is the 'yet' of syncretism:

Yet languageless. Mouth always a gauze, words locked behind tongue, stopped
in and out, what's she saying, what's she want, why's she mad, this woman –
silence stuck, struck, stopped – there and back, English and Chinese churning
ocean, her languages caught in that loving angry rip tide of children and coercive
tradition and authority. Yet. (5)

This quotation refers to Wah's 'double grandmother', but also in a
broader sense to the experience of 'migrant-tongued' women and the
deeper silences and injuries of both original and host culture gendering.
Diamond Grill is a work of translation and interpretation, speaking for,
with, to and of migration in the quest for a new discourse of hybridity – a
third language stripped of a simplified and racialised ethnification. As
Stephen Slemon has pointed out (in private correspondence) the doors in
the restaurant are an extended central metaphor for the condition of
being Chinese-Canadian. The doors are double exits and entrances, from
the café to the kitchen, from the kitchen to the café, to the café from the
kitchen, and to the kitchen from the café. The 'Chinese' move in and out
of the swing doors, the 'Canadians' are fixed in the café. Food, and the
preparation of food, becomes an important signifier of ethnic identity,
particularly at a time when, in all other senses, the Chinese were under
threat – from the Chinese Immigration (Exclusion) Act, subject to
Detention Hospital, and effectively disenfranchised until the late
1940s. The hyphen is the door which swings between the Occident
and the Orient.

    For Fred Wah's family, hybridity was often a negative, silencing and
excluding experience. For the author himself it is, literally and metaphorically, his embodiment – the routes, roots, bloodlines and ocean
crossings enter, become his body, as the text itself is a bodying forth of
hyphenation, of hybridisation and syncretism: 'parts folding into body
after body' (36). The book is about all kinds of crossings and intersections, stylistic and generic as well as ontological and physiological.
Hybridisation is a survival strategy for the individual, as well as a
new shared and syncretic trajectory, the opening up of the possibility of
place in a history and family of fragments and displacement. Place
becomes an affective zone, a grounding and earthing. The diamond of
the Diamond Grill is a shape, a talisman and a precious metal – a
synthesis of superstition, material practice and fantasy. The restaurant is
Wah's father's continuous narrative in a sense, as the text we read is his:

an investment and an investiture. For the son the restaurant is a site which partly defines the ambivalence of hybridity – 'things we don't always taste willingly but forever after crave' (46), rather as identity was what he was not, or could not join, or feel, or understand. Wah argues that hybrids are the only Canadians, exposing the racism of ethnification and underlining the fact that 'national' identity is always a contestation. His comment on his mother pithily says it all: 'She has been half-erased and her English is good, it's blond' (61), reminding us that the Canadian government once passed legislation forbidding white women from working in Chinese places. The legislation enacted the fear of miscegenation, the negation of a possible hybridisation, the 'dissonance of encounter' (68). The dissonance of encounter is, in many ways, what this chapter has been addressing throughout.

At one point in the text, Fred Wah footnotes a reference to important concepts developed by Mary Louise Pratt which, for my purposes, help to focus on particular aspects of hybridity. The first concept is that of 'code-switching' in which speakers switch seamlessly between two languages and derive a sense of ownership and cultural power in an otherwise unempowered and 'othered' context. Properly understood, multi-culturalism can be seen as a code-switching resource, a fluid and hybridised discourse and material practice, of simultaneous difference and not-difference. This is the process I have called syncretism – the cultural practices of hyphenation/hybridity. The other concept outlined by Pratt is that of the 'contact zone' which, she acknowledges, is a space heavily determined by colonisation, radical inequality and conflict but also capable of being seen as the 'spatial and temporal copresence of subjects previously separated by geographic and historical disjunctures, and whose trajectories now intersect' (Pratt 1992: 6–7).

As long as the 'radically asymmetrical relations of power' (Pratt) are never erased from our understanding of the process, it is very helpful to see hybridity and syncretism as the consequences of the intersecting and interactive experiences of the 'contact zones' of globalised cities. It is a continuing improvisation, a place to be as well as a narrative of a possibly new belonging, a renewal of agency. This new agency would be a way of overcoming the racialised identity 'quantifiers' mocked by Wah at one point where he refers to the racial percentages (such as 75 per cent Chinese) of the family's 'stock exchange'. Living in the hyphen is a qualitative experience, an affective cultural consciousness.

While not presenting his experience as representative, Wah shows how it does represent a potential absurdity: 'You and I have done alright, our genealogical trajectories compounded or diluted enough into the white middle class to put us over the blue line'. (105). This is a point made by several of the writers in *Under Western Eyes* ; visibility, freed from class and gender oppressions, is not necessarily an insurmountable problem for 'acceptability'. No doubt is left, however, that 'living white' is the hegemonic norm and model. What Wah and others are trying to shape is a counter-hegemonic process whereby hybridity and syncretism are positive choices, forms of cultural agency and empowerment, a (literally) living alternative; not a looking back, nor a looking up, but a looking forwards to a code-switching future in which white is only one ethnicity among others. Wah's achievement is to explore all these issues in the form of the material anchorage provided by the nexus of food/family/history/memory, the economic and cultural capital provided by the restaurant as a resource, a centre and location for interactive exchange. It is the contact zone for the book's improvisations, play, lexical and syntactical riffs and genre-crossing encounters. Identity is not a game, but rooted in particularity and physicality – 'the details under foot' (121).

One particular problem that Fred Wah highlights is also dealt with by Friedman and Ahmad. This is the issue of the appropriation of immigrant identity by 'the dominant white cultural landscape'. Wah complains of being inducted into someone else's story or project. It is certainly true that the uncritical and unreflexive celebration of hybridity could be recruited to serve a hegemonic function, usurping the bi-cultural experience and diluting yet again the distinctiveness and difference of a 'migrant' configuration of identity: figured out of their own space/s. The specificity of the diasporic communities can be erased by style politics. As Wah says, 'the hyphen always seems to demand negotiation', a negotiation which leads to the unsettling of white settler Canada. Appropriation is an attempted reconquest (evidenced in the Canadian government's top-down host-guest model of multi-culturalism) in which the migrant comes to inhabit an emptied space. I make this point as a way of reminding ourselves that the original settlements of Canada and Australia, in particular, were considered to be of empty spaces. Not that Wah does not acknowledge that, at times, he is tempted to exploit the 'transpicuous' nature of near-whiteness, to become the gun not the target for once. The Vietnam War – 'we should nuke those chinks' someone says to him – helped him decide never to be an 'American We'.

Throughout Diamond Grill language and food are the primary sources of connection and continuity – the conduits of time and place and memory, both metaphors and the resources of metaphor. The whole book localises and specifies place – the restaurant in particular – as something inhabited and navigated, moved in and through, bodied and embodied. Hyphenation is metaphor (which, in its classical usage, means being at home in a strange place), but also more than metaphor; it has a material, almost kinetic, presence articulated through the continuous dialectic of inside and outside: 'the door clangs and rattles a noisy hyphen between the muffled winter outside and the silence of the warm and waiting kitchen inside' (176).

I have stressed throughout the localising and specifying activity of this text because it is through this that a form of migrant agency is achieved. The Diamond Grill restaurant is the epicentre of a geographical, historical, economic, social and political process of globalisation which began in the nineteenth century and precipitated the long, and continuing, diaspora of peoples decentred and displaced, racialised and subordinated, by the demands of Western capitalism. This globalisation has taken, and continues to take, many forms so that, paradoxical though it may seem, we need to speak and think of many 'globalisms' not one homogeneous process. If cultural hybridity is one phenomenological consequence of this diaspora, and syncretism its practice, then these must not be allowed to float free of the political, economic and social particularity of their traces in the history of violence and expropriation.

A STORY FULL OF HOLES

Reference has already been made to the exploitation of the Chinese in Canada, to exclusion acts, immigration laws, disenfranchisement and continuing histories of discrimination and racism. Settled in Canada since the middle of the nineteenth century, it is only in the past fifty years that citizenship rights, the franchise and access to professional occupations have been made available. Segregated and subordinated, bounded and placed in 'ethnic enclaves', a distinctive culture of overseas, or diasporic, Chinese has nevertheless developed. In the past twenty years a number of writers have attempted to articulate that culture in fictional forms which also historicise the legacy of exclusion and racialisation. As has so often been the experience of the non-white settler in British or North American society, as it was the experience of the colonised in their own countries, the history and culture learned at school was that of the dominant white social order:

What has characterized our experiences growing up Asian Canadian has been a sense of separation from all things Asian Canadian. We learned little about our ancestors, the pioneers who had made this land grow, 'caught silver from the sea', laid the rails that had bound British Columbia to Canada. Our school books didn't deal with the Vancouver racial riots of 1887 and 1907, or the World War Two expulsion, incarceration and later dispersal of the Japanese Canadians, or the disenfranchisement of both peoples until the late 1940s. (Chu 1979: viii)

In the remainder of this chapter I want to look briefly at two examples of Asian-Canadian writing, one by a writer of Chinese family origin, the other of Japanese origin. Sky Lee was born in British Columbia, while Hiromi Goti was born in Japan and emigrated with her family to Canada when she was three years old.

In Sky Lee's *Disappearing Moon Café* (1990) the epicentric narrative

figure is Kae Ying Woo who pieces together the tangled and hidden history of the Wongs which starts in 1892 when Wong Gwei left China for British Columbia. The novel is based primarily in Vancouver's Chinatown. It is an interpretative and transformative narrative, giving voices to a legacy of the repressed and the silenced. Like many of the texts referred to throughout, this one is both contemporary and historicised, opened up narratively to an informing and transforming past; it is situated in those moments which dynamite the continuum of the present. It explores, among a host of other things, the role of the Chinese immigrant in the industrial expansion of North America, and finds a language for those one-dimensionalised, broken monosyllabled stereotypes of 1950s Westerns – victimised, sacrificed and bloodied.

The narrative is a work of reclamation and of recovery but there is no stable or originary past, home, or a continuous story. It is crossed temporally and spatially by difference, as fact and metaphor endlessly produced; the text is split, partial, suppressed and incomplete.

The work is structured around a Prologue, followed by seven chapters with intersections, and an Epilogue. The Prologue is a 'bone-searching expedition' as is the whole narrative: 'This was in 1892, the beginning of the retrieval of bones, which lasted well into the 1930s' (*Disappearing Moon Café*: 16) and 'Like them he would piece himself together again from scattered, shattered bone and then endure' (13). As with so many diasporic narratives, the piecing together from dispersed and fragmented selves and histories is both an individual and a collective project. Sixteen specific years are isolated in the narrative trajectory which spans 1892–1987. Many of the specified years recur, are returned to again and again, each time with a different inflection. The whole text is a revisionary project, working with and across four generations of migrants, native born, and bi-racial people, with a focus on the doubly exiled women.

The principal figures are Kae's great-grandfather and great-grandmother, her grandmother, and her mother; each one is articulated differentially but always with reference to their gendered and racialised oppression.

The first relationship described is between a Chinese man and Kelora, half Caucasian-half native American (but brought up by a Chinaman), whose language is neither purely native American nor Chinese, but a patois. This relationship, and Kelora's split identity, announces and articulates the transnational, transcultural, nomadic and diasporic trail of the narrative. Their son – complexly hybridised and hyphenated – An Ting becomes the lover of Fong Wei (and father of her three children), the daughter of Gwei Wong and his Chinese wife, and subsequently the father of the man who makes Fong Wei's daughter Suzanne pregnant.

Kae's first chapter is called 'Waiting for Enlightenment'; she charts her genealogical roots in an act of remembering, but

I'm so very disappointed – I've been brought up to believe in kinship, or those with whom we share. I thought that by applying attention to all the important events such as the births and the deaths, the intricate complexities of a family with Chinese roots could be massaged into a suant, digestible unit. Like a herbal pill – I thought I could swallow it and my mind would become enlightened. (19)

The actual complexities prove far more intractable to a univocal transcription or translation. The narrative is polyphonic, multi-accented, full of reversals, doublings, code-switchings and fractures. There is no singular equivalence between 'experience' and its recording (for example, 'Let's just say for now that Gong Gong died in 1972, maybe 1942 – the family tree gets tricky here'):

At funerals, full-month parties, graduations, it was easy to see an inevitable logic underlining life, a crisp beginning and a well-penned conclusion, nice and neat, and as reassuring as receiving a certificate for good attendance or a gold star at the top of the page. (20)

As the narrative becomes more tangled, striated and recessive the 'inevitable logic' eludes the telling and the narrator is forced into a search for a model of formlessness to overcome the limits imposed by form. The writing is never an expressive transcription of an already there, anterior 'real', but, as the text shows, a continuous (or discontinuous) rewriting, almost like the café itself, divided into a nostalgic replica Chinese teahouse dining room and a modern counter and booth section. The structuring moments described are parenthetical and peripheral, mere strategies of anamnesia, not the 'messy truth' of transformative memory.

The story that is told – 'the well-kept secret that I had actually unearthed years ago – finally begins to end for me with the birth of my son, Robert Man Jook Lee, on April 29, 1986' moves backwards and forwards in time across almost the entire century (23). Throughout the narrative, the birth/writing analogy is invoked; it is a *becoming* Chinese-Canadian which is being shaped, not simply the chronicle of an already existing set of characters and events.

The narrative traces a dialogical relationship between a Canadianised individualism – locked into the mercantile – and a residual Chinese collective:

'Bah, who needs them!' she [Lee Mui Lan, Kae's grandmother] muttered to herself, not realising that she referred to a faraway home in her heart that had disintegrated over the years – her old home in the village, made up almost entirely of women . . . All of them desperately weaving tenuous, invisible threads over the ocean, to cling cobweblike to their men and sons on the Gold Mountains'. (25–6)

Without her society of women, Mui Lan lost substance. Over the years, she became bodiless: 'she relied heavily on him [she is a merchant's wife] for her identity in this land'. It is this insubstantiality, and a corresponding silence, which the narrative seeks to give form and voice to.

Dress, language and other cultural hybridisations (mini-skirts and rabbit-fur jackets) are mixed with nostalgia, replications and homesickness. Lives and lines flow together in the memory of the primary narrator – the writing 'I' (born in Canada, studied in Beijing) – directly and indirectly piecing the bones together of an endlessly storied culture: 'women's strength is in the bonds they form together', Kae's friend, Hermia, an overseas Chinese from Switzerland, tells her. The China of tradition and memory has been turned inside out in search of radical truths, and the narrative uses a blend of first- and third-person voices, letters and other forms of evidence.

The narrative becomes a destabilising, risk-taking activity (pebbly and jagged) where the legitimate, traditional and conventional are all opened up, de-essentialised, and all identity is seen as fluid and defective, on the verge of breaking out – a process of becoming, emergence and presencing: 'our lives belong to strangers'.

What a coward I was! I was afraid of risks, and I had to cling to the ground, pebbly and jagged. I wallowed in petty detail and ignored the essence. Legitimate, traditional and conventional were the adjectives to wear in those days, especially when I suspected my own identity might be as defective. (41)

The gender fate of the first-generation women, turned in upon themselves, enslaved by their displaced presence in Canada and subjected to the misogynistic vernacular of Chinese men, is opened up to question by their daughters and granddaughters, looking back, not in nostalgia, but in order to disinter and give voice to buried and silenced experiences. The narrator has moments when she is uncomfortable with 'Chineseness' as she tries to 'pass' as 'Canadian' but, as she and her male cousin research their histories through newspaper cuttings in the library, she comes to realise that, for gender reasons, although their pasts may converge at times they can never be the same story. The cousin, Morgan, researches a public history of racism and discrimination ('guest people'), and the sexual 'anxiety' of the white community about Chinese men, focused on the murder in 1924 of a young white female, Janet Smith. In respect of this event, as so often, the Chinese were victimised but, for the first time, fought back: there was no going back, they were rerooted, rerouted permanently – the 'old villages had faded into a vague distance, too far to retrace now' (71). It was the first step on a long journey away from China and towards Canada; old ways were fast disappearing but citizenship took another quarter of a century: 'Overseas Chinese were like derelicts, neither here nor there, not tolerated anywhere' (77).

For Kae, the narrator, her history has to be carved out of a more private realm: 'I am quite uncertain as to what I need to see between the blind slats which hide and hold me . . . why is it so hard to get answers to questions I've been asking all my life?' (121). Her narrative is agonistic, a struggle with a series of complicated knots which defy unravelling, knots of race, racism and gender. Her work is more archaeological than historiographical, the careful excavation and intricate piecing together of hundreds of dispersed and shattered fragments, layered across generations and convoluted relationships. Kae's nanny, Chi, is symptomatic of this process, an ethnically Chinese woman who grew up as a Hindu and learned her cultural 'Chineseness' from Kae's mother. There are no straight lines or pure sources, Kae realises, as she constantly 'sees double' and constantly comes up against masks, role-playing and duplicities in trying to trace her family history: 'Chinese bought and sold their identities a lot in those days' (232). What the narrative discovers is that there is no prior, essential or authentic identity 'back there' to be accessed, but, rather, a trail of shifting performances and variable disguises. So if the narrative bears a resemblance to the conventions of the 'family saga', it is also written very much against the grain of the genre, peopled by ungrounded and displaced women and men, storying their survival in episodic ways which, for the women in particular, attempt to 'form a bridge over the abyss'. In a woman-hating culture, each generation of women realise in their different ways that whenever they ventured out of 'their place . . . they came back fractured' (164).

This fracturing is a feature of the text's form as well as being a condition of its narrated experience, a symptom of all the split figures in the text and of its temporal organisation. The section 'Feeding the Dead: 1986', is technically a departure from the overall narrative shape in the ways in which, in speculative and hypothetical form, it experiments with a range of codes and media for configuring the members of the family. These range from television interview, through séance and film, to domestic melodrama and Greek tragedy. The question that is being posed by using these various styles and media is the familiar one in diasporic fictions: how, if we live in an endlessly storied world, can any one form adequately represent the complex histories of displacement, exclusion, racialisation and dispossession? How far is it possible to think in terms of an individual self, or of personal identity in the context of so many tangled lines and confused belongings? What does family, blood, inheritance mean in 'A story full of holes' (160)? The process of anamnesis, that which can neither be remembered nor forgotten, figures once more as part of the diasporic imagination.

The narrator's friend, Hermia, asks her a crucial question which refers not just to the issue of identity but also to the wider problem involved in narrating the diasporic: the limitations of the realist novel, particularly the *bildungsroman*, as a hegemonic paradigm designed to privilege and prioritise an individualist model of development. The novel raises, in its formal structures and in its themes, questions related to the production of spaces for the overlooked, forgotten and marginalised collective self:

Do you mean individuals must gather their identity from all the generations that touch them – past and future, no matter how slightly? Do you mean that an individual is not an individual at all, but a series of individuals – some of whom come before her, some after her? Do you mean that this story isn't a story of several generations, but of one individual thinking collectively? (189)

INSCRIBE MY NAME ACROSS THE COUNTRY

In the process of re-telling personal myth, I have taken tremendous liberties with my grandmother's history. This novel is a departure from historical 'fact' into the realms of contemporary folk legend. And should (almost) always be considered a work of fiction. (Goto 1994)

The (almost) is a crucial modification which refers us to the tradition of ethnic autobiography where another 'almost' allows the intrusion of the fictional, so that the epistemological status of the writing is put into question. The narrative in *Chorus of Mushrooms* is, like the identities of the grandmother (Naoe) and of the granddaughter (Murasaki), both a deconstruction and something made up as it goes along. The autobiographical framework is spliced with the fictional processes of reflection, speculation, invention, meditation, recollection and, above all, imagination. Whilst not referring specifically to the orderings, linearity and diachrony of autobiography, there is nevertheless an implicit inter-textuality, a resonating cultural 'quotation'. In a sense, the text is autobiographical: the self, the life and the writing are all pluralised, split, interwoven, multi-accented and a hybrid construction. Bakhtin's concept of hybridisation is useful in locating this particular feature of the text:

A hybrid construction is an utterance that belongs, by its grammatical (syntactic) and compositional markers, to a single speaker, but that actually contains mixed within it two utterances, two speech manners, two styles, two 'languages', two semantic and axiological belief systems. (Bakhtin 1981: 304)

This particular aspect of hybridisation is especially appropriate because the text is dominated by language, both as subject and medium, readable and audible – spoken and silent. Against the grain of the unitary assimilationist ideology which has evacuated Japanese-ness linguistically and culturally from her home, Murasaki introduces the internally conflicted and multiple, produced by, and through, complex and variable syntactic, lexical and compositional markers. Displacement, temporal and spatial rupture, and confusions and conflations of the grammatical 'person', all embody the themes of the text as well as formally generating its disruptive narrative: *'There isn't a time line. It's not a linear equation. You start in the middle and unfold outward from there. It's not a flat surface that you walk back and forth on '* (132; italics in original).

Murasaki appropriates the 'double consciousness' of always looking at themselves through the eyes of dominant others (her parents' position) for her own ends by 'writing back' through her own eyes, ears and mouth: a process of learning, listening to, speaking and reading Japanese, reclaiming a suppressed ethnicity as part of a complex, dynamic and positive identity and not simply an ethnicity conferred on a racially and racialised visible minority group. By so doing she does not cease to be Canadian, but affirms herself against a definition of Canadian that excludes whoever is not white. While Murasaki enhances her identity in a pluralist fashion by 'becoming' Japanese, her grandmother enhances hers by 'becoming' Canadian in an extended moment of cultural fantasy where she participates as a rider in a rodeo.

The text constantly undermines reductive, exclusionary and static models of identity, nationality and narrativity. It is a work of reciprocity and recognition for Murasaki in relation to her grandmother, parents, unnamed partner, and, ultimately, her self/selves. Murasaki's parents, by their silence, accommodation, exclusive use of English and abandonment of all but their physical traces of Japanese-ness, live out the dominant society's stereotype/caricature of the Asian-Canadian as the 'model minority'. To paraphrase the title of a 1960s autobiography by a Japanese American, they are 'Canadians in disguise'. Individualised, nuclearised and marginalised they are gradually, and only partially, brought into 'chorus' by the narrative, acknowledging an existence that is bi-cultural.

Many ethnic autobiographies follow a similar trajectory, climaxing in a coming-of-age in the host society. The novel 'knows' this convention, partly uses it and partly turns it against itself by having the young, second-generation migrant coming of age by travelling away from the host society, and the grandmother fully immersing herself into it after thirty years of passivity and silence. James Clifford has called culture 'a site of travel' (1992) and it is in this sense that Murasaki is leaving her 'home' town, Nanton, another means of extending her cultural under-standing and commitment to continuous change. Her father asks her if she is going to Japan but she says: 'No, no. That's too literal a translation, I think' (209).

Her answer shows that she is not interested in any idea of cultural essences or pre-given identities. It also brings to mind something that Avtar Brah has said about diaspora, home and the ideology of return. Brah describes home as a mythic place of desire in the diasporic imagination and argues that, in this sense, it is a place of no return, even if return literally is feasible, as in the case of Murasaki, and it is possible to visit the specific geographical location seen as the place of descent or origin. Against the commonplace, and racist, perception that the first-generation immigrant is a sojourner, motivated by an ideology of return, the grandmother Naoe wishes to travel in Canada ('culture as a site of travel'); she has no desire to return to Japan, wanting instead to: 'inscribe my name across this country' (108), rather than being inscribed/ racialised by the country. Similarly, for Murasaki, going to Japan would be 'too literal a translation' of her 'homing desire' (Brah 1996) which has also been throughout a critique of discourses of fixed origins, identities or narrative modes. Her 'homing desire' is not a desire for a homeland – she has no problem in belonging locationally in Canada – but for something which she expresses as a 'a sound I can almost hear, just slightly outside my hearing range. And I want to know what that sound is. What I'm missing' (209). Experienced as silence, absence, loss even, in terms of her current understanding and phenomenological reality, this homing desire is part of a continuing process, ever pluralising, against fixity and essence, incapable of literal translation or prescriptive articulation: it is 'not here', beyond, an othering experience. Perhaps it might be thought of as something emergent, not yet come into language, a becoming; in Brah's terms a multi-locationality within and across territorial, cultural and psychic boundaries: part of diasporic identity formation. The work of translation is not an iterative but a reiterative production or performance.

The shifts in person, time, space, location, narrative regime and genre which characterise the narrative are all part of what Brah has in another context called 'creolised envisioning'. The text's structure, style, character and themes are all forms of inter-sectionality: diverse, multiple, hybrid and heterogeneous.

While the novel takes up and echoes some of the most prominent themes of 'ethnic autobiography', its primary relation to these is one of 'adulteration' (with some punning on 'adult' given the coming-of-age trope), a concept developed by David Lloyd as 'stylisation of the hybrid status of the colonised subject as of the colonised culture' (1993: 110). This text does not strictly address the colonised subject, more precisely the hegemonised, mediated and othered subject, but the text's stylisation, parodic practices and disruption of fixed identities all contribute to disidentification and the unsettling of a culture of 'settler dominance', as well as those assimilationist fictions and autobiographies complicit with it.

Chorus of Mushrooms is also written against the grain of the representative or representational authority of the 'ethnic' eye, against prescriptive models of roots or authenticity, and against the idea that each particular migrant trajectory is necessarily and always already allegorical. As the last line of the novel suggests: 'You know you can change the story' (220). Illusioned and voluntarist though that may be, it does indicate that there may be more than one means of cultural integration, an alternative to the 'multi-cultural voice' modelled by her mother in the local newspaper, a space for cultural difference and 'the juggling of two cultures'. The narrative is divided into five parts, of which Part 3 is in many ways the most interesting, as well as being the most fragmented. It is entitled 'An Immigrant Story with a Happy Ending', but it is no more than a series of brief and incomplete notes and jottings, the outline of a story that cannot be told, close to what Lloyd meant by saying that the writer should be 'manifesting absence, incarnating emptiness' (1993: 56). It is here that the longing of belonging resides, where remembering and forgetting are problematised, and the separation between beginnings and endings, endings and beginnings thrown into doubt. Linearity and temporality are violated. Part 3 is the silence or absence of the narrative, that which cannot be spoken; the missing, lost and hidden. It is, in the terms used by Lyotard and referred to a number of times in this book, 'that which can neither be remembered (represented to consciousness) nor forgotten (consigned to oblivion). It is that which returns uncannily' (Readings 1991: xxxii). While Keiko/Kay announces in the newspaper interview that she is at home in this country (Canada), for Murasaki/ Muriel the uncanny and the unhomely shape her experience. Part 3 is the 'missing part' of the narrative, its singularity, lost between voice (multi-cultural representation/happy ending) and silence.

The text also can be understood in relation to a number of problems raised by Trinh Minh-ha, specifically the insider/outsider binary and the ways in which the 'outsider' is repeatedly seen in essentialist terms:

This is not to say that the historical 'I' can be obscured or ignored, and that differentiation cannot be made; but that 'I' is not unitary, culture has never been monolithic, and is always more or less in relation to a judging subject. Differences do not only exist between outsider and insider – two entities – they are also at work within the outsider or the insider – a single entity. (Trinh Min-ha 1991)

When the novel begins, Murasaki is Muriel (insider), Keiko is Kaye (insider), while Naoe is Naoe (outsider). Muriel, Kaye and Sam (Shinji) speak no Japanese, only English (insider), while Naoe speaks only Japanese and no English (outsider). The very categories, of course, presume and privilege the dominant white Canadian discourse ['thinking she was as white as her neighbour'], a process highlighted when Murasaki/Muriel is chosen to play the lead in *Alice in Wonderland* at school, and her mother and teacher eagerly discuss her transfiguration into a blonde. This moment, 'over-colluded' in by Kaye/Keiko, only serves to reinforce the fact that in a racialised and racist culture, however much the outsider subscribes to the insider-dominant, skin colour disrupts the assimilated, unitary 'I'. Murasaki's parents erase almost all traces of

'Orientalism', subordinating themselves willingly to the dominant. Murasaki takes the 'almost' in order to story the contingent and historically specific construction of white hegemony, while simultaneously bodying forth (the 'Alice' moment coincides with the onset of puberty) the hyphenated identities and hybrid realities of her, and her family's, Japanese-Canadian existence. Murasaki's father's mushroom-growing plant is an obvious metaphor for their situation. The mushrooms, fungi of rapid growth, are grown in artificially produced humid conditions, transplanted from their originating soil and produced in isolation, on the margins. Interestingly, most of the workers are immigrants, not co-ethnics but recently arrived Vietnamese. Figuratively speaking, a mushroom is also a person or family that has suddenly sprung into notice; an upstart.

Chorus of Mushrooms 'springs' the family into notice through narrative; telling a story against the grain of the erasures, silences and concealments of Murasaki's parents: their attempts to render invisible their visible 'difference'. They chose the 'great Canadian melting pot' (175). Murasaki's stories are her mushrooms: 'stories grow out of stories grow out of stories' (172). Confined to her chair, bound by her 'language-lessness', separated from her family, Naoe has no story, neither hers nor others of her: 'What is surprising is that most town folk were unaware that the old woman was even living with the Tonkatsus' (88).

As I have been arguing throughout, *Chorus of Mushrooms*, although a work of recovery, is not a narrative of return: its emergence is too ambivalent for such a formulation. As Bhaba says, 'the important thing about the hybrid site is to see that the contenders in any antagonistic interaction are never unitary . . . and their interaction therefore has the possibility always of setting up other sites' (1991: 61).

The antagonistic interaction in the narrative is only superficially generational and intracultural; the narrative resonates with the effects of larger histories, conflicts, cultural presumptions and appropriations and relations of power. Assimilationist ideologies are unitary (as are multi-culturalist ones, arguably), while they also suppress racism and exploitation. In dismantling the unitary, the novel constructs the hybrid site in the form of a narrative which has built into it the possibility of setting up other sites through its processes of rearticulation, split forms and syncretised/creolised 'envisionings'.

5

Knowing Your Place: Becoming Black/Asian-British (1): *Song of the Boatwoman, The Map-Makers of Spitalfields* and *Fruit of the Lemon*

'I'm not really a liar, I just learned very early on that those of us deprived of history sometimes need to turn to mythology to feel complete, to belong.'

(Syal *Anita and Me*: 10)

Although it is a common misunderstanding that non-white immigration to the United Kingdom began in 1948 with the *Empire Windrush*, there is considerable evidence that immigration is a longstanding phenomenon. Nevertheless, it is in the post-Second World War period that a significant migrant presence established itself in the UK to such an extent that the majority of non-white residents are now British born. The minority ethnic population is just over 3.5 million, or 6.3 per cent of the total population. They are highly concentrated in the areas of their settlement, with almost 80 per cent living in the south-east region and the Midlands. The minority ethnic population consists of approximately 1.5 million people of South Asian origin, 0.88 million of Black African-Caribbean origin, and 0.64 million of Chinese or other ethnic groups. The cultural narratives – visual and written – to which I shall be referring throughout this chapter and the following one, will be drawn from each of the segments of this population. Some are by British-born non-whites, others by those who have spent a significant part of their childhood and adult life either in Britain or outside their country of origin. All of them are people whose situation has been described, variously, as 'marginal' or 'between cultures'. Both terms assume fixed centres or clearly defined, and absolute, discourses of boundary. However, what the narrative practices suggest is that, in a multi-racial and multi-cultural society, despite widespread institutional and 'procedural' racism, it is possible to achieve points of convergence which do not simply serve a hegemonic purpose. Against the logics and histories of separation and exclusion, braiding and mutuality can take place. Spaces of difference can be dialogical and not simply a site for producing new essences or absolutes. Iconographic and scriptural traditions can intersect with new configurations to cross boundaries and open up new frontiers/territories.

Opening up new territories has depended to a considerable extent upon the availability of cultural resources for articulating unrecognised or 'hitherto unspoken and often unknown' stories:

On a personal level, a dim sense of the story must be told to the self. How easy this will be depends on the cultural resources available to support the story and to enable it to be assembled. For many, stories are clouded in defences and repressions which simply do not allow any articulationthe actual experiences were simply not open for recognition. (Plummer 1995: 58)

Plummer is speaking of what he calls 'narratives of intimacy', coming-out stories of various kinds, but 'migrant writing' is of a comparable nature.

As Linde and others have pointed out, even the concept of a 'self' to be articulated is not a universally available cultural resource (Linde 1993: 98–9). Given that categories of 'self' and 'identity' are not unproblematic, but culturally and linguistically specific, the narratives I will consider are not simply ones in which a specific sense of story had to be developed to express a self, but rather, they are equally concerned with developing appropriate metaphorical resources for constructing a self through tropes of agency, cohesion and continuity which are not simply recognised as 'ethnic', or 'different'. Storying is a process of self and other recognition, sustained and mediated through cultural vocabularies, freshly shaped legibilities and 'linguistically expressible' histories (ibid.: 101). This is not just a matter of finding a voice or articulating new models of cultural literacy in a counter-hegemonic fashion, but of understanding the specific social and historical conditions within which narrative forms are both produced and consumed. 'Migrant' writing, a product of flux, moving identities and sometimes conditions of near illegibility, works with what might be called 'an archaeology of identity' – culturally, temporally, and spatially multi-layered.

I use the concept of the 'archaeology of identity' to try to suggest that migrancy can produce a self which is, simultaneously and not unproblematically, both individualised and community-orientated – specifically realised as well as being drawn from the resources of a cultural and historical repertoire. Arguably, all selves constructed in narratives are constituted in this way but the conditions of migrancy – colonialism, displacement, marginalisation and racism – mean that these constructions are articulated in a more transparent and legible fashion. Singularity is never possible, if desirable even, in such a marked and over-determined situation of power. In speaking of the historic relation between the sexes, Georg Simmel used the analogy of master and slave, saying that:

It is part of the master's privileges not to have to think continuously of the fact that he is the master, while the position of the slave carries with it the constant reminder of his being a slave. It cannot be overlooked that the woman forgets far less often the fact of being a woman than the man of being a man. (quoted in Linde 1993: 113)

Whereas for me, the cultural categories of being male, white, middle class and heterosexual were not even perceived as being cultural categories until twenty years or so ago, for the 'migrant' who is non-white, British born or not, the position of being in an 'ethnic minority' or of 'mixed race' is thought of continuously as an identity defined by a dominant white culture and living at the margins of that culture. The unlawful killings of Stephen Lawrence, Ricky Reel and of Michael Menson are but three reminders 'of being a slave'.

Recent research carried out by Muhammad Anwar (1998) on ethnic minorities and the British electoral system found that three times the number of ethnic minorities compared with whites felt that race relations in their area and nationally were getting worse, and also the majority of Black, Asian and other ethnic minorities felt that the ethnic minorities status/position in British society was worse compared with that of white people. Unexpectedly, perhaps, this was also recognised by a significant minority (41 per cent) of whites.

The foregoing section may seem unnecessarily negative, but it is designed to show that for all the talk of a third space, hybridity and new ethnicities, some caution needs to be exercised before any of these conditions are uncritically celebrated. The majority of non-white people in Britain live their daily lives framed by racial disadvantage and discrimination. At a cultural level, however, it is also true that there are distinct signs that for many migrants their very location in displacement and at the margins, and their continuous reminder of 'being a slave', has also given rise to a condition of the possibility of agency in a new historical situation. In the dialectic of belonging and not belonging a new agency may be shaped which contests the available cultural resources / categories of identity and power. The migrant's 'double vision' (Said) may be the legacy of a specific and irreversible history, while the negative material realities of most migrant experience are very evident, but this does not mean that these constraints preclude forever the liminal presence of alternative identifications which render boundaries unstable and 'repressed others' articulate. The very process of narration creates the conditions of reflexivity which is one of the properties of the 'double vision'. Never forgetting the fact of 'being a slave', thinking continuously of this condition, can lead to a situation of anamnesis, in which the categories under which one is obliged to live cease to be thought of as iconic, and the years of living out an identity relationally and subordinately are put into question. The condition of reflexivity, the ability to relate to oneself externally and, by so doing, recovering that continuously 'othered' self narratively and bringing it into language or image ready for evaluation and negotiation other than in the terms of the dominant cultural categories, has been extensively demonstrated. From this point on, it is possible for the migrant to cease 'walking around in a world of others who appear to have proper boundaries and effective armor' (Linde 1993: 121).

Not only does the migrant possess Said's 'double vision', but he or she can also create, in terms of what Bakhtin has called 'double-voiced discourse', a merging of voices. Bakhtin uses the concept variously but, in this particular context, it is its use in relation to what he calls a 'hidden polemic' that I wish to deploy it. In a hidden polemic, Bakhtin argues, the author's discourse is directed towards its own referential object but, 'at the same time every statement about the object is constructed in such a way that, apart from its referential meaning, a polemical blow is struck at the other's discourse, at the other's statement about the same object' (1984: 195). Bakhtin stresses that the other's discourse is not itself reproduced, but that the 'other's words are treated antagonistically' and it is this antagonism 'which determines the author's discourse'. What I am arguing, by analogy, is that narratives of the 'migrant othered' are always articulated in antagonism with the othering discourse (colonialism, racism, hegemonic whiteness or Western values for instance) which forces the narrative 'to alter itself accordingly under [its] influence and initiative.' Given the conditions of writing/creating from subordination, the 'migrant' narrative will not speak from its 'own' cultural discourse in any essentialist sense, nor simply in the voice of the 'othering' culture, but what emerges is a situation of 'intense dialogicality'. It is this intense and 'hidden' dialogicality which is what I think of as a profound, and defining, characteristic of the so-called 'third space'. Such a discourse, Bakhtin says in a memorable phrase, 'draws in, as it were, sucks in to itself the other's replies, intensely reworking them' (197).

The 'third space' narrative is an intensive reworking in which the text presupposes, without necessarily articulating, a dialogue 'in which the statements of the second speaker are omitted' but which are present invisibly, leave deep traces, and penetrate deeply inside what is, nevertheless, an *active* reworking and reversal of the historical legacy ('of being a slave') in which the other has been oppressively dominated by the 'othering' discourse. The silenced speaks, the other 'writes back' in an internal dialogisation of discourse in which the hegemonic script 'loses its composure and confidence, becomes agitated, internally undecided and two-faced' (198). Bakhtin argues that such discourse is not only double voiced but also double accented. One of the effects of colonialism and, subsequently, metropolitan racism is monologisation, hence transitional narratives which attempt to break with expected models of otherness have to negotiate deep silences and unspeakability as it is difficult to speak aloud, 'for loud and living intonation [the available and dominant cultural resources] monologises discourse and cannot do justice to the other person's voice present in it' (198). In transition, therefore, the traces of monological othering are present as the unuttered voice of intense dialogicality, but no longer determining or dominating in what emerges as an internally undecided, 'in between' narrative.

GAINING GROUND: MIGRANT FICTIONS

Although many of the writers treated in this, and the following, chapter situate their work in the past, or in a space other than that currently lived in, this is not an act of nostalgia, but of anamnesis, a process of fabulation in which a particular time or place is not so much recovered, or even discovered, but brought into being, invented, made and unmade. In his essay, 'Imaginary homelands', Salman Rushdie speaks for a range of writers:

It may be that writers in my position, exiles or migrants, are haunted by some sense of loss, some urge to reclaim, to look back . . . But if we do look back, we must also do so in the knowledge – which gives rise to profound uncertainties – that our physical alienation from India almost inevitably means that we will not be capable of reclaiming precisely the thing that was lost; that we will, in short, create fictions, not actual cities or villages, but invisible ones, imaginary homelands, Indias of the mind. (1991: 10)

For such writers, their identity may, in Rushdie's terms, be conceived of as 'at once plural and partial'. However, this urge to 'reclaim' is not simply 'archaeological' as it 'renews the past, refiguring it as a contingent in-between space, that innovates and interrupts the performance of the present' (Bhabha 1994: 7). More important even than this, perhaps passive, process is not just an act of renewing but of reworking, by second-generation immigrants in particular: 'reworking the past exposes its hybridity, and to recognise and acknowledge this hybrid past in terms of the present empowers the community and gives its agency'. So, not only is the 'migrant's' belonging split between a family experience (language, religion and culture of origin) and a 'street' experience (that of the culture of current location), but the past becomes a complex, multi-layered and hybrid phenomenon also. The outcome of this interaction between present and past, this reworking, is the production of cultural identities that, in Stuart Hall's term, are 'in transition' and also, one might add, negotiation and transformation. Mapping this transition is one of the tasks of a number of cultural works, in particular Syed Manzurul Islam's 'The Map-Makers of Spitalfields', but also, to a less specific extent, Levy's *Fruit of the Lemon*, Meera Syal's *Anita and Me*, and the writings of Hanif Kureishi. Not surprisingly, journey metaphors proliferate in these works and, in Said's phrase, 'homes are always provisional', borders crossed, and identities are formed 'on the move'. Literally, in some cases, and metaphorically in others, these fictions construct figures in the borderlands, bi-focal and bi-local, with complex and multiple belongings: 'deterritorialised', living through difference but not necessarily marginalised.

Before moving to a closer analysis of some of the texts in question, it may be as well to attempt to clarify what precisely is meant by migrant or diasporic writing in the British context. Many of the writers are British born, all are British subjects, but are part of what a combination of political, social, and cultural forces have designated an ethnic minority. As Smaro Kamboureli has argued, 'ethnic subjectivity is never utterly free and of itself', but is always part of, and explicitly or not, in dialogue with the larger social formation (1993: 211). For many, the 'British', like 'Canadians' in Kamboureli's example, are implicitly other than the ethnic minorities who are permanently consigned to a condition of otherness. Hence I prefer the term 'migrant' writing, with its double meaning; as it suggests transition and, possibly, transgression – a questioning of absolute 'otherness'. It also interrogates the hegemonic assumptions about whiteness as invisibility and not an ethnicity. Migrant writing enters, disrupts and destabilises the settled and dominant categories of the larger cultural narrative and refuses marginality: 'the problem of outside/inside must always itself be a process of hybridity' (Bhabha 1994: 4). Hybridity is always a threat to the dominant culture which seeks to 'ethnicise' difference and render it static and exotic, rather than seeing it as a condition of the culture as a whole, always in transformation, always subject to modification.

To adapt Kamboureli's argument slightly, what these texts do is start from a position where ethnic subjectivity is only a point of departure; the point of arrival, provisional and deferred, is hybridity as agency in so far as it interrupts the prevailing relations between power and knowledge by bringing into question the problems of the representation of otherness as a conflicted and contestable site of struggle, internal to, and not separate from, the articulations of a national culture. This culture is always, it will be argued, situated in 'in-between' spaces, in narratives of transition and negotiation, antagonism and critique. To summarise this section, a quotation from Homi Bhabha's introduction to *The Location of Culture* should help to focus the argument so far and prepare for the analysis of particular texts:

The social articulation of difference, from the minority perspective, is a complex, on-going negotiation that seeks to authorise *cultural hybridities that emerge in moments of historical transformation*. The 'right' to signify from the periphery of authorised power and privilege does not depend on the persistence of tradition; it is resourced by the power of tradition to be reinscribed through the conditions of contingency and contradictoriness that attend upon the lives of those who are 'in the minority'. The recognition that tradition bestows is a partial form of identification. In restaging the past it introduces other, incommensurable cultural temporalities into the invention of tradition. (Bhabha 1994: 2; my italics)

I would argue that the post-1945 emigration to Britain of significant numbers of people from Asia and the Caribbean is such a moment of 'historical transformation', and that culturally in the past decade or so many writers and film-makers (especially 'second-generation' migrants) have claimed the right to 'signify' and, as a consequence, have reinvented and reinscribed tradition from the perspective of their multiple and partial identifications. It is some of these reinscriptions which will now be examined. Several of these work within already existing narrative traditions – the autobiography and the picaresque – to revisit or 'rewrite' the story of childhood and early adolescence and/or of the arrival of parents. In the words of Onyekachi Wambu, 'they also began, uniquely, to map the contours of their own identity as black British people, not as rejected outsiders, but as critical insiders. We moved from post-colonialism to multi-cultural Britain' (Wambu 1998: 28). The sometimes acerbic comedies of Kureishi and Syal show just how critical and far inside they are.

Even those who seem simply to be repeating standard narrative forms also work with a certain level of displacement, the insider's critical question. This is what has been called 'repetitions with a difference'; such a repetition uses an already existing form 'in order to transform it from within, deterritorialize it' (Deleuze and Guattari 1987: 349). These are, to a greater or lesser extent, *texts of becoming*, in the sense conveyed by Deleuze and Guattari:

One reterritorializes, or allows oneself to be reterritorialized, on a minority as a state; but in a becoming, one is deterritorialized. Even blacks, as the Black Panthers said, must become-black. (291)

In this chapter, and in Chapter 6, a number of texts of becoming, texts of deterritorialisation, in which we see a process of becoming-Black British, will be examined in order to establish ways in which they 'turn the gaze of the discriminated back upon the eye of power' (Bhabha 1994: 112).

GOING HOME

Meiling Jin, a writer of the Chinese diaspora, was born in Guyana and
now lives in London. Her collection of short stories, *Song of the Boatwoman* (1996) ranges across locations in London, China, California,
Malaysia and the Caribbean. In the story, 'Short Fuse', Gladys – the
central figure – has lived five years of 'exile' from Guyana, and in London:
'She knew the look that said: no coloureds, no children, no animals, and
bore each insult, each act of hostility, as a mark of exile' (89). The exile is
not only from Guyana and within London from the 'host' society, but also
within Guyana as a person of Chinese antecedents caught between
African-Caribbeans and East Indian Caribbeans. Home – 'If I move is
home I going' – then becomes a complex and conflicted space, her
temporariness in England – 'she never intended to stay' – opening out
into a wider sense of instability and of permanent transience, alienated
by colour, dialect, race and cuisine from the localised and ordered spaces
of the host nation.

Home is initially a place to be dreamed of, never one of the few places
Gladys has lived in over five years. Her current existence, her present
dwelling, is a palimpsest – beneath it is her mother, her absent husband
Sidney, her home on Subryanville where the fruit, trees, windows and
floors become the readable spaces of her multiple location and split or
doubled identity. Everything she does, thinks or imagines is predicated
upon return: the more money she earns as an outworker brings her closer to
home – 'she stitches each lining with precision, each stitch being exactly
the same' (93). The garment being stitched is an analogue of 'home' and
when her plan to go home is shattered and she is resigned to living under
the gaze/stare 'that tells her all she needs to know about white and
coloured' (96), she devises a plan to kill her neighbour's dog who becomes
the only visible symbol of power over which she can exercise any control.
The dog 'polices' her every movement in and out of her house; it even
immobilises her – 'caught like a trespasser'. The overcrowded space in
which she lives with her two sons causes her 'to permanently shrink
inwards', and this inward shrinking is paralleled by a similar external
contraction in which her whole world is reduced to the scale of negotiating
the entrance to her house and her conflict with the dog as a hostile
gatekeeper: a functional contact zone. Condensed and miniaturised into
this conflict is an image of her otherness, her not belonging, and displacement. Even her dream of 'home' is reduced to the yellow mango – symbol of
both home and return which has caused her to forget her usual strategy of
dog avoidance – which is misshapen through its fall from her bag when she
is attacked. The misshapen mango both prefigures her realisation that
there will be no return, and configures her 'contentless' trespass and exile:
'a middle-aged Chinese woman in an ill-fitting coat' (88).

As food is one of the markers of difference – the landlady has isolated Gladys's gas supply to prevent the cooking smells – it is fitting that she kills the dog with a poisoned black pudding, another symbol of home. That she can only function at the level of the dog confirms one of the primary characteristics of racism - its refusal to the other of the status of human. As has already been discussed in the Introduction, the migrant arouses in the host neighbour a range of ontological anxieties – indistinction, temporariness, transience, instability, contingency and the arbitrary, the absence of sameness and self-identification – which have been relieved by investments in whiteness and Englishness. The visibility of the non-white migrant threatens these investments with exposure and transparency, and thus she has to be 'stared' back into invisibility by an unreturnable gaze. Gladys is forced to live her difference in a context of 'indifference', a condition of her subhumanity.

So many writers (Caryl Phillips, Andrea Levy, Meera Syal, Meiling Lin) locate their fictions in the Britain of the 1960s and early 1970s as a way of focusing upon that extended moment of 'encounter' which was marked most dramatically by the 1948 *Windrush* journey. It is the restaging of this encounter which is designed as a process of anamnesis, of bringing into awareness, not simply auto/biographical tropes, but also the continuation into the 1990s of racist cultural formations which, in the face of the provisional, the contingent and the transitory, convert emotional boundaries into essences and ethnic absolutes which reject the diasporic communities and seek to cleanse and expel them beyond the borders of the host imaginary of coherence and meaningfulness. Figures like Gladys live their invisibility in the interstitial and unreadable spaces of dream, memory and the consumption of objects of home, an uncelebrated and non-celebratory hybridity. The very titles of this particular story, 'Short Fuse', and the following one, 'An Uneasy Life', embody this insecurity.

Most of the stories in the collection feature women who are in some ways marginal, either because of their race or their sexuality, often both. The story 'Homecoming' features a Westernised Malaysian woman, Margret, living in London but on her first visit home with her English lesbian lover, Jack. 'Home' starts out as a physical location – 'This was home, even though she had long ago ceased to belong' – but in the course of the three-week visit it alternates between being a complex space of identity – 'it was good to be home' – a place of nostalgia and childhood memory, part of her 'imaginary', and a locus of change, conflict, and splitting – 'It's like two sides of me coming together and they don't fit'. Wanting to tell her mother that she is a lesbian, Margret finds herself unable to do more than engage in small talk. Significantly, there is no word in her family language for 'lesbian' and this absence/lack shapes the 'contentless' discourse of the return home. Displaced from one centre – 'my mother is old-fashioned Chinese' – she is unable to name or give voice to the centre of her sexual identity and lapses into silence, a silence which relates to both her mother and to Jack. The 'home-coming out' is infinitely postponed but in the airport restaurant, prior to her return to England, Margret tells her mother that she is thinking of living together with Jack on her return, and her mother refers to their friendship – 'Early days! Maybe you still courting – lah' (123). The word which does not exist in their Chinese language is never spoken – 'The two women looked at each other in silence' – but there is a sense, finally, that Margret's 'home' is no longer a place of regression but a new space in which the two centres of her life can meet; her mother is able to look at her, not as a child, but as a woman with her own sexual identity. Interestingly, the text places the sentences 'the two women looked at each other in silence', and 'the two women made their way to the departure lounge' in close proximity to articulate a stage in growth which has not yet come into language. As combined subjects of both sentences, the distance between them which the story charts, even if the text reverts to the banal and the safe at the end, has been narrowed. The departure lounge is also a place of arrival. The first of the two sentences is an encounter and an exchange, the second a coming together in a shared activity – there is a semantic shift and the breath which Margret held as the plane landed at Penang airport can now be let out. A double distance – cultural and sexual – has been travelled.

STRATEGIES OF REPOSSESSION

As is obvious from the title, Syed Manzurul Islam's short story, 'The Mapmakers of Spitalfields' is concerned with a cartographic imagination. Unlike Kureishi's Karim in *The Buddha of Suburbia*, who is journeying away from a particular location, the central figure in this story constructs, in complex ways, a place-bound identity. It is an attempt to localise and contextualise the 'nomadic', to ground it in a particularising and specific experience of difference: diasporic but also resident, with abode signifying the often forgotten past tense of abide. The story traces a process of cultural translation in which hybridity, rather than being seen as a point of arrival, is but the condition of the possibility of a creative and productive third space. I mean this in the sense captured by Salman Rushdie: 'It is normally supposed that something always gets lost in translation; I cling, obstinately, to the notion that something can always be gained' (1991: 17).

Adapting a phrase from de Certeau, it will be argued that what Islam, or his character Brothero-Man, creates is a migrational, or metaphorical, Spitalfields which 'slips into the clear text of the planned and readable city' (de Certeau 1993). What is created is not simply a cultural space; the very choice of the location, Spitalfields, opens up a history of displacements and migrations, of a genealogy of changing material practices. Throughout this analysis I will be drawing extensively on de Certeau's 'Walking in the city' and Derek Gregory's *Geographical Imaginations* (1994), in particular the section 'Strategies of dispossession' (168–74). Most of the texts referred to so far have been concerned with what Gregory calls 'a leitmotif of all post-colonial literatures': place and displacement. This particular story could almost be seen as a 'synecdochal allegory' of this leitmotif. Brothero-Man, the map-maker, does not seek an identity in memory, in the past, or in 'categorical ethnicity' (the phrase is Ien Ang's: 1994) but in 'a strange new city, always at the crossroads, and between the cities of lost times and cities of times yet to come' (Islam 1997: 69).

In de Certeau's terms, Brothero-Man's endless traversing of the spaces of the locality is part of a fiction, a practice that 'invents spaces': 'what this walking exile produces is precisely the body of legends that is currently lacking in one's own vicinity' (de Certeau 1993: 160). The text charts what is, simultaneously, a migrant reading and a writing of the city, an opening up of spaces to a 'new' difference: mapping another land of belonging, another image of Englishness. As has been argued elsewhere in this book, post-war immigration has helped to pull 'Englishness' out of shape, and to push it in new directions, clearly differentiated formations. Despite the 'new' racism of the 1970s and 1980s, and all the efforts of Thatcherism, Britain in the 1990s is a place in which 'the surface of this order [undifferentiated ethnicity] is everywhere punched and torn open by ellipses, drifts and leaks of meaning' (ibid.). The story adopts a style of ellipses, drifts and leaks as part of its structure, but the order which is punctured is not only that of 'Englishness' but also of 'Bengali-ness'. While the blond-haired men in white overalls with red Doc Martens pursue Brothero throughout the narrative in order to arrest and incarcerate him, several of his fellow Bengalis seek to defend themselves from his irreverent and dissenting boundary crossing, and are complicit with the white judgement of 'madness'. In making a home out of 'here' (and not out of a 'faraway home') and in carving out of the local space a time of becoming, he is creating a legend, a point of legibility. De Certeau reminds us of the etymology: '*legenda* what is *to be read*, but also what *can be read*' (ibid.). Brothero-Man travels across generations and gender, enters and exits musical, spiritual and culinary cultures and subcultures, dehomogenising the undifferentiated spaces of the Bengali 'other'. He approves of the youth who are 'neither here nor there', in Harlem, Kingston or Brixton. His mystery, his elusiveness, his twilight singularity, make him not a 'roots' man but almost an 'uproots' man, challenging, by his presence and hybrid use of an 'Engali' or 'Benglish' idiolect, both English and Bengali essences. In the terms used earlier, he is erasing the 'or' and mapping the 'and', liberating spaces for new routes and occupations. The fact that many cannot understand his 'babbles' indicates that what Brothero-Man is doing is developing a style which is based upon a 'peculiar processing of the symbolic' in which words as conventionally understood 'operate in the name of an emptying-out and wearing-away of their primary role' (ibid.: 158–9). There is, as de Certeau says, a rhetoric of walking and it is this which the story produces; a rhetoric in which it becomes apparent that the map is not the territory. The mapping process detaches itself from the spaces it was supposed to define and creates, instead, a series of 'imaginary meeting-points' or thresholds on his 'nomadic' itinerary.

Spitalfields in some ways does not exist, it is an idea or it becomes an imaginary. Against those fixed points and already inscribed places on the map, Brothero-Man's deterritorialising activities constitute procedures for remembering, coming to terms, not with the past, but with the future. In spatialising, in weaving seemingly disparate places together, he repossesses and reappropriates in such a way that does not simply restore, or give back, spaces to its residents (threatened, as they are, by the constant menace of racist skinheads), but 'unbricks' and transforms them in the process. What Brothero-Man presents is not a gift, or a given, but a set of procedures, a model of entering and grounding the local against passive models of 'return' or fatalistic marginalisation. The white men in overalls are vestigial bearers of power and knowledge, but this relationship is undermined and rendered transparent and arbitrary by the central figure's strategic 'invisibility'. The strategy is enabling and empowering, not on behalf of the individual but of the wider community; it is a political act, a way of making psychic, cultural and material spaces habitable: 'ways of going out and coming back in.'

The men in white overalls 'haunt' Brick Lane because Brothero-Man bears all the traces of madness – discursively categorised – signs that 'the strange, the alien, the other' (Gregory 1994: 72) are 'massing outside the gates of Reason'. It is part of 'white mythology', its power–knowledge continuum, that whiteness and reason are coterminous. What the story shows is that the strange, alien and other are always already constitutively inside the gates, displacing and subverting the boundaries and binaries and surveillances which seek to dispossess them. Derrida is valuable in respect of these insights because he has, in Gregory's words, an 'uncanny (unheimlich) ability to show us that at the heart of what we take to be familiar, native, at home – where we think we can find our center – lurk (is concealed and repressed) what is unfamiliar, strange and uncanny' (ibid.). Even though the white men in overalls increasingly seem to behave like figures in a Whitehall farce or a Chaplin movie, the story does not simply replace one set of binaries with another, as the 'Bengaliness' of the 'Asian' figures is also opened up to critique and interrogation. In rendering himself 'unreadable', out of the sight of his pursuers, and slipping through the nets of hegemonic categories, he is, by analogy, modelling for the dispossessed and 'othered' a series of strategies of refusal and resistance, what de Certeau calls 'sly multiplicity' – an apt description of Brothero-Man.

This modelling faculty is crucial because, although I have talked throughout of Brothero-Man as a distinguishable character in a narrative, it is clear that this distinctiveness is itself a narrative strategy as his key role is exemplary, a 'condition of the possibility' of cultural translation, of sliding against the masks of newer selves, of mobilising against 'dispossession through othering', displacing the scopic regime of whiteness, stepping out of the slide/side show of colonialism and its racist legacies. In other words, Brothero-Man's almost shamanic role is designed to demonstrate, by visiting and revisiting the sites and interstices of Brick Lane in a totalising strategy, that 'space itself was a text that had to be written before it could be interpreted' (Carter, quoted in Gregory 1994: 172). Brothero-Man, at an individual cognitive level, 'writes' the local spaces on behalf of the community and also acts as interpreter. At a symbolic and ethical level he is the 'becoming-black' of the community in the sense discussed earlier: he embodies the community in the process of becoming, of disavowal, of differentiation, of teaching the local spaces 'how to speak'. It is, in Carter's terms, 'an epistemological strategy, a mode of knowing', a process of nomination and ex-nomination, shaping a spatial grammar, 'forms of spatial punctuation'. Above all, and indebted to Lefebvre's claim that 'space had to be produced before it could be read' (Gregory 1994: 172), Carter speaks of the language of naming, the language of travelling (the rhetoric of walking): 'What was named was not something out there; rather it represented in mental orientation, an intention to travel' (ibid.). If anything, Brothero-Man's journey is precisely a travelling against the 'something out there', the prescribed, always already known, the certainties of 'white mythologies': 'White invasion was a form of spatial writing that erased the earlier meaning . . . the absence of a shared intentional space in which translation could occur' (ibid.: 173).

What Islam is doing in 'Map-makers' is not simply replacing 'white invasion' by 'black invasion' but setting in train a narrative process of undecidability, in which the erased and the effaced can proactively, and from a position of limited empowerment, help to reconstitute a shared intentional space in which white is not translated into black (racist liberalism) or black into white (colonialism), but a third space can emerge from the continua of translation, out of a complexity of becoming – identities, a new belonging which exceed, go beyond 'the spaces that border hybridity' (Venn 1999: 263).

The use of the plural in the story's title alerts us to the fact that each generation of immigrants to Spitalfields (from the seventeenth century onwards) has had to 'sing the country', bring it into existence and ownership, within the horizons of new expectations and new intelligibilities. The text deconstructs the effects of an anterior, and superior, ordering truth and places into question, under erasure even, that which in the 'white mythology . . . stands apart from the world itself, as the meaning that things themselves represent' (Gregory: 174). In the narrative, truth, nature, meaning and the obvious are all given histories, situated and contextualised, as Brothero-Man 'went back and forth, sketching delicately, with the skill of a miniaturist, a map at the very heart of this foreign city'. Structurally, the text never fully separates the map-maker from the narrating voice (something which is made clear at the end), so much so that, contrary to the traditions of the first-person (singular) narrative, this becomes a multi-accented, polyvocal, 'we' narrative, in which everyone becomes Brothero-Man. In tracing Brothero-Man, the narrator also becomes a map-maker. Not only is he the map-maker entering the local spaces, the streets, the homes, the shops, the mosques, but, metaphorically, he is also insinuating, 'brothering' himself into the spaces of the narrative: a process of textualisation is taking place – he is 'entering a secret zone in another country', neither Bangla Desh nor England in any simple sense, but living 'by bending the English tongue to the umpteenth degree'(69), and 'drawing the secret blueprint of a new city', neither a copy of the migrants' city left behind nor in the likeness of the host inner cities. The men in overalls are determined to stop him completing his map, because they know it is more than an ordnance survey, but a cartography of values, of histories as oppression and dispossession, of ideologies, of violences. An incomplete map, a fragment, would leave the hierarchy of the prior, offering truth intact and still apart from the world itself. A complete map would incorporate white mythology, render it visible, transparent, and contingent – deauthorised. It is Brothero-Man as potentially authorising a new set of future possibilities – neither here nor there, inside nor outside, ethical and political – that is menacing and which has to be discursively bound and gagged, placed in the asylum. At all costs he must be prevented from biting off 'a chunk of your land' and 'wearing a parchment of a map at one with his body' (75) because white power survives partly through alienating the body of the 'other' from the 'other inside him/her'.

In the final section of the story, there is an extended, italicised passage which synopsises the whole mapping process, not only literally in retracing Brothero-Man's journey in which 'our' city is repossessed from within 'their strange city', but also by the way in which structurally its ellipses, drifts and leaks of meaning (signified typographically by gaps and breaks) break down and break up what Bhabha has called the authority of the sentence, as in slow motion Brothero-Man melts and completely vanishes: a figment of the white men's imagination perhaps, or paranoia. What they do not realise is that they had been witnesses at a birth: that of a potential succession of map-makers, liberated from spaces that could now be reoccupied in new and complex ways.

EXPECTATIONS OF RETURN

In 'A Coney Island of the Mind', Ferlinghetti wrote that 'Home is the place one starts from'– it is a point of departure. Home will be discussed later in terms established by Avtar Brah and in connection with *Anita and Me*. It is also at the centre of Andrea Levy's third novel *Fruit of the Lemon* (1999). Her two previous novels were set in the 1960s and 1970s respectively; this one never specifies a precise time, but it seems to be centred on the early 1970s. Andrea Levy was born in London of Jamaican parents and the parents of her first-person narrator, Faith, came to England on the Jamaica Producers' banana boat.

To some extent, Levy is still working within the trajectory of the biographical narrative (two academic books are cited in the Acknowledgements as offering assistance in her research) but in its focus on both England and Jamaica a doubly articulated storying takes place which becomes multi-voiced and polyaccented. A brief opening section sketches the outline of the narrator's parents' journey to England, the birth of their two children, and the purchase of their first house: 'We finally arrive home' (*Fruit of the Lemon*: 11). This initial experience bears some traces of the 'stock' migrant genre mocked by Meera Syal, but for many families from the Caribbean entering Britain when 'British identity was still wrapped up in the concept of empire and imperial destiny' (Phillips 1998: 430), poverty, unemployment, over-crowding, separation, and racist violence were widely shared.

The first part of the novel – England – is mostly taken up with Faith's experience as a young woman starting her second job after leaving art college, leaving the family home, and sharing a flat with three white friends. Much of this section is taken up with her work in the costume department of BBC Television Centre, the vicissitudes of flat sharing, and attempts to 'leave home' in a more than literal sense. Though conscious that both at college and at Television Centre she is exploited for her token ethnicity, the novel is only rarely directed outwards to the wider social and political context of the time, but is primarily concerned with coming to terms with her identity, not as migrant like her parents but as 'diasporic' and living a multiple life in a hybrid, syncretic culture. Although Faith experiences what George Lamming has called 'the consolation of freedom', nevertheless she is also aware of the missing dimensions of her parents' 'narratives and subjectivities' (Chamberlain 1998: 49), as neither says very much about their early life in the Caribbean.

According to Mary Chamberlain, for many first migrants to Britain from Barbados, ' "home" was the physical space in which they found their primary identity and Barbados became for most the site of un-ambiguous allegiance' (ibid.). For Faith's parents their allegiance is much more ambiguous, and they live comfortably within the moral and social horizons of respectable British working-class/lower middle-class life. It is their relative silence about their past lives which motivates Faith's search for a time and space before her time and space. As Marianne Hirsch says in 'Past Lives: Postmemories in Exile': 'None of us ever knows the world of our parents. We can say that the motor of the fictional imagination is fuelled in great part by the desire to know the world as it looked and felt before our birth' (1996: 419). Faith's own search for agency and identity is focused by her parents' decision to return to Jamaica: 'We're thinking of going home to Jamaica' (44). It is this decision – initially prompting Faith to ask the question 'why'? – which precipitates the second half of the narrative in which Faith 'returns' to a place from which she has not come. As with so many of the fictions examined here, the metaphor of the journey forms one of the axes of the narrative. Like Haroon and Anwar in The Buddha of Suburbia, Faith's parents had 'lived English' with her mother in particular regularly saying, mantra-like, 'You couldn't get this in Jamaica', whereas the opposite would be true of the person living nostalgically with a persistent fantasy of return. Her parents, on the contrary, had never been back, preferring to holiday in Devon. Given the silence of the past, and Jamaica as an absence, Faith is compelled to interrogate her mother's simple, and seemingly uncomplicated utterance, 'Because we from Jamaica'.

Much of the narrative is taken up with Faith's 'why', and with the complexities of 'going home', 'here' and 'there', 'another country', and with precisely what 'from Jamaica' means beyond its geographical sense. Her brother's apparently unquestioning endorsement of their parents' decision leads Faith to view both him and them as 'strangers', suddenly existing separately from her, out of context. Not only does she begin to question her own belonging, but comes to sense also that the 'fences and gates and barbed wire' of England's 'green and pleasant land' (56) are not simply material presences but extend into cultural, social and political dimensions. When she considers applying for a post as dresser in the BBC, one of her colleagues says: 'But they don't have black dressers' (71). When she applies and is appointed, she is told by Carl's girlfriend, Ruth, that it is just tokenism and she must do something about it.

Whether or not her appointment is tokenism is impossible for Faith to resolve but, after her parents' decision to return home, she becomes increasingly aware of how extensive is the racism of the society in which she lives as she experiences the coarse and abusive language of her friend Marion's working class family, the genteel and well-spoken racism of her friend Simon's 'quintessentially English' village, the unthinking and 'well meaning' discourse of her liberal flatmates, and the physical violence meted out to a black woman in a radical bookshop. Add to this the fact that the frequently asked question 'Where are you from?' is never fully answered to the satisfaction of her white interlocutors until she points to her parents' origin, and the complications of the Black Power militant Ruth's *white* family, and it begins to dawn on Faith what her parents are migrating *from*: an England in which a black person can only ever be seen as guest, stranger, transient, always belonging elsewhere. As Marion tries to explain – reminding us of the so-called 'new' racism – 'it's a cultural thing'.

From relative invisibility to becoming-black, Faith begins to wonder what it is that people see when they look at her, and she slowly enters into an awareness of her body as a multi-layered, striated identity. It is this striature which forms the second part of the narrative, following Faith's breakdown precipitated by the dizzying confusions of a contradictory and conflicted identity:

I could not see where I was stepping. I got into bed. But as my eyes adjusted to the dark I could see my reflection in the wardrobe mirror. A black girl lying in a bed. I covered the mirror with a bath towel. I didn't want to be black any more. I just wanted to live. The other mirror in the room I covered with a tee shirt – *Voilà!* I was no longer black. (160)

Throughout the first part of the novel, Faith has been an autodiegetic narrator, the protagonist of the story she narrates, although towards the end of this phase of the narrative she becomes increasingly passive and spectatorial, reduced ultimately to the confines of her room. In order to understand this process, it may be helpful to draw upon an observation by Lefebvre in respect of the problematics of space which he sees as 'composed of questions about mental and social space, about their interconnections' (Lefebvre 1991: 413). The space of Part 1 – 'England' – is not just cartographic or locational, but also mental and cultural. Faith is not only produced in, and by, that space but also partly produces it as her belonging/not belonging. The section I have just quoted from the novel can be linked with Lefebvre in the way in which he brings together the mental and social: '[space] is first all *my* body, and then it is my body counterpart or "other", its mirror-image or shadow: it is the shifting intersection between that which touches, penetrates, threatens or benefits my body on the one hand, and all other bodies on the other' (ibid.: 184).

The whole of part one has presented this 'shifting intersection' between Faith's body and her body counterparts, or others, in a space representationally designated as 'England'. This social space is a space of white hegemony; by covering her mirrors, Faith is becoming-white, as her body can no longer be 'seen' by its counterparts or others. She enters England, England enters her in an act of reciprocal invisibility (as 'whiteness' is invisible as an ethnicity). If, therefore, as Lefebvre also says, 'The whole of (social) space proceeds from the body', then, in this act of veiling, Faith is symbolically removing the black, the 'multi', from the body of England. It becomes ethnically undifferentiated. However, this is only the end of one part of the overall narrative, an illusory point of arrival (the 'punctual ego' thinking it can 'see itself seeing itself') but also a point of departure, a prelude to another shifting intersection between a different space and a different body: 'Child, everyone should know where they come from' (162). The use of 'child' in that sentence is not accidental, even if it is a familiar/familial usage.

This willed invisibility, this act of erasure, can never be complete, it is only a stage in the formation of identity; a stage in which traces of the marks of the originally visible body remain and persist. As Derrida points out, such 'traces do not indicate the marks themselves but the absence of the marks' (Childers and Hentzi 1995: 99). In other words, Faith's black body, from which the whole of social space proceeds, is not an absolute, or essentialised and unchanging presence, but 'under erasure' is the site of the very absence of such a fixed identity. Jamaica is a space in which another specular counterpart is possible, is producible. The second part of the narrative is the production of this space and its mental/social interconnections in which a second 'alienation' takes place between the 'child' and her own self-image. Faith journeys away from the paranoiac space of her England/self towards a new cultural imaginary, another scopic regime. Faith's 'England self' can also be helpfully understood in terms described by Merleau-Ponty:

Since the seer is caught up in what he [sic] sees, it is still himself he sees: there is a fundamental narcissism of vision. And thus, for the same reason, the vision he exercises, he also undergoes from the things, such that, as many painters have said, I feel myself looked at by the things, my activity is equally passivity – which is the second and more profound sense of the narcissism: not to see in the outside, as the others see it, the contour of a body one inhabits, but especially to be seen by the outside, to exist within it, to emigrate into it, to be seduced, captivated, alienated by the phantom, so that the seer and the visible reciprocate one another and we no longer know which sees and which is seen. (1968: 139)

Faith collapses under this 'fundamental narcissism of vision', and it is perhaps not too fanciful to see this phase as an appropriate way of codifying the 'England' narrative: white skin, white masks. The point I made earlier about the autodiegetic narrator becoming spectatorial is reinforced by the phrase 'my activity is equally passivity'. Faith has literally, and metaphorically, come to exist within, to emigrate into, and be seduced, captivated and alienated by the 'phantom': 'I was no longer black'.

The 'real' Jamaica, however, where 'they come from', is not simply available in any originary sense. It has to be made, produced, performed even, not recovered from some pre-existing state. As Elizabeth Grosz writes: 'It is our positioning within space, both as the point of perspectival access to space, but also as an object for others in space, that gives the subject any coherent identity' (Grosz 1988). It is this positioning as, and at, the centre of her own space – mainly as an object for the voices and vision of others in space – that forms the basis of Part 2 of the novel. In Grosz's terms: 'The subject's relation to its own body provides it with basic spatial concepts and terms by which it can reflect on its own position'. At the end of Part 1, both perspective and reflexivity have been entirely undermined. Covering the mirrors returned Faith to 'the borderless space of the body in fragments' (Burgin 1996: 129). Jamaica will provide location, dimension and orientation; home, almost, in a Jamaica with its own time and enunciative space. What Jamaica yields, in Faith's quest for origin and the tracing of a history, familial and national, is best described by Foucault: 'What is found at the historical beginning of things is not the inviolable identity of their origin; it is the dissension of other things. It is disparity' (1977: 142). A differential history, as Bhabha has called it.

It is important to note that the narrative constructs Jamaica temporally as well as structurally, for, as Burgin comments: 'The fabric of self-identity – individual, ethnic, or national – is woven in time and space, history and geography, memory and place' (1996: 190). Its historicity is a crucial dimension of Faith's present, and future: a cognitive mapping, or allegory, in Jameson's terms (1992). As Burgin also says, 'Identification is the privileged mechanism by which other histories and memories become our own' (ibid.: 234). This is why the narrative shifts from the first-person, autodiegetic narrator to the voices of other histories and other memories, as Faith's identification takes both transitive and reflexive forms, a binding and a bonding. The real object loss of Part 1 is supplemented by the partial identification – 'substitute gratification'– of Part 2. The journey to Jamaica is a journey away from non-differentiation – the erased black girl lying in a bed – towards some kind of perception of distance/difference. The journey has been precipitated by an inaugural loss at a metaphorical level, but literally it is the splitting away of the parents from her 'home', her country, a reverse-migration or return. Faith's voyage is an act of spacing, in all senses of the word, a diacrisis. It is also a process of rememoration, in so far as the principle of identity (according to Kierkegaard) is based upon repetition.

As a process of itineration as well as of iteration, Faith's visit to

Jamaica is also interrogative as she has to discard any previous assumptions: 'everything was a little familiar but not quite'; ' "Can you fasten
your seatbelt", a stewardess said to me in a broad Jamaican accent . . .
She was white' (168). It is the 'not quite' which constitutes the distance
which Faith has to travel on her initiatory journey through 'astonishing
strangeness'. The strangeness is not just the unfamiliar, but also the
unexpectedly familiar; her Aunt Coral's house reminded her of home,
while the aunt has 'the aura of kin'. At first she converts and translates
Jamaica into home, her bedroom in London, but gradually she comes to
listen to other stories, other voices: 'Coral's Story told to me by Coral'
(189). Part 2 is punctuated at times by diagrams of family trees as Faith
comes to know about counterparts and others, past and present. Coral
becomes a secondary narrator, gatekeeper and interpreter making the
spaces of Jamaica readable. Each new story leads to an extension of the
family tree (pp. 190, 212, 228, 240, 258, 280, 306) which becomes
increasingly complex at a temporal and spatial level as the layers of
the family unfold, intersect and crossover. With one exception each story
is a woman's story. The family is characterised by transnational mobility
as narratives of migration to Cuba, America and Panama overlap with
memories of labour exploitation, eviction, 'miscegenation' and internal
racisms based upon differentiated shades of black ('She wanted to know
was Mildred a quadroon, and octoroon, a half-breed or just black') (288)).
    Faith's visit to her mother's childhood home is, at first, compared with
other historic places she has been to as a tourist, but they were sites of
public time, public narrativity. The visit is a landmark in the recognition
of distance and difference: 'This was where my mum grew up and kept a
goat called Columbine – on this land! It was so far from Crouch End clock
tower, Dunn's bakery and the W3 bus' (255). What is happening is
similar to what Ricoeur refers to as private narrativity or history: 'As
soon as the individual comes up against the finite limits of its own
existence, it is obliged to recollect itself and to make time its *own*'
(Ricoeur 1995: 221). This is what the narrative is doing, enabling the
autodiegetic figure to make time, and space arguably, her own. It is close
to demography, the 'kernel of history', and the succession of family trees
graphically represent 'the regeneration of generations' (Ricoeur), the
story of the living and the dead, made up both of anecdotes and
genealogies, and slavery and colonisation: the meeting point of private
time and public time.
    Faith's relatives laid out a past out in front of her: 'They wrapped me in
a family history and swaddled me tight in its stories' (326). The birthing/
rebirthing imagery is obvious. What Faith comes to experience is 'the
shifting intersection between that which touches, penetrates, threatens
or benefits my bodyand all other bodies'(Lefebvre 1991: 184); a shared
private and public (Jamaica/England) past emerges and Faith imagines a

new 'childhood' in which she is now articulate where, originally, she was silent and 'contentless':

Let those bully boys walk behind me in the playground. Let them tell me, 'You're a darkie. Faith's a darkie.' I am the granddaughter of Grace and William Campbell. I am the great-grandchild of Cecelia Hilton. I am descended from Katherine whose mother was a slave. I am the cousin of Afria. I am the niece of Coral Thompson and the daughter of Wade and Mildred Jackson. Let them say what they like. Because I am the bastard child of Empire and I will have my day. (327)

This counterpoints the covered mirrors of Part 1 – 'I was no longer black' – as she has come to recognise her specular counterpart, to conceive of a new imaginary, and to achieve a transformation of personality based upon a new prototype or model: 'the bastard child of Empire', spatialised, historicised, syncretised. This 'enunciative agency' (Bhabha) has resulted from a social process, a reinscription and relocation, an act of revision, spoken from 'outside the sentence':

It is the disjunctive, fragmented, displaced agency of those who have suffered the sentence of history - subjugation, domination, diaspora, displacement - that forces one to think outside the certainly of the sententious. (Bhabha 1992: 56)

A different cultural temporality is produced from the experience of social marginality. This new temporality emerges from a narrative shaped by what Marianne Hirsch has called, 'post-memory'. Post-memory is not mediated through recollection, or prompted by return, but 'through an imaginative investment and creation' (1996: 420). This is a very important concept which Hirsch develops with specific reference to the offspring of holocaust survivors, but it has a particular salience also for second-generation diasporic memory. Actively or passively (as in Faith's case) dominated by narratives that preceded their birth, post-memory is applicable to those 'whose own belated stories are displaced by the stories of the previous generation, shaped by traumatic events that can be neither fully understood nor re-created' (ibid.). *Fruit of the Lemon* presents both the belated story and the story of the previous generation dialogically; there is both displacement and renewal as the structure of the novel also has a Part 3: 'England', in which the narrator returns from Jamaica on the same day (Guy Fawkes') that her parents came to England: 'I was come coming home. I was coming home to tell everyone' (339). The iteration structurally synopsises the complete narrative process, it is a repetition with a difference, opening up alterity and hetero-geneity, becoming-other. The family tree on the final page of the novel graphically embodies and repeats this.

Faith's condition at the end of Part 1 is a kind of exile, 'from a completed time which would have been that of identity itself' (ibid.:

421). This condition of exile from the space of identity Hirsch describes as characteristic of post-memory, or, in a phrase adopted from Nadine Fresco, 'an absent memory'. This apparently contradictory phrase is linked by Hirsch with another concept, that of 'empty memory', developed by the French writer, Henri Raczymow who speaks of 'memory shot through with holes'. Virtually all of the second-generation diasporic narratives examined throughout this book are working with a similar concept of memory, not in order to recover or fill in, but to connect/intersect on a secondary level. On the contrary, as Hirsch says, 'It creates where it cannot recover. It imagines where it cannot recall. It mourns a loss that cannot be repaired (ibid.: 422). Paradoxically, for Faith, Jamaica becomes the country of memory, the space of 'deep and residual cultural knowledges, overlaid with more present practices' (ibid.: 439). In Phil Cohen's terms, England as a nation has been continually founded from outside itself, by the advent of strangers (Cohen 1998: 20). 'Here' – England – can finally be shaped 'in relation to an elsewhere'. England has, so to speak, expanded its own borders by 'opening up the territory of a possible "encounter", a *road* which invites us to rethink our stable positions, to cross our own boundaries, and to take a journey towards diversity' (Yocum 1996: 227). This opening up of the territory of a possible encounter, this crossing of boundaries and journeying towards diversity characterises not just the narratives which have formed the objects of analysis in this chapter, but also multi-cultural Britain of the 1990s, that 'dangerous crossroads', in Colin Prescod's phrase, which challenges ideologies of undifferentiated ethnicity, and has slippages and leakages of identity, 'breaking ground for a new territory of *differences*' (ibid.). Maybe it is possible to think of a future in which a double, or multiple, belonging is not necessarily a burden but can also be a condition of possibility, 'outside the sentence' in Barthes' formulation, or part of a 'more dialogic process', in Bhabha's, that attempts

to track the processes of displacement and realignment that are already at work, constructing something different and hybrid from the encounter: a third space that does not simply revise or invert the dualities, but *revalues* the ideological bases of division and difference. (Bhabha 1992: 58)

I mentioned earlier that, with one exception, each story told in Part 2 is a woman's story. This gendering of 'rememoration' and the fact that it is Faith's mother who says: 'Child, everyone should know where they come from', indicates quite strongly that *Fruit of the Lemon* is not only 'migrant' writing but is also operating in the spaces of the body and of the unconscious: the public in the private, and the private in the public. As Burgin puts it, 'the subject of individual biography is not socially unique' (1996: 211), and so Faith's journey can be recoded in psycho-analytic terms, as part of a wider experience:

The country from which we come is always the one to which we are returning. You are on the return road which passes through the country of children in the maternal body. You have already passed through here: you recognise the land-scape. You have always been on the return road. (Cixous 1976: 544)

6

Britain's Children Without a Home:
Becoming Black/Asian-British (2) –
The Buddha of Suburbia, Anita and Me,
Bhaji on the Beach and *East is East*

The title of this chapter is taken from Hanif Kureishi's 1986 'The rainbow sign', in which he discusses the conflicts and contradictions experienced by people born in Britain but whose families originated from the Indian subcontinent. Part of the essay focuses on a visit the author made to Pakistan, his father's birthplace and the home of many of his relatives, a place in which he was forced to confront his split identity as both an Englishman and a Paki ('We are Pakistanis, but you, you will always be a Paki') without automatic claim to either belonging. To further confuse matters, Kureishi says that he only felt patriotic when he was away from England. As a 'double stranger', Kureishi becomes aware of the closeness of the two societies which have shaped his identity and, at the same time, of the distance between them. Home, in a sense, was like no place. Referring to Roger Scruton's racist formulation of immigrants as the 'alien wedge', and his notion of the desire for 'the company of one's kind', Kureishi asks what this phrase means precisely, particularly in the case of people with multiple and partial belongings. Ideas like Scruton's are still very much often thought in Britain but perhaps less frequently expressed today (at least in public); but although changes have taken place since Kureishi wrote this essay, the situation for the people he is describing has not radically altered. The third-generation immigrant children in the school where I am a governor in inner-city Nottingham are still 'Pakis' when they enter the predominantly white spaces of the city centre or the football grounds of the local professional clubs. In this context, it is not surprising that, as Kureishi says, he knows:

Pakistanis and Indians born and brought up here who consider their position to be the result of a diaspora: they are in exile awaiting return to a better place, where they belong, where they are welcome. And there this 'belonging' will be total. This will be home and peace. (Kureishi 1996: 100)

A conflicted sense of home and belonging, partly but not entirely inter-generational, forms the basis of the fictions explored in this chapter.

PARTITION

As mentioned earlier, much of migrant writing is concerned with con-cepts of 'home'. Indeed, Avtar Brah has claimed that the concept of diaspora embodies a subtext of 'home' (Brah 1996: 190). Brah's work, a rare combination of theoretical material and empirical research, is a major contribution to the understanding of the politics of diaspora in post-war Britain. The subtitle of the book, 'Contesting identities', clearly locates its focus on difference and diversity but above all it indicates how identities are actively constructed, challenged and performed in an agonistic sense. In terms of *Anita and Me*, Brah's concept of diaspora is of value in so far as it 'offers a critique of discourses of fixed origins while taking account of a homing desire, as distinct from a desire for a homeland' (ibid.: 16). Although using different terms, this 'homing desire' is what Kureishi is also trying to describe. Brah describes home as a 'mythic place of desire in the diasporic imagination' and as such might be considered as 'a place of no return', comparable perhaps with Rushdie's 'Indias of the mind'. Certainly, for many first-generation emigrants to Britain, 'going back' remained a strong desire, if not possibility, for a number of years until 'there' became a mythic place of desire while they, and their children, came to terms with the lived experience of 'here', a specific locality and place of residence.

For Meena, the narrator of *Anita and Me*, her conflicted and contested belonging involves a process of conceptualising her parents' place of origin in both a temporal and spatial sense, and of translating, rerouting, that 'origin' into the 'vernacular' of her own split location as a British-born Asian. As she comes under pressure from what slowly unfolds as a racist community, the more she needs to learn of the history, politics and languages of her parents' India, not as a place to retreat to, but as a cultural space to start out from in order to contest the fixed, racialised identity inscribed in her localised experience in the rural West Midlands. Initially distanced from her parents and their extended family, Meena longs to identify with the local, white working-class community embo-died in the figure of the precocious role model, Anita.

As Brah argues: 'The identity of the diasporic imagined community is far from fixed or pre-given. It is constituted within the crucible of the materiality of everyday life; in the everyday stories we tell ourselves individually and collectively' (1996: 183). Meena, the nine-year-old child, begins by fixing her parents in a pre-given reality which she measures against the 'norms' of the surrounding village community. In the distance between 'home' and 'community' she endeavours to insinuate herself through a process of cultural and linguistic mimicry, increasingly bringing her learned demotic back into the home with its mixture of Punjabi and Received Pronunciation English. At one point, she is punished because she says that she likes a song so much that she could 'shag the arse off it'. For much of the narrative Meena is, or desires to be, a devoted supplement to Anita but as the village breaks up, marginalised by the building of a motorway, the closure of the local school and new housing developments, so Meena disengages from this supplementary role and a 'dense self' emerges. I take this useful term from William Connolly's book *Identity/Difference*: 'My identity is what I am and how I am recognised rather than what I choose, want, or consent to. It is the dense self from which choosing, wanting, and consenting proceed' (1991: 64). The 'dense self' in the novel is doubly constructed/ articulated: first as the simulacrum of Anita, her ethnicity under erasure, the outsider masquerading as an insider; second, as the complex child of her parents and her grandmother, a blend of a culture of origin with the culture of location: a critical, and knowing, insider/outsider.

Anita and Me, like so many semi-autobiographical first novels, is an initiation narrative, a rite of passage and transition from the rural idyll of an eternal summer perspective to the dark and conflicted experience of a racialised and sexualised world. Having said this, the novel begins by distancing itself from the stereotypical migrant narrative which it mocks in a prefatory section by staging and stylising the 'Windrush' moment: deference, impoverished housing, sweated labour, pregnancy, exclusion. In some ways, this has become a staple documentary, the obligatory realism of the migrant narrative.

In *Anita and Me*, it is made clear at the outset by the narrator that this is a work of invention, and even if, tonally, it often sounds like a document of observation and synthesis, its positionality (including that of the narrating voice) is put into question by the flux of the text, the point of intelligence destabilised and disestablished. This is not only a matter of form but can also be related to the construction of identity in the narrative, an identity which places itself, and is placed, at constant risk:

Multiple identifications within the same subject can compete with each other, producing further conflicts to be managed; identifications that once appeared permanent or unassailable can be quickly dislodged . . . It is a profoundly turbulent history of contradictory impulses and structural incoherencies. (Fuss 1995: 49)

The novel works with a series of multiple and contradictory identifica-tions as Meena and her family negotiate a conflicted space in which, individually, they are treated with respect but as part of a larger category of racialised 'others', they are excluded. Their experience, as sole Asian immigrants in a rural English situation, is atypical of this particular period – the late 1960s – and is one of the few 'migrant' texts not set in an urban context. In some senses, the family's uniqueness gives them an elected role as exemplary representatives: 'It was her duty to show them that we could wear discreet gold jewellery, dress in tasteful silks and speak English without an accent' (*Anita and Me*: 25). All of the white British figures in the village, of course, speak English with a very strong accent. The village and its inhabitants are only seen from the perspective of the narrator and they are often constructed as figures in a Dickensian gallery of working-class stereotypes, identified in terms of what Barthes called the semic code, a major device for thematising persons, objects or places. A reverse stereotyping or caricaturing takes place as the con-trolling gaze is Asian British. In a similar reversal, the Asian family gently poke fun at the habits of their English friends. Although the narrative is multi-voiced, all the voices are filtered through the mimicry and simulation of the narrator; the white British characters have almost no voice of their own. Conversely, when Meena tries to imagine India it is in the tropes and images of her locality plus 'a few cows lounging around on the corners' (32). For her parents, on the contrary, Tollington is chosen precisely because its fields, trees, light and space 'could almost look something like home' (35). Both parents and daughter in a sense 'find' themselves in translation. Food is a particular example of this. Meena longs to eat the local fish fingers and chips, while her mother spurned the instant or the takeaway: 'This food was not just something to fill a hole, it was soul food, it was the food their far-away mothers made and came seasoned with memory and longing, this was the nearest they would get for many years, to home' (61). Meena successfully navigates the two worlds and is not caught 'in between cultures', because both are fluid and subject to change, but instead creates a new culture, a third space, which is a synthesis of both worlds. What the novel does is trace the highly particularised and differentiated process of one specific form of hybridity as identity, as a lived social reality. It is, in Friedman's terms, 'emic', an 'experienced hybridity' emerging from a thick description, but with the tensions and contradictory forces left unresolved.

What emerges in the narrative is Meena's gradual realisation that she, and her generation of British-born Asians, embodied all the unfulfilled desires of their parents' generation. With this realisation comes a series of adjustments and recognitions, including an awareness of the fact that, despite her exaggerated Tollington accent, 'there was a corner of me that would be forever not England' (112), even if her Punjabi is spoken with a

Birmingham accent. Her characteristic lying is part of an endeavour to endlessly create a self. As Brah says, 'the "individual" narrator does not unfold but is produced in the process of narration' (1996: 10). It is the plural and partial Meena that is produced in a double process: the Meena that journeys towards her family and multiple identifications and away from the monological local culture. Anita embodies this local culture, initially a 'cosy village idyll', but progressively fractured and hollowed out to expose a cross-section of an impoverished, sidelined and dead-end world in which Meena is the only child who passes the eleven-plus, and her family are one of the few with a future beyond the village.

On or around her tenth birthday, Meena experiences her deepest sense of alienation and separation from her home culture, expressed graphically in the following way:

I wanted to shed my body like a snake slithering out of its skin and emerge reborn, pink and unrecognisable. I began avoiding mirrors, I refused to put on the Indian suits my mother laid out for me . . . I hid in the house when Auntie Sheila bade fond farewells in Punjabi to my parents from the front garden, I took to walking several paces behind or in front of my parents when we went on a shopping trip, checking my reflection in shop windows, bitterly disappointed it was still there. (146)

This is an eloquent description of what I previously called ethnic erasure, a ceremonious refusal or willed nullification of the 'mirror stage' which annuls both self and other, a desire for dedifferentiation in all senses. It compares with Faith's veiling of the mirrors in *Fruit of the Lemon*. The repeated subjective pronouns are metaphorically buried by a series of negatives (avoiding, hid, refused). From 'I began avoiding mirrors' to 'it was still there' is a lengthy, inclusive sentence which syntactically and simultaneously enacts the exclusion of Meena from her parents' world in all senses, and excludes them from her. The inclusiveness, however, shows grammatically (structurally) how this desired exclusion will not happen. The worlds of 'India' and Tollington, both epic and banal, are part of a cultural continuum. Meena may see Anita as a passport to acceptance, her entrée to invisible and non-ethnic whiteness, but, later, she becomes aware that Anita is not an entrance but a cul-de-sac, part of a thwarted and blunted class fraction, powerless, excluded and marginalised: her name, Rutter, defining and confining her future. For Meena for whom 'living in the grey area between all categories felt increasingly like home', there is a way out; for Anita, 'worshipped' initially as 'a real Tollington wench', there is only immiseration. Meena can shed skins, try on roles, mimic voices: Anita is Anita, a terminus identity. Anita, by virtue of her whiteness, is reflected in, and by, the dominant culture which only grants Meena's world an exaggerated and exotic walk-on role, but, ultimately, Meena can cross boundaries, journey through the dominant territory if only on sufferance and subject to racist violence. Anita and her peers are going nowhere, they are immobilised: their endless scooter journeys are circular.

Naively, Meena throws herself into the world of the local, walking side by side with Anita, equal and power-sharing: seemingly an insider. The village fete proves to be a turning point, the moment when the familiar turns into the unknown and Meena becomes aware of 'how many strangers did indeed live amongst us' (173). This marks the second stage of her double estrangement: first from family as described earlier, now from her 'elected' community. This transformation is marked by the physical reincarnation of the local youth as skinheads armed with a new-found racist discourse, articulated by the Wolverhampton MP, Enoch Powell, although not in his well-bred, classical tones: 'We don't give a toss for anybody else. This is our patch. Not some wogs' handout' (193). Up to now, the narrative has told of friends being made out of strangers, of a young girl shuttling between the world of 'stranger' and 'friend'; from this point on, change, loss and upheaval drive a narrative in which strangers are made out of friends and the narrator comes to realise that she did not live under the same sky as most people. She becomes a 'minority', an ethnicised 'other', a figure of partition, only able to reclaim her Tollington 'sky' through the agency of her Nanima, her mother's mother visiting from India. From her, she begins to learn Punjabi and retraces, mentally, her parents' 5,000-mile journey from the Partition that has irreversibly shaped their lives.

Meena's Nanima also helps her to focus on her displacement, her urge to reinvent herself, 'to be someone else in some other place far from Tollington' (211), like the people Kureishi spoke of. Nanima's presence contextualises Meena's estrangement, produces a 'denser' self, both rerooted and rerouted. This re-education was to have been completed by Meena's first visit to India, but this is delayed by prolonged hospitalisation. This delay has symbol value because it postpones/defers the conventional 'return' and also enables Meena to complete this stage of her transition journey within her 'culture of residence' with all its contradictory articulations. This is part of the agonistic process, the need to confront ambiguity and ambivalence, the complex and conflicted spaces of her 'summer' phase. Part of this confrontation is the racist attack by Meena's local hero, Sam Lowbridge, on an Asian man; an attack which was 'too close to home, and for the first time, I wondered if Tollington would ever truly be home again' (275). This returns us to Brah's concept of diaspora. Meena's becoming British Asian is an active process which erases the racist Anita and Sam (a racism of powerlessness and of a downward spiral), at the same time as her location 'unbecomes' home to be replaced by a 'homing desire' which 'signals these processes of *multi-locationality across geographical, cultural and psychic boundaries*' (Brah 1996: 194; italics in original). She is relocated, reconfigured along an 'Asian' continuum, at least at the level of intention.

The whole of Meena's final year in Tollington is compressed into a few pages, pages which mark her 'unbelonging', her return to observer/outsider status, uncoupled from Anita and the local. This separation is marked symbolically when she tells the racist Sam: 'I *am* the others, Sam. You did mean me' (314). Significantly, the narrative does not move to a triumphalist ending, with the rebirth of the lower middle-class, upwardly mobile Asian female. There is throughout the text a 'second', or shadow, narrative – edged with allegory suggested by the name Tollington – which marks the closure not just of a period of time, but the foreclosure of possibility for a generation of rural working-class youth, abandoned in a former mining village, prospectless in the face of urbanisation, speculation and the loss of space. That an Indian property owner, Harinder Singh, is party and willing agent to these metamorphoses complicates Meena's sense of displacement. As Sam says, however: 'But you wos never gonna look at me, you won't be stayin will ya? You can move on. How come? How come I can't?' (314). This neatly summarises the whole of this 'shadow' narrative: the beached white males and females of a deskilled working class, whose 'whiteness' is their only vestigial link with the dominant relations of power. For Meena, as she notes, 'the place in which I belonged was wherever I stood and there was nothing stopping me simply moving forward and claiming each resting place as home' (303). At last she has a body which 'fitted me to perfection and was all mine!' (326).

Anita and Me is a narrative about race and class. Sam and Anita never find bodies which fit them to perfection. In the final paragraph of the text Meena writes a note: ' "Dear Anita, We're moving on Saturday. I'm going to the Grammar School, so at least you won't be around to tease me about my tam-o-shanter." She never replied, of course' (328). The active verbs in the note, 'moving' and 'going' mark off Meena from Anita who only ever existed as a 'narrative' supplement to, and construct of, Meena with her 'moving' identity. Fixed, silent, invisible, erased, Anita never could reply: the narrative dialogue has broken down.

THE ENIGMA OF SURVIVAL

Arguing against the notion that cultures automatically correspond to 'homogenous national states', Gilroy writes (1993) of the 'rhizomorphic, fractal structure of the transcultural', and it is this formation which is at the root of much of Kureishi's writing, both the essays and the fiction. Although located exclusively in suburban and metropolitan London, *The Buddha of Suburbia* explores a complex cultural terrain which extends far beyond its immediate geographical space. Not, of course, in any obvious way a response to Stuart Hall's 1988 essay, 'New ethnicities', the novel nevertheless traces a range of diverse and contradictory subject positions – speculative, innovative and essentialist – social experiences and cultural identities which constitute the life of the seventeen year old, Karim Amir, 'an Englishman born and bred, almost' (The Buddha of Suburbia: 3). As every critic has remarked, it is the 'almost' which is at the basis of the novel's conflict, and of its comedy. Rhizomorphic and fractal, Karim is an 'odd mixture of continents and blood, of here and there, of belonging and not, that makes me restless and easily bored ' (3). In the course of the novel, the locational certainties of 'here' and 'there' are unsettled and disrupted, as are the identitarian assumptions of 'belonging'.

In the process of the novel's exploration of how to construct a 'bi-racial' identity, existing categories of 'white' and 'black' are exposed as political and cultural constructs, and not, in Hall's terms, as 'transcendental racial categories grounded, or guaranteed, in Nature' (Hall 1988: 28). Faced with a society which is prepared to patronise or tolerate the non-white 'other' in so far as they accede to ethnic white hegemonic norms and values, Karim is caught between mimicry and subversion. To compound the problem, he is also bi-sexual, so he is doubly 'transgressive', a crossroads person, unable to seek refuge in a given, or unproblematic, subjectivity. Living in his homeland, speaking his 'mother tongue', he is, nevertheless, situated in the space of what Freud called that other locality between 'perception and consciousness'. Published in 1990, at the end of a decade in which nationalism in Britain was given a fresh twist and inflection by identifying it with Victorian values, the Second World War, and not being swamped by people from other cultures (Scruton's 'alien wedge'), The Buddha of Suburbia interrogates the paranoia which was, arguably, at the root of this new nationalism shaped, in many ways, during the 1970s. The rhetorical terms of Margaret Thatcher's speech to a Conservative rally at Cheltenham racecourse on Saturday, 3 July 1982 (in the aftermath of the Falklands War) indicates what I mean. The speech is bound together by references to 'our country', 'our people', 'this nation', 'the real spirit of these times', and 'Britain's recovery, which all our people long to see' (Barnett 1982: 150). On the face of it, this is an inclusive speech with its repeated use of the first person plural, but it also contains an unspoken excluded. The Falklands 'victory', Thatcher argued, showed that those who thought 'we could never again be what we were' were wrong. Ideologically, Thatcherism was predicated upon a series of representations of 'what we were'. It is an ideal past, ethnically undifferentiated and white, and situated in a time prior to mass immigration, 'people from other cultures'. Economically neo-liberal, culturally Powellite, Thatcherism constructed a paranoia around welfare scroungers, militant strikers and immigrants.

It is this context which provides yet another 'location' for Kureishi, with Karim being part of a minority within a minority – 'between cultures'. As has been argued by Barker and others, racism in this period took a cultural turn (Barker 1981).

In terms referred to earlier, Kureishi's Karim, and his cousin Jamila, possess a 'double vision' (perhaps in both senses of that term), and the text is, throughout, a multiple-voiced discourse. There is also what Bakhtin called a hidden polemic. As demonstrated above, Bakhtin argued that in such a polemic, the author's discourse is directed towards its own referential object – in this instance,the journey of a bi-racial teenager from the suburbs to the metropolis – but 'at the same time every statement about the object is constructed in such a way that, apart from its referential meaning, a polemical blow is struck at the other's discourse, at the other's statement about the same object' (Bakhtin 1984: 195). The complexity of the novel is such that the other's discourse is not simply 'hegemonic white Englishness', although this is the text's primary 'antagonist', as the situation of 'intense dialogality' (Bakhtin) is further complicated by the existence of another antagonism, a second determination, which also articulates its own statement about the referential object in the terms of Indian culture, or a 'remembered' version of it. Karim's 'place', his 'people', his 'heritage' are doubly presented (even if his father initially 'lives English' in the style of one of Macaulay's 'native' civil servants), and in antagonism, and the text 'draws in, as it were, sucks in to itself the other's replies'. The Buddha of Suburbia intensely reworks both sets of reply, and, in a sense, the whole text can be read as an extended response to a series of spoken, anticipated or misspoken replies, hegemonic scripts which lose their composure and confidence, partly by being discovered, recovered as scripts, or constructs. Kureishi's displaced subject, 'restless and easily bored', comes to occupy a contingent space, transcultural and cosmopolitan. It is both a psychical and a physical space, a space in which Karim is able to confront the possibility of 'being an other', of living 'the cosmopolitanism of the excoriated', in Kristeva's phrase. Metaphorically, layers of skin are stripped or peeled off, but, of course, it is his very skin colour which 'others' him as 'Paki' or 'wog'. In this sense, his skin colour locates him in a biologically constructed racial category, despite what I said earlier about racism taking a culturalist turn in the 1980s. The biological category was always retained as an option, particularly for use with reference to someone like Karim: British born, English accent, culturally signified through the dominant registers of dress style, music, food and so on.

To adopt Stuart Hall's terms, Kureishi is trying to establish 'a different logic of difference' to one which is based upon the binary 'black or British' (Hall 1992: 472). Karim is constantly moving, positioning and repositioning himself, negotiating spaces which eliminate the 'or' and make way for the 'and' with its opening up of the possibilities of new identities, new ethnicities. In attempting to secure that 'or', Thatcherism endeavoured to place the signifier 'British' (and 'we', 'our', 'us' for that matter) 'outside of history, outside of change, outside of political inter-vention' (ibid.). To a limited extent, and far less significantly, certain figures in the text also try to do the same to the signifier 'home', or 'India'. Identity for Karim is a continuous, and never settled, cultural, historical and political contestation. As Kureishi put it, in another context:

If there is to be a serious attempt to understand Britain today, with its mix of races and colours, its hysteria and despair, then writing about it has to be complex. It can't apologise or idealise. It can't sentimentalise and it can't represent only one group as having a monopoly on virtue. (1985)

It is in this sense that The Buddha of Suburbia is much more than an 'ethnic' novel, but is very much a novel about the 'shift and difficulties' of Britain in the 1970s, about the horizons of the suburban lower middle class, and about attempts to essentialise categories of race and sexuality. It also challenges a hegemonic politics which sought to reinscribe difference as 'a radical and unbridgable separation' in the face of a difference 'sliding against the masks of newer selves'. It is this difference, in Hall's words 'positional, conditional and conjunctural', which the novel produces narratively, at the level of form and theme. Seduced by the temptations of invisibility and marginality at times, it also resists them.

Thatcherism as a discourse forgot that 'Englishness' was a complexly positioned narrative and 'tried to speak everybody else' (in Hall's phrase) from an imperial and universal place. What Kureishi tries to do in this novel is to 'oblige us to recognise that enunciation comes from some-where' (Hall 1991: 36). Throughout the novel, and in many of his essays, Kureishi is trying to ground that 'somewhere', position it in all its contradictory locations/territories. The point is that it is never simply in one place or in one time, especially for 'migrant' writing with its complex take on the politics of address, and its need to go beyond the construction of the mimetic self designed by colonialism and desired by hegemonic whiteness, so that the 'other is not where it is' (ibid.: 39). Despite this, however, Karim's father returns metaphorically to a fixed belonging – 'I have lived in the West for most of my life, and I will die here, yet I remain to all intents and purposes an Indian man. I will never be anything but an Indian' (263) – to such an extent that he shifts religion and becomes a Western-imaged guru, and his friend Anwar, who has come to England with him, lives out an increasingly paranoid existence fantasising about return.

Hailed by some critics for its autobiographical and picaresque qua-lities, seen by others as a bildungsroman, there has been a tendency to see *The Buddha of Suburbia* as a necessarily representative text, a voice from the margins. Its apparently realist style seems to reinforce these categories of inscription. Although the text has 'beady eyes' and is satirical of Anglo-Saxon attitudes, it is also more than just a fable or ethnic narrative. It is a complex and densely mediated text which mocks and challenges the very model of realism as representation: the writing up, or the writing in, of an anterior, pre-existing reality.

The opening sentence of the novel, and the use of the first-person narrator, is disturbed immediately by the qualifier, 'almost'. It alerts us to the fact that what we will read will undercut the subject as, and at, the point of intelligibility, and that this point is not a given, but an endlessly created and recreated becoming, a series of improvisations, to use a theatrical metaphor which Kureishi works with. It could be argued that no point of intelligibility is ever reached which is not also questioned by the flux of the text with its sliding of signifiers. The very concept of 'signifier' is itself thrown into doubt by that 'almost'. What we experience is the putting on and off of masks, the casting and recasting of roles, and the construction of copies which are part of the struggle 'to locate myself and learn what the heart is' (284). This takes us beyond the cognitive genre, and outside of the representational as anything more than the articulation of existing, and dominant, cultural codes.

Playing with the concept of mimicry as double vision, Karim is capable of replaying a form of narcissistic identification produced by dependent colonial relations (Bhabha 1994: 88) and also 'the *menace* of mimicry [which] is its double vision which in disclosing the ambivalence of colonial discourse also disrupts its authority' (ibid.). He can represent, and subvert through ironic compromise, 'authorized versions of otherness'. This is achieved not just in his theatrical performances – although it is at its most articulate here – but also through the 'staging' of what Bhabha calls the repetition of partial presence, a desire which 'articulates those disturbances of cultural, racial and historical difference that menace the narcissistic demand of colonial authority' (ibid.). This at a time (or shortly before) it must be remembered, when Britain was being culturally reimagined as a form of colonial authority (selectively, of course: the sovereignty of the white Falklands demanded a British Task Force; that of black Grenada, an American invasion). In a context of paranoia at 'being swamped by people of other cultures', 'our' culture required 'mimic men', hard-working Asians and 'model minority ' Chinese. Karim, almost an Englishman but not quite, embodies mimicry as an active process, not the passivity of tolerated 'copies'. As an actor he partly reverses the colonial appropriation:

By now producing a partial vision of the colonizer's presence; a gaze of otherness, that shares the acuity of the generalogical gaze which, as Foucault describes it, liberates marginal elements and shatters the unity of man's being through which he extends his sovereignty'. (ibid.: 89)

By analogy, migrant writing is, in some ways, a form of mimicry in so far as it is, also, 'always produced at the site of interdiction' (ibid.), the space of prohibition – Karim, almost English, almost the same, but not quite/ white. What the novel does is make apparent the visibility of mimicry in particular ways, ways which displace and decentre the controlling gaze by liberating marginal elements: 'the Other that belongs inside one' (Hall 1991: 48). This, Hall says, is 'the Other that one can only know from the place from which one stands. This is the self as it is inscribed in the gaze of the Other' (ibid.). It is this positioning, this textual strategy, which enables Kureishi both to construct, and break down, conventional boundaries 'between outside and inside, between those who belong and those who do not, between those whose histories have been written and those whose histories they have depended upon but whose histories cannot be spoken' (ibid.). How this 'doubleness' is expressed in the ranges of this particular text I will try to show by analysing two particular narrative sequences. These occur in Chapters 10, 11, 12 and 15.

As has been shown, the novel opens with a displacement, and a displacement–reconfiguration dialectic continues throughout the text. Object throughout of a racist, displacing gaze, the narrator seeks to become its subject, to return what was always authorised as an un-returnable gaze. In the process, something of the nature of narrative itself is revealed. In saying this, I am thinking of Paul Ricoeur's idea that the 'notion of self relies on narrative identity and not on the formal identity of an unchanging thing' (Venn 1999: 270). Self, Ricoeur argues, knows itself 'only indirectly by the detour of the cultural signs of all sorts which are articulated on the symbolic mediations which always already articulate action and, among them, the narratives of everyday life' (Ricoeur 1991: 198). These mediations and articulations, described by Venn as 'mobile', are what constitute and motivate Karim who is refigured, and seeks to refigure himself, through the processes of narrative. Karim is placed at the intersection of a number of stories which he, and others, tell about themselves. It is in, and through, these sometimes contradictory, often antagonistic, stories that narrative is said to have a recognition (or, in some cases, misrecognition) effect. If, as Ricoeur suggests, 'subjects recognise themselves in the stories they tell about themselves', then in a novel like *The Buddha of Suburbia* this is rendered problematic by the fact that what might be called already existing 'spaces of recognition' for the (almost) English subject, who is non-white, have been thoroughly colonised. The available narratives have to be refigured, disfigured even, and transformed through the construction of 'scripts for staging particular selves' (Venn 1999: 270–1), a process of becoming. In Raymond Williams's terms, this involves narratives and figurations which may be, simultaneously, residual, dominant and emergent, a project of complex negotiation.

Split, in transition and emergent, Karim shifts among spaces of 'undecidable belonging' (a dentist with a South African accent asks at one point 'Does he speak English?': ' "A few words", I said' (258)).

> But I did feel, looking at these strange creatures now – the Indians – that in some way these were my people, and that I'd spent my life denying or avoiding the fact. I felt ashamed and incomplete at the same time, as if half of me were missing, and as if I'd been colluding with my enemies, those whites who wanted Indians to be like them . . . So if I wanted the additional personality bonus of an English past, I would have to create it. (212–13)

This, precisely, is narrative as a 'recognition effect', an acknowledgement that self is not something which can simply be formed by changing his accent, leaving the suburbs, and escaping from his family, but is, in Foucault's terms, genealogical and ontological, 'a philosophical life in which the critique of what we are is at one and the same time the historical analysis of the limits that are imposed on us and an experiment with the possibility of going beyond them' (Foucault 1991: 50). Making himself up, creating a self, is not simply a matter of addressing the question 'who am I in the present?' but also of a cultural analysis of the proscriptions and prescriptions belonging, historically and politically, to being at one and the same time, English, Indian, white and black. It is, at once, the enigma of arrival and departure, of limits and excess.

A little earlier I quoted the phrase, 'scripts for staging particular selves', and this is particularly appropriate for this text as, at two crucial points, Karim, as a professional actor, has to script and stage two particular 'ethnic' identities. Strictly speaking, for the role of Mowgli in Kipling's *Jungle Book*, he, initially, is scripted – literally and meta-phorically written into a part – and staged. In the second play, an improvisation, he is 'free' to script and produce his 'self', but still within an 'ethnic other' definition. The differences between the two productions stake out the territory of his emergence, the project of becoming and the possibility of going *beyond*, not just of historical limits but also of the splits, the transitionality, 'the spaces that border hybridity' (Venn 1999: 263).

The theatrical metaphors enable Kureishi to examine the structure of identification which, as Hall, Bhabha and others have pointed out, is always produced through *ambivalence*: 'always constructed though splitting' (Hall 1991: 47). Hall quotes the moment in *Black Skin, White Masks* when Fanon describes his experience of a white child saying: 'Look, Mama, a black man'. Fanon goes on to say: 'For the first time, I knew who I was. For the first time, I felt as if I had been simultaneously exploded in the gaze, in the violent gaze of the other, and at the same, recomposed as another' (ibid.: 48). Karim, covered in 'shit-brown cream' and with a loin cloth and fake Indian accent, acts Mowgli in, and through, the violent and 'authenticating' gaze of the other: 'splitting between that which one is, and that which is the other' (ibid.). His racialised 'self' is relayed through the position of the 'other', as that 'other' has been constituted in colonial, racist discourse. It is a narrative of identity which is not, at this stage, performed or narrated in terms of his 'Orpington' self, only the 'Indian' extracted from his complex bi-raciality: exotic, like a figure from the *Black and White Minstrel Show*. It is assumed he will not have to *act*. The acting, the staging, and the make-up, however, all stress how much identity is a matter of performance and narrativity, of a story being told. For all of the contradictions, Karim nevertheless relishes being 'the pivot of the production' and tries to displace the 'gaze of the other' in some respects. To a limited extent he partially recomposes himself by recognising the 'other' that is inside him and achieves a small measure of 'alienation' from the part by, occasionally, lapsing into a Cockney accent. However, his militant feminist cousin, Jamila, condemns the clichés about Indians and the accent while Karim, overtly critical of the role, enjoys the recognition the role brings. A complex splitting is taking place which Karim, for all his knowingness, does not command or control; he has been reduced to a stereotype, literally in terms of the play, but also metaphorically in terms of the larger narrative project of belonging/not belonging:

As someone on the margins, Karim cannot achieve his goal of reaching the centre but when this marginality becomes exotic and eccentric, he can. To arrive at the centre, he must become eccentric, exit from the circle, the structure of social and class relations. (Doyle 1997: 110)

Lacan spoke of mimicry in the following manner:

Mimicry reveals something in so far as it is distinct from what might be called an itself that is behind. The effect of mimicry is camouflage . . . It is not a question of harmonizing with the background, but against a mottled background, of becoming mottled – exactly like the technique of camouflage practised in human warfare. (Lacan, quoted in Bhabha 1994: 85)

In the course of the narrative, Karim does succeed in becoming mottled, but at the *Jungle Book* stage he is only able to operate at the level of 'an itself that is behind'; moreover, it is an 'itself' imposed by colonial discourse – he is camouflaged (by the 'shit-brown' cream) passively – as he has no agency, and 'willingly' applies the cream. Mimicry comes later, in his second production, where he is allowed to script and produce his character. As Bhabha demonstrates, 'in order to be effective mimicry must continually produce its slippage, its excess, its difference . . . a process of disavowal' (Bhabha 1994: 86).

The director asks Karim to model himself upon someone from his own background, 'Someone black' (170). At this stage he is still being constituted in the terms of an essentialised other: the Mowgli narrative which confines him to the way his position in society has been fixed. Karim assents and develops a character around his father's friend, Anwar. He had wanted to focus on his 'hero' and friend, Charlie, but he is not 'someone black'. In developing and presenting the character of Anwar, on hunger strike to force Jamila into an arranged marriage and behaving violently in the street, Karim has his representation rejected by the other black member of the company, Tracey, precisely because it will be seen as 'representative'. It is an arguable position, and one that comes from Kureishi's critical perception of Black politics of the time, but given his minority status and his ambition, Karim is vulnerable to being 'flattered, appropriated and used' (Alibhai 1991). Even if his performance is designed to 'displace' the gaze, it is not something which he can determine on an entirely voluntaristic level.

His second choice is Jamila's husband, Changez, a character rendered absurd and risible throughout much of the text – part of Kureshi's satirical intention to balance the stereotypes perhaps, as both white and Asian figures are caricatured. Sometimes, it has to be said, these stereotypes are the products of Karim's own distorting and distorted gaze.

In the first production, the audience has a referential context in which it places Mowgli, a known figure from an authorised discourse: 'white truth'. Karim has to be constructed in accordance with this prior reference. In choosing to develop a character based upon Changez (the name is phonetically interesting), Karim has no anterior, cultural pre-text: simply the man himself. This is where an interesting representational gap opens up. Karim says to Changez: 'I'll show you just as you are' (183), compounding the realist fallacy. For his part, Changez asks Karim 'not to enter by the back door and portray me in your play' (185). Setting aside the obvious sexual innuendo, this is exactly what Karim does try to do by constructing a bizarre and monstrous figure which he calls Tariq, and in the process reproducing the characteristics Tracey had objected to earlier. Pyke, the director, welcomes the portrayal because it has 'class, race, fucking and force', and as with Shadwell, the *Jungle Book* director, he fixes Karim in a role which fits the mimicry of colonial desire, cutting out, and against, the possibilities of ambivalence:

When in character, playing not me, you have to be yourself. To make your not-self real you have to steal from your authentic self . . . The closer you play to yourself the better. Paradox of paradoxes: to be someone else successfully you must be yourself. (220)

In playing an immigrant fresh from a small Indian town, Karim assembles a costume which renders Tariq 'a wretched and comic character'. What he is not aware of is that, in representing Changez, the audience is not laughing at the original (to which it has no access), but at the other that belongs inside him, Karim. The audience are recomposing Karim as another, not approving a performance. Meanwhile, the real Changez has been subject to racist violence, one of numerous attacks in the area. A protest is planned and Karim fails to show, as he is too busy rehearsing his role as Changez, 'getting behind his peculiar eyeballs'. He performs this role, finally, in front of 400 white people who, with the critics, judged Karim as 'hilarious and honest', true, that is, to *their* knowledge of the 'native other'. Only his mother sees him as not an Indian: 'you're an Englishman'. 'Be what you are', she tells him which, of course, is the dilemma at the centre of the whole narrative. To his fellow-actor Eleanor's friend, Heater, nevertheless, he is a 'Paki cunt', actor or not. Ironically, Changez sees the role as 'fundamentally autobiographical' and is glad that Karim did not try 'the leap of invention into his character'.

As virtually no one in the audience, except Jamila, knows Changez, he is able to sustain his illusion 'that I am not a person who could be successfully impersonated' (231). He does not recognise 'himself' and all that Karim has succeeded in doing is representing, not a particular figure, but a caricature who confirms white prejudices. The changing, shifting, mobile Changez eludes Karim's essentialising and the intended mockery rebounds. The cool, sophisticated, ambitious and socially mobile Karim is cemented in, hoist by his own petard, authorising the very discourse that has authorised him as 'other'. This is confirmed when, in his next role, he is offered the part as the rebellious student son of an Indian shopkeeper in a television soap opera, another complex sedimentation as a 'contemporary issue', a token black as a rare 1970s television presence. As far as Karim is concerned he has 'fixed' Changez but he fails to understand the cracks which are appearing in ethnic absolutes and that:

'identity effects' are always crucially *split*. Under cover of camouflage, mimicry like the fetish, is a part-object that radically revalues the normative knowledges of the priority of race, writing, history. For the fetish mimes the forms of authority at the point at which it deauthorizes them. (Bhabha 1994: 91)

As narrator, Karim could be assumed to be the point of intelligibility of the narrative, but his staging of Changez acts as a metaphor of a wider situation. As the 'mobile', adaptable Changez de-authorises the narrative representation constructed by Karim, this scenario radically revalues 'the normative knowledges' of the priority of Karim's ordering of the narration and renders it fallible. In other words, as the text as a whole challenges the codes and canons of Englishness, it also undermines the authority and presumed 'representativeness' of its central figure as the categorical and definitive 'hybrid'. In this way, the narrator's gaze is partly displaced and space made for other versions of diasporic and syncretic experience – that of Haroon, Anwar, Jamila and Changez.

A GOOD DAY OUT

Apart from *My|Beautiful Launderette*, Gurinder Chadha's *Bhaji on the Beach* (1993) has reached a wider audience than any other film dealing with British Asian experience. *East is East* (1999), directed by Damien O'Donnell and adapted by Ayub Khan-Din from his West End stage play, is likely to play to even larger audiences but, at the time of writing, it has not yet gone on general release so it is too early to say. Its enthusiastic reception at Cannes, Edinburgh, and a range of other festivals, suggests that it will be an international box-office success. My observations on this film towards the end of this section are based upon a single viewing, of the UK premiere at Edinburgh in August 1999.

Bhaji on the Beach is based almost entirely upon the differences within a small section of an Asian community based in Birmingham, rather than on the difference between the community and the dominant white society. The film is more an exploration of gender issues than those of race, but these are articulated within a number of set-pieces related to a range of codes shaped by a specific ethnicity and cultural practices. Sex, pleasure, food and family, are all subject to transcoding within the film which transfers its cast of characters from a recognisably 'Asian' enclave in Birmingham to Blackpool, the quintessentially white, working-class English seaside resort, which becomes a metaphorical site for exploring the transformations of 'Asianness' brought about by the pressures of migration and inter-generational gender conflicts. All the events take place in the course of a single day which is used to focus, synoptically, on a wide number of ongoing problems which are magnified by this time–space compression. The potential changes brought about by the day and the mode of resolution make the film a comedy, but the dilemmas posed suggest levels of conflict and tension beyond the comic.

The film establishes a number of symptomatic, if not necessarily representative, themes which are a source of conflict brought about, as initially presented, by female behaviour (later seen as choices). Unlike a number of cultural fictions which treat only the situation of second generation non-white immigrants, the film opens with a prefigurative scene in which Asha, first generation, 'hallucinates' on images of a Hindu Goddess and of herself as a 'model' Indian wife serving an 'ideal' son, husband and daughter. An abrupt shift is produced by a number of camera shots from above showing Asha terrified and dwarfed by the swirling detritus of the retail store – cans, videos, newspapers, ice lollies.

This shot opens onto another in which her daughter, sons and husband fill out a very limited space and demand breakfast. This is a perspective which the feminist Simi, whose Sahili Women's Centre has organised the outing (which it becomes in more than one sense), is probably unaware of as the first generation is seen as part of the problem. Initially, there are two peer-based group affiliations seemingly irreconcilable, but slippages and overlaps occur.

Although the white presence is muted throughout the film, or features in highly stylised ways such as the 'mooning', the male strippers, and the absurdly theatrical relic Ambrose Waddington, there are nevertheless signs – in the form of graffiti and racist language (in the Blackpool café) – which indicate the wider context in which, although narratively the women are symbolically central, their 'real' belonging is marginal. The 'aunties' conservatism is signified as perhaps more than just a condition of their being unable to leave India culturally, but also as a reflex of an earlier more manifest and publicly normative phase of racism. It is also a defensiveness brought about by displacement and subordinated gender roles sharpened by the relative contextlessness of their present situation. They are confined to rhetorical and symbolic 'flourishes' within an exaggerated 'exile' patriarchy. The Westernised relative from Bombay explodes any comforting myths about India and suggests that the British-based aunts are twenty years out of date and living in a fantasy of 'home'. Despite this, the film does not allow any easy positions to be automatically endorsed as the 'mediating' role of Asha shows.

As I have said, *Bhaji on the Beach* is about transcodings and negotiations. From a starting point of certain 'absolute' positions, subtler and more flexible perspectives emerge. The traditional working-class seaside holiday developed in the mid- to late nineteenth century, as an increasingly urbanised and time-disciplined workforce, with small amounts of disposable income, made its way out of time and its customary space to recreate itself. Similarly confined spatially and culturally disciplined, the women enter a different temporality – festive or carnival – in which the everyday is seen through a different lens and each set-piece issue – Ginder's divorce and her experience of domestic violence; Hashida's cross-racial relationship and pregnancy; Madhu and Ladju's 'promiscuity' and absorption in teenage culture; and Asha's headaches and low self-esteem – are all given fresh inflections by exposure. Each situation is represented in a stylised manner, as a point of extreme, as a way of focusing not just upon the immediate or symptomatic local instance but upon the wider prescriptions of race and gender.

I have stressed 'gender' on more than one occasion as a focus of the film, but this is not confined to women. Initially, Ranjit (Ginder's husband) is seen as 'typically' (Asian) male, absorbed with his self-image, violent and chauvinist. Deeper focus does not excuse this but situates it in a wider patriarchal family context. Ranjit is shown, behaviourally, as a mid-point between the excessive sexism and macho violence of his older brother with his contempt for women, education and 'weakness', and the younger brother's sensitivity, insight and power-lessness. Family-driven ('she was too dark; you can't trust the dark ones' his mother says of Ginder), his son valued for his 'maleness', Ranjit models himself upon a set of conventional patriarchal expectations about 'a woman's place'. He cannot see Ginder, only his wife. When it is mentioned that he used to beat her up, one of the aunties says, 'she must have done something', a familiar blaming the victim refrain. Although technically a 'love marriage', the choice of a 'modern couple' (seen as a cause of the failed relationship by the older generation), both Ginder and Ranjit are rendered virtually choiceless by unreflexive social and cultural structures, Asian-centred for the purposes of the narrative but by no means only an 'Asian' problem.

Females are seen either as those who make the family what it is, or as community tokens – 'one of our girls we can be proud of' – like Hashida, the prospective medical student. Blackpool opens up spaces and reflex-ive time, a site for play where alternative, liberating possibilities can be explored, not in order simply to reverse, or turn upside down, the absolutes of the quotidian world, but to negotiate 'differences' between the 'differences-within'. Oliver, Hashida's African-Caribbean boyfriend, breaks with the counsel of his separatist friend and his own egocen-tricity, and approaches her in a spirit of commitment, while she decides against an abortion. Ginder, vacillating between returning to her violent husband or resolving to be a single parent, chooses the latter. Asha, flattered momentarily by the courtship of the effete sexist and racist Ambrose Waddington, who offers to exchange her family bondage for an exotic, ethnic, walk-on part in his Raj romance (he had played an Indian in *Bhowani Junction*), resists his blandishments while, at the same time, moderating her judgmental treatment of Ginder and offering positive support, and realising that, setting aside the content of Ambrose's fantasy (in black face his make-up runs), there are spaces for her other than those hollowed out by her family: 'I wasn't born selling bloody newspapers'.

What the film does not do is suggest that a whole set of ready-made solutions have now been made available, but, instead, it starts out from a premise of fixity and stasis in which a range of people are frozen into poses, roles, attitudes and frames: the demobilising 'clichés' of British Asian culture. It then proceeds to puncture and tear open the initial certainties to reveal gaps, drifts and leakages (even Cliff Richard's anodyne 'Summer Holiday' is given a fresh lick of paint by its Punjabi lyrics). Roles are seen as roles not life sentences; both males and females are 'stripped' to a point where identity is seen as performative and negotiable. The film leaves us at a point of departure, not of arrival. The possibilities that have been animated and mobilised by the narrative are still highly conditional, but each person, in a sense, is returning to a centre and not a refuge. A limited degree of transcoding has taken place, inter-cultural and intracultural. It has been possible to enter an arche-typal 'English' space and, if not occupy it, at least deterritorialise it. Moving freely in and out of 'English' spaces (bingo, fish and chips, fairground) – all of which are hostile in some measure – enables the figures to negotiate, but not be assimilated; to open up a narrative of identity in which both Bhaji and beach, initially extra and other, can co-exist. The film proposes its own logic and rhetoric; it does not simply represent or reflect, but 'individuates and makes ambiguous the "legible" order' (During 1993: 151) of both 'bhaji' and 'beach' in their synecdochal forms. In all senses of the word, it is a motion picture.

In keeping with the conventions of Shakespearean comedy, *Bhaji on the Beach* takes its characters out of the time and space of the everyday and into the 'timeless' and boundless realm of the excursion, the world of 'play' in which the crises and stalemates of the quotidian are magnified, distorted and seen as contingent. It is a trip taken for pleasure and, importantly, for 'cultural' health; it is a journey away from the site of contestation and conflict but always with the intention of returning to it, recreated and activated. An excursion is a means by which presents become futures, achieve a forward momentum. *East is East* (1999) is more of an incursion as the Khan family under siege (mostly from itself) remain in place, Salford, and in time, 1971. It is also a film about gender and patriarchy, with the emphasis upon forms of male socialisation.

It is a witty and, at times, outrageously funny film but almost all the jokes are at the expense of the overbearing first-generation patriarch, George Khan, married to a white woman Ella, but with his first wife in Pakistan. It is also, at times, a sexist film. At its premiere, Ayub Khan-Din said that he set the play/film in 1971 for autobiographical reasons, but there is both internal and external evidence which gives the moment wider significance. In the immediate post-war period, up to the early 1960s, labour shortages in Britain were made up for by migrant workers from the New Commonwealth, the so-called 'visible minorities' (George Khan came before the war). Immigration was relatively unrestricted but the Immigration Act of 1962 severely curtailed this, confining access mainly to dependants. Nevertheless, in the late 1960s and early 1970s East African Asians came to Britain from Kenya (1968) and Uganda (1972). In this period also, a racist candidate (Peter Griffiths) won a seat at the General Election for the Conservatives in Smethwick, and Enoch Powell made his infamous 'Rivers of Blood' speech in 1968. Racism took a cultural turn and repatriation entered the agenda. The film shows posters for a Powell meeting and a Powell speech on television, and the Khans' neighbour is a fascist activist. It is a recurring theme, though it is muted by the idiosyncratic representation of the caricature 'Nazi' neighbour who has an increasingly token presence. His daughter, Stella, goes out with Tariq Kahn, and his grandson, Ernest, 'worships' the only Khan daughter and is the closest friend of the youngest son.

The main focus on the film is on the bi-racial family. Figures released in 1997 indicate that half of British-born Caribbean men, a third of Caribbean women and a fifth of Indian and African-Asian men have a white partner, but in 1971 the incidence of bi-racial families would have been considerably smaller, and a white woman marrying a black partner in 1946 (when the Khans married) would have have been likely to be called a 'whore', and the children 'half-caste'. There are a number of themes and a number of tensions, but the main conflict revolves around arranged marriage; unusually, and against conventional representations, it is the males who are the subject of these arrangements. Arranged marriage is less important as an issue itself, but more as the centre of a struggle for command between father and sons. It is also presented in such a way that privileges, unquestioningly, Western models of marriage (choice) and forms of romantic love. By turns, sad and funny, George, who has in many ways abandoned his culture and feels increasingly isolated, strives to be 'Pakistani' and Muslim by the only means left to him – insisting on his youngest son's circumcision and arranging marriages for his sons with the daughters of Pakistani immigrants living in Bradford.

One son rejects his father's plans on the scheduled wedding day, and seeks a career in fashion with a 'camp' partner. His portrait is removed from the living-room wall and he is declared dead. Another son is at college ostensibly studying to become an engineer but is, in fact, an art student. Fashion and art would be seen by George as unmanly, and much of the film is taken up with the interrogation of essentialist gender roles. Penises and pudenda are played with as ways of detaching gender identities from absolute belongings, as well as underlining/undermining the phallocracy of patriarchy.

A mass of contradictions (he runs a fish and chip shop) George constantly tries to withdraw, metaphorically, from the conditions of his bi-racial marriage. He constantly threatens to bring his first wife from Pakistan (she is likely to be more compliant) as Ella tactically outmanoeuvres him again and again. Notionally subject to his authority, Ella stakes out a more even relationship than George might wish for and supports her children in their commitments to 'Englishness'. They refer to the Bradford family that comes to visit as 'Pakis' but their own 'visibility' as non-white places them in a conflicted situation which, although the film does not really confront this, cannot just be wished away. As I noted earlier, all the laughs are on the father who, at times, seems to be 'living' in Pakistan worried about his family living on the border at the time of the East Pakistan breakaway to become Bangla Desh, aided by India. His British family is also living on the border – a place which they happily inhabit – and he is constantly trying to pull them back and fit them into a Pakistani enclave against their frequent transgressive and transcoding activities (alcohol; bacon and sausage; mini-skirts; and the small boy's eternal parka).

Lacking community – Salford is not Bradford – George Khan is forced to imagine one which he and his sons inhabit as 'good' Pakistanis, whereas they, with the one exception who is a dutiful Muslim, immerse themselves intensely in the local, adopting English names and lifestyles when it suits them. The sons do not speak Urdu and know little of Islamic culture, but, despite the Kiplingesque echo of the title, the 'twain' do meet in Salford and alternatives to the Bollywood romance are seen as possible.

In the latter stages of the film when the sons discover their 'engagements' – arranged by the father without their knowledge – a series of confrontations bring into articulation a number of buried themes, many of them based upon the contradictions of George's own experience. Presumably his wife in Pakistan was an arranged marriage, but in England he chose a 'love' marriage to a white woman, a circumstance which may well have been a source of unacknowledged shame. The Pakistani woman from Bradford refers to his 'family of half breeds'. When Tariq says, 'I am not a Pakistani, I speak English, not Urdu', George says, in his 'broken' English, 'English people never accepting you'. It is then that we realise the 'tyrant' is trying to restore his sons, by a regressive act, to a cultural identity in which they will be acceptable, will not be always 'in-between'. Authoritarian, wrongheaded and violent though he is, a logic comes through, emergent from barely articulated years of racism, a nostalgic and impossible logic shaped from a vanished and abandoned past to propose a possible future. In a sense, it is not an arranged marriage for his sons which he has set up, but, symbolically, a 'rearranged' marriage: his own. Nevertheless, at the end Ella and George achieve a semblance of reconciliation: 'He's my husband and he's still your father'. With the arranged marriages exploded in farce, the film creates a space for an intercultural, bi-racial future in which neither half of the binary needs to dominate or be the source of regression, but, in setting the film in 1971, this means that 'the phenomenon of migration, displacement, life in a minority group' (Rushdie 1991: 20) in the intervening period cannot be discounted. Between the memory event and the moment of filming (1999), racism in Britain has taken many different directions and 'acceptability by the English' is still highly conditional. Writing in 1997, Mohan Luthra says:

Overall the British-born black and ethnic minority groups face a society in which institutions are highly marketised and inclined towards a closed culture . . . Unlike their parents and grandparents they face a more fragmented, casualised and marketised spectrum of institutions as well as a system endowed with magistracy, networks and patronage in which gaining of qualifications appears to offer little protection from discrimination. (1997: 47)

It could be argued that *East is East* is likely to be such an 'acceptable' film precisely because it is set in the past and because the images the bi-racial figures inhabit are in no way threatening or transgressive. In other words, there is a potential incorporation of their apparent differences, a recuperation which, in part, answers Sara Ahmed's question, posed in 'Passing through hybridity', 'How do ambiguous bodies get read in a way which further supports the enunciative power of those who are telling the difference?' (1999: 89). It is a large question and one which, potentially, destabilises the premises upon which this book has been based. Have many of the fictions which I have examined crossed over from minority to mainstream status because the images they represent are not transgressive; are they marketable because, in some ways, they support the enunciative power of those (the cultural brokers of power relations) who are 'telling the difference'? To adapt Ahmed's terms, are they 'passing' precisely because of a certain class-based (professional, lower middle) model of hybridity which they produce. While this may be true in some respects and perhaps the fictions cannot be seen as counter-hegemonic, or resistant, at the same time their very currency could also exceed the enunciative power of those who are telling the difference and become popular – in the sense of finding, or perhaps even founding, a public – on their own terms, or at least in terms which render secure power relations around race and gender ambivalent and problematic: the project of both a new future-orientated narrative and the possibility of unthinking some of the received categories, and certainties, around ethnic identity.

CONCLUSION: THE UNBELONGING

Almost all of the narratives discussed in this book have been concerned with settled first- or second-generation immigrants, and the concept of boundary or border has been used extensively as a metaphor in many cases. Neil Bissoondath's short story, 'On the Eve of Uncertain Tomor-rows' (1990) presents a range of characters, mostly exiles from oppressive regimes, for whom migration into liberal, multi-cultural Canada is beset with profound difficulties. For them a border existence is more than a metaphor, and similarly their 'in-between' status has no positive or celebratory features. Confined to a rooming-house, Joaquin, the central figure, exists on the edge of an unknown life beyond him embodied in the few tall buildings of an unspecified city. His situation is both intensively local, compressed in time and space, and also symptomatic of the wider experience of the political refugee. Images of confinement recur through-out the narrative. He and his fellow asylum-seekers exist on the other side of the frontier of identity: the territory of the unbelonging.

Another figure in the rooming-house, Amin, has learned already that multi-culturalism means converting into the currency of a Canadian tomorrow; he plans to change his name to Thomson (a rich and bright name – respected he thinks, but not feared; D.C. perhaps?) and for his immigration interview wears a simple white shirt, pleated trousers, and dark socks in order to produce the 'genteel poverty' look styled by the refugees' lawyer, Jeremy Windhook, to offset any possible brigand-like characteristics. The lawyer knows that acceptance means the scaling down of difference, assimilation and translation into the symbolic imagery of the Anglo-Canadian host culture. The refugees' future de-pends upon an effective performance, a set of representations which erase the traces of their original belonging and alterity, and their political threat. Their task is to shape an effective narrative of unbelonging, an empty, passive space ready to be filled by Canadian images of belonging. The fact that Amin is refused entry, as he is classified as an economic refugee, indicates that 'Amin Thomson, Canadian' – with its suggestion of choice and agency – is an insupportable (unsustainable) contradiction in a country propagating its liberal credentials by receiving asylum seekers from repressive political regimes (Joaquin is from Central Amer-ica) and thus enhancing its democratic image in the face of the alien other. Economic refugees 'shorten' the distance between the host and the country of origin because they implicate the beneficiaries of a global capitalist economy. The fact that for his interview Windhook offers Joaquin the jacket worn by Amin for his, indicates both a level of interchangeability (indifference, even) and the need to perform at the expense of another refugee, to invent a marketable self.

There are seven people in the rooming-house – a Vietnamese couple and five single men – all caught between belongings. Suspended in empty time and empty space, each day has no dawn and each figure devises different tactics for coping with their isolation, unaware of the uncharted territory ahead, mapless tomorrows. For Joaquin the 'dawnless' days means that he is confined, not only in space and time, but also by the darkness of his memories of torture offset only by occasional fantasies of tomorrow. His internal space offers no reassuring identity, no space of safety, no scope for semiotic individuation; instead it is a hostile, dangerous and chaotic place, the space of the enemy. Canada holds out the hope of a renewed internal space, a fresh site to construct a first-person form, a 'my own', an 'ours'. This offer is highly conditional and based upon a profound asymmetry. In a sense, Joaquin's 'tomorrow' depends upon the effective construction of a clearly staked-out boundary which represents his past belonging as 'their space', 'other', 'hostile', 'dangerous', and 'chaotic'. The more convincing the boundary is, the more likely the binary division between 'other' and Canada will be interpreted in his favour. Undecidability in representation will cause him to suffer the fate of Amin.

In a way Joaquin's presence on the border could be conceived of as being analogous to a 'text' in Lotman's model where he tracks 'the flux of energy that follows every criss-crossing of a boundary' (Papastergiadis 1995: 14). In developing this analogy I will be following closely Papastergiadis's lucid explanation of Lotman's model in which a text arrives from the outside and 'a dialogue occurs in the context of difference'. As Papastergiadis points out, 'the precondition for dialogue is the mutual attraction of the participants' (15), which is why Joaquin, and his lawyer, have to begin by building a boundary predicated upon absolute difference (the oppressive regime) and then proceed to make him 'attractive' to the host culture so that it will perceive his potential for restructuring. In this context, unlike in the Lotman model, it is the receiving culture which is imbued with 'salvific qualities' and by being integrated into this culture his 'tomorrow' can be realised, his distinctive presence and difference dissolved. It is by no means a fully dialogical process as the 'new model' Joaquin will only be internalised, restructured and allowed to re-enter time and space on the terms of the receiving culture. Hence the 'representational' coaching by the lawyer and the attention to details of style and performance.

In Joaquin's case his hands, ironically, are the main props in his identity performance. Tortured to the point where he will never again practise his skills as an electrician, his hands will be used by the lawyer to the fullest theatrical effect as evidence of his authenticity, proof of his necessary suffering to meet the criteria of the 'salvific' culture. The scars are his stigmata, marks of credibility, signifiers ruptured from their past signifieds, redesigned to overcome 'uncertain tomorrows', the doubting Thomases of the immigration office. In a sense, the scars are also metonyms of that other nation. The marks on the hands and the scars on back, chest, buttocks are, potentially, emblems of a sufficient disfigurement, and erasure, of the political body which prepares it for 'dialogue'. Simultaneously embodied – for dramatic purposes – and disembodied – for political purposes – Joaquin has to undergo a reconfiguration and transformation in order to continue on his migrant's journey to make himself legible. The anal violation, organ disruption and bodily dysfunction graphically imaged for the hearing (the seeing?) by Windhook, are, literally, signs of the regime's 'monstrosity', and, metaphorically, signifiers of the condition required by Canada's 'humanity', and an adequate 'disfigurement' for entry. In the process, the identity and body of the man vanish, are erased, displaced by a tradeable 'commodity'.

Contextless, Joaquin makes one journey to the poor margins of the city where he 'relocates', or reorientates, himself in 'the shadowed cocoon of La Barricada' ('On The Eve of Uncertain Tomorrows': 13), an eclectic, hastily constructed space decorated with bits and pieces of his country and continent – a refuge for refugees. It is a zone which 'narrates' the dialectic of belonging and unbelonging. The bar is also a form of security, a fortification against the 'enemy' for illegals; it is a borderland. On one wall, there is a painting which represents a vision of 'a rural paradise in which humans are trespassers' (14). The iconography suggests, at one and the same time, both the 'lost' country of memory and Canada. To Joaquin this is a work of despair and he always sits with his back to it. The comparison with his own situation is obvious, as in both his home country and in Canada his 'humanity' is trespassing; the one broke his body, the other needs it as evidence: both evacuate the person. The bar itself also signifies one of the conditions of immigrant eligibility, 'spirit broken into timidity', a place where 'yesterday becomes forever'. On the one hand, Canada – the space whose edges he occupies – is an ever-receding tomorrow, a vague and uncertain landscape; on the other, La Barricada represents an over-detailed, 'excessive' enclave: the 'past interior', and anterior. Despite this, the word 'back', as in 'they're sending him back', is a word which produces terror. There is a sense in which neither the bar, nor Canada, are places in which Joaquin would come if he had a choice.

Everyone in the bar is torn between there and here, spatial and temporal 'lepers', forced to carry out their own medical care, inventing and reinventing identities as part of their transitional and illegal status. Just the recall of a name returns Joaquin to his torture and the memory of his sister's dismemberment. Remembering and dismembering merge into the same process and are reconfigured in the present with the attempted suicide of the young mother and widow, Tere, whose life Joaquin has helped to save; it is the only 'act of his own' in this city and it momentarily enlivens and empowers him, a tiny step towards the creation of an internal space, the form of the first person. It is a healing, and self-healing moment, particularly as he had used his otherwise useless hands. These hands, no longer only props in a testimonial, symbolise a wider anima-tion in which he begins to trace a journey through streets never before followed, looks in the windows of bars, cafés, and restaurants, and, for the first time, starts to internalise, absorb the domestic spaces of the city, takes on an active 'tense', mobilised again in time and space.

This mood of self-figuration is momentary and dissolves when he returns to the tensions and distances of the rooming-house, and is further punctured and revealed as illusory when Windhook, handing over Amin's sombre grey jacket (a 'tactical' choice of colour) to Joaquin for his interview the next day, tells him that Amin has been refused entry. Not able to qualify under the UN definition (like Flavio, a figure at *La Barricada* who had been sent back), Amin is scheduled to be deported, not to his country of origin, but to Germany, his last point of departure. The news hollows out the entire space in which Joaquin stands, nullifies the previous 'act of his own' and renders lifeless the earlier animation and movement. He is a 'refugee' again, in retreat, on the eve of a spectacle in which he is the decentred performer forced to stage a presence, dependent upon finding a plausible persona, or mask, to screen his dispossession, his unbelonging. Pushed to the side of his life, represented by another, the story is an act of mourning for his own bereavement, the loss of his 'own', forced to masquerade as the very model of passivity. It is, in Elleke Boehmer's phrases, both a narrative of 'not quite' and 'in-between' (Boehmer 1995: 232). As Amin's fate shows there is no 'third space between a name and its alternate' (Papastergiadis: 17), no scope for agency or self-definition in the pre-immigrant moment, other than that identity conferred by the fixed terms and conditions of nation-state and race, of inter-national agreements, rhetorics and bureaucracy. The whole narrative is about legitimation and the justification of cultural imaginaries and national discourses; a conflict between physical/material and symbolic–ideological regimes of value and control, contested and contesting, finalities, against slippage and binarised. Unbelonging is the permanent condition of being on the eve of an uncertain tomorrow.

Written against the grain of the 'diasporic romance' of endless hybridity as well as being a kind of anti-national allegory, Bissoondath's story forces us to reflect upon the political realities of a global culture in which the 'developed' countries simultaneously talk up human rights while ruthlessly policing boundaries so that those of us invited 'to imagine beyond the binary' (Clark 1995: 43) can do so only in highly determined and coded ways.

Bibliography

Agamben, G. (1998) *Homo Sacer: Sovereign Power and Bare Life*, trans. D. Heller-Roazen, Stanford: Stanford University Press.

Ahmad, A. (1995) 'The politics of literary postcoloniality', *Race and Class*, 36, 3: 1–20.

Ahmed, S. (1999) '"She'll wake up one of these days and find she's turned into a nigger": passing through hybridity', *Theory, Culture and Society*, 16, 2, April, pp. 87–106.

Alibhai, Y. (1991) *New Statesman and Society*, 15 February, pp. 17–18.

Allen, P. G. (1987) 'The autobiography of a confluence', in Swann and Krupat (eds.), *I Tell You Now*, Lincoln: University of Nebraska Press.

Amin, S. (1989) *Eurocentrism*, trans. Russell Moore, London: Zed Books.

Andermahr, S., Lovell, T., and Wolkowitz, C. (eds.) (1997), *A Glossary of Feminist Theory*, London: Arnold.

Ang, I. (1994) 'On not speaking Chinese: postmodern ethnicity and the politics of diaspora', *New Formations*, 24, Winter, pp. 1–19.

Anwar, M. (1998) *Ethnic Minorities and the British Electoral System*, Coventry: Centre for Research in Ethnic Relations, University of Warwick.

Anzaldúa, G. (1987) *Borderlands/La Frontera: The New Mestizo*, San Francisco: Aunt Lute Books.

Bakhtin, M. (1981) *The Dialogic Imagination*, trans. C. Emerson and M. Holquist, Austin: University of Texas Press.

Bakhtin, M. (1984) *Problems of Dostoevsky's Poetics*, ed. and trans. by C. Emerson, Manchester: Manchester University Press.

Bambara, T. C. (1985) 'Salvation is the issue', in Evans (ed.), *Black Women Writers*, London: Pluto Press.

Barker, M. (1981) *The New Racism*, London: Junction Books.

Barnett, A. (1982) *Iron Britannia*, London: Allison and Busby.

Barthes, R. (1976) *The Pleasure of the Text*, trans. R. Miller, New York: Cape.

Berger, J. (1984) *And our Faces, my Heart, Brief as Photos*, London: Writers and Readers.

Bhabha, H. (1991) 'The post-colonial critic: Homi Bhabha interviewed by David Bennett and Terry Collits', *Arena*, 96.

Bhabha, H. (1992) 'Post-colonial authority and postmodern guilt', in Grossberg, Nelson, and Treichler (eds.), *Cultural Studies*, New York: Routledge, pp. 56–68.

Bhabha, H. (1994) *The Location of Culture*, London: Routledge.

Bissoondath, N. (1991) *On the Eve of Uncertain Tomorrows*, London: Minerva.

Boehmer, E. (1995) *Colonial and Postcolonial Literature*, Oxford: Oxford University Press.

Brah, A. (1996) *Cartographies of Diaspora*, London: Routledge.

Burgin, V. (1996) In/Different Spaces: Place and Memory in Visual Culture, Berkeley: University of California Press.

Butler, J. (1993) Bodies that Matter: On the Discursive Limits of 'Sex', New York and London: Routledge.

Canclini, N. G. (1995) Hybrid Cultures, Minneapolis: University of Minnesota Press.

Canevacci, M. (1992) 'Image-accumulation and cultural syncretism', Theory, Culture and Society, 9, 3, pp. 95–110.

Cha, T. H. K. (1982) Dictée, New York: Tanam.

Chadha, G. (1994) (dir.) Bhaji on the Beach, London: Channel Four/Umbi Films.

Chamberlain, M. (1998) 'I belong to whoever wants me', New Formations, 33, Spring, pp. 47–58.

Chambers, I. (1996) 'Signs of silence, lines of listening', in Chambers and Curti (eds.), The Post-Colonial Question, London: Routledge, pp. 47–62.

Chambers, I. and Curti, L. (eds.) (1996) The Post-Colonial Question: Common Skies, Divided Horizons, London: Routledge.

Childers, J. and Hentzi, G. (eds.) (1995) Columbia Dictionary of Modern Literary and Cultural Criticism, New York: Columbia University Press.

Childs, P. and Williams, P. (1997) An Introduction to Post-Colonial Theory, London: Harvester Wheatsheaf.

Chu, G. et al. (1979) Inalienable Rice: A Chinese and Japanese Canadian Anthology, Vancouver: Powell Street Revue and the Chinese Canadian Writers Workshop.

Cixous, H. (1976) 'Fiction and its phantoms: a reading of Freud's "The Uncanny"', New Literary History, 7: 3, Spring.

Cixous, H. (1988) Writing Differences: Readings from the Seminar of Hélène Cixous, S. Sellers (ed.), Milton Keynes: Open University Press.

Clark, Vèvè A. (1995) 'Developing diaspora literacy and marasa consciousness', in Spillers (ed.), Comparative American Identities: Race, Sex, and Nationality in the Modern Text, New York and London: Routledge.

Clifford, J. (1992) The Predicament of Culture, Cambridge: Harvard.

Cohen, P. (1998) 'Who needs an island?', New Formations, 33, Spring, pp. 11–37.

Cohen, R. (1997) Global Diasporas: An Introduction, London: UCL Press.

Connolly, W. (1991) Identity/Difference: Democratic Negotiations of Political Paradox, Ithaca: Cornell University Press.

Cunningham, S. and Nguyen, T. (1998) 'Floating Lives: the Media of the Vietnamese Diaspora', unpublished paper.

Danticat, E. (1995) 'Caroline's Wedding', in Ford (ed.), The Granta Book of the American Long Story, London: Granta, pp. 651–86.

de Certeau, M. (1984) The Practice of Everyday Life, Berkeley: University of California Press.

de Certeau, M. (1993) 'Walking in the city', in During (ed.), The Cultural Studies Reader, London: Routledge.

de Man, P. (1984) The Rhetoric of Romanticism, New York: Columbia University Press.

Deleuze, G. and Guattari, F. (1988) A Thousand Plateaus, trans. B. Massumi, Minneapolis: University of Minnesota Press.

Doyle, W. (1997) 'The space between identity and otherness in Hanif Kureishi's The Buddha of Suburbia', Commonwealth Essays and Studies, Special Issue No. SP4, pp. 110–18.

During, S. (ed.) (1993) The Cultural Studies Reader, London: Routledge.

Eng, D. L. (1997) 'Out here and over there: queerness and diaspora in Asian-American studies', Social Text, 52/53, pp. 31–52.

Fanon, F. (1986) Black Skin, White Masks, London: Pluto.

Fischer, M. (1986) 'Ethnicity and the post-modern arts of memory', in Clifford and Marcus (eds.), *Writing Culture: The Poetics and Politics of Ethnography*, Berkeley and Los Angeles: University of California Press.

Foucault, M. (1977) 'Nietzsche, genealogy, history', in *Language, Counter-Memory, Practice*, Oxford: Blackwell.

Frank, A. (1991) 'For a sociology of the body: an analytical review', in Featherstone, Hepworth and Turner (eds.), *The Body: Social Process and Cultural Theory*, London: Sage.

Freud, S. (1899) 'Screen memories', in *Standard Edition*, vol. 3.

Friedman, J. (1997) 'Global crises, the struggle for cultural identity and intellectual porkbarrelling: cosmopolitanisms versus locals, ethnics and nationals in an era of dehegemonisation', in Werbner and Modood (eds.), *Debating Cultural Hybridity*, London: Zed Books, pp. 70–89.

Fukuyama, F. (1992) *The End of History and The Last Man*, London: Penguin.

Fuss, D. (1995) *Identification Papers*, New York: Routledge.

Galloway, D. (1980) *The Absurd Hero*, Austin: University of Texas Press.

Garcia, C. (1992) *Dreaming in Cuban*, London: Harper Collins.

Gates, H. L. (1997) *The Guardian*, 19 July.

Gilroy, P. (1993) *The Black Atlantic: Modernity and Double Consciousness*, London: Verso.

Giroux, H. (1992) *Border Crossings: Cultural Workers and the Politics of Education*, London: Routledge.

Goldberg, D. (ed.) (1995) *Multiculturalism: A Critical Reader*, Oxford: Blackwell.

Gómez-Peña, G. (1992–3) 'The new world (b)order', *Third Text*, vol. 21, Winter.

Goto, H. (1997) *Chorus of Mushrooms*, London: The Women's Press. Originally published 1994.

Gregory, D. (1994) *Geographical Imaginations*, Cambridge, MA and Oxford: Blackwell.

Grosz, E. (1988) 'Space, time, and bodies', *On the Beach*, 13 April.

Hall, S. (1987) 'Minimal selves', in ICA *Documents 6: Postmodernism and the Question of Identity*, London: ICA.

Hall, S. (1988) 'New ethnicities', in Mercer (ed.), *ICA Documents 7: Black Film, British Cinema*.

Hall, S. (1991) 'Old and new identities, old and new ethnicities', in King (ed.), *Culture, Globalization, and the World-System*, London: Macmillan.

Hall, S. (1992) 'New ethnicities', in Donald and Rattansi (eds.), *Race, Culture and Difference*, London: Sage.

Hall, S. (1993) 'Cultural identity and diaspora', in Williams and Chrisman (eds.), *Colonial Discourse and Post-Colonial Theory*, Hemel Hempstead: Harvester Wheatsheaf.

Hall, S. (1995) 'Negotiating Caribbean identities', *New Left Review*, 209, pp. 3–14.

Hall, S. (1996a) 'When was the "post-colonial"? Thinking at the limit', in Chambers and Curti.

Hall, S. (1996b) 'Who needs "identity"?', in Hall and du Gay (eds.), *Questions of Cultural Identity*, London: Sage.

Harjo, J. (1983) 'Anchorage', in *She Had Some Horses,* New York: Thunder's Mouth Press.

Harris, W. (1985) 'Adversarial contexts and creativity', *New Left Review*, 154.

Hicks, D. E. (1991) *Border Writing: The Multidimensional Text*, Minneapolis: University of Minnesota Press.

Hirsch, M. (1996) 'Past lives: postmemories in exile', in Suleiman (ed.), *Exile and Creativity*, Durham, NC and London: Duke University Press.

Hongo, G. (ed.) (1995) *Under Western Eyes: Personal Essays from Asian America*, New York: Anchor Books.

hooks, b. (1984) *Feminist Theory: From Margin to Center*, Boston: South End Press.

hooks, b. (1989) 'The politics of radical black subjectivity', in *Talking Back*, Boston: South End Press.

Islam, S. M. (1997) *The Map-makers of Spitalfields*, Leeds: Peepal Tree Press.

Jameson, F. (1992) *The Geopolitical Aesthetic: Cinema and Space in the World System*, Bloomington and Indianapolis: Indiana University Press.

JanMohamed, A. R. (1992) 'Some implications of Paulo Freire's border pedagogy', *Cultural Studies*, Winter, 107–17.

Jen, G. (1992) *Typical American*, New York: Plume/Penguin. First published in the USA 1991.

Jen, G. (1997) *Mona in the Promised Land*, London: Granta.

Jen, G. (1999) *Who's Irish?* London: Granta.

Jin, M. (1996) *Song of the Boatwoman*, Leeds: Peepal Tree Press.

Kamboureli, S. (1993) 'The technology of ethnicity: Canadian multiculturalism and the language of law', *Open Letter*, vol. 8, nos. 5–6, Winter–Spring, pp. 202–17.

Kim, E. (1990) ' "Such opposite creatures": men and women in Asian-American literature', *Michigan Quarterly Review*, Winter: 68–93.

Kingston, M. H. (1981) *The Woman Warrior: Memoirs of a Girlhood Among Ghosts*, London: Picador. First published in the USA 1975.

Kolodny, A. (1992) 'Letting go our grand obsessions: notes toward a new literary history of the American frontiers', *American Literature*, 64.1, pp. 1–18.

Krause, D. (1984) 'Reading Bon's Letter and Faulkner's *Absalom, Absalom!*', *PMLA* 99. 2, March: 225–41.

Kureishi, H. (1985) 'Dirty washing', *Time Out*, 14–20 November.

Kureishi, H. (1990) *The Buddha of Suburbia*, London: Faber and Faber.

Kureishi, H. (1996) 'The rainbow sign', in *My Beautiful Launderette and other Writings*, London: Faber and Faber.

Lee, A. (1994) *Eat Drink Man Woman, The Wedding Banquet*, New York: The Overlook Press.

Lee, C-R. (1995) *Native Speaker*, London: Granta Books.

Lee, S. (1992) *Disappearing Moon Café*, Seattle: The Seal Press. First published in Canada in 1990.

Lefebvre, H. (1991) *The Production of Space*, Oxford and Cambridge, MA: Blackwell.

Levy, A. (1999) *Fruit of the Lemon*, London: Review.

Linde, C. (1993) *Life Stories: the Creation of Coherence*, New York: Oxford University Press.

Lloyd, D. (1993) *Anomalous States: Irish Writing and the Post-Colonial Moment*, Dublin: Lilliput.

Loomba, A. (1998) *Colonialism/Post-colonialism*, London: Routledge.

Lotman, Y. (1991) *The Universe of the Mind*, trans. A. Shukman, London: Tauris.

Lowe, D. (1995) *The Body in Late-Capitalist America*, Durham and London: Duke University Press.

Lowe, L. (1996) *Immigrant Acts*, Durham and London: Duke University Press.

Lull, J. (1995) *Media, Communication, Culture: A Global Approach*, Cambridge: Polity.

Luthra, M. (1997) *Britain's Black Population: Social Change, Public Policy and Agenda*, Aldershot: Arena.

Lyotard, J-F. (1986) *Le Postmoderne Expliqué aux enfants*, Paris: Galilée.

Lyotard, J-F. (1984) *The Postmodern Condition*. Minneapolis: University of Minnesota Press.

Martin-Barbero, J. (1993) *Communication, Culture, and Hegemony*, London: Sage.

McGuigan, J. (1999) *Modernity and Postmodern Culture*, Buckingham: Open University Press.

Merleau-Ponty, M. (1968) *The Visible and the Invisible*, Evanston: Northwestern University Press.

Min, P. G. (ed.) (1995) *Asian-Americans: Contemporary Trends and Issues*, Thousand Oaks, CA.: Sage.

Mukherjee, B. (1991) 'A Four Hundred-Year-Old Woman', in Mariani (ed), *Critical Fictions*, Seattle: Bay Press.

Mukherjee, B. (1991) *Jasmine*, London: Virago Press, 1991. First published in the USA 1989.

Nealon, J. T. (1998) *Alterity Politics: Ethics and Performative Subjectivity*, Durham and London: Duke University Press.

Ng, F. M. (1994) *Bone*, New York: Harper Perennial. First published in the USA 1993.

O'Donnell, D. (1999) (dir.) *East is East*, London: Film Four Limited/Assassin Films.

Ozeki, R. L. (1998) *My Year of Meat*, London: Picador.

Papastergiadis, N. (1995) 'Restless hybrids', *Third Text*, 32, Autumn, pp. 9–18.

Payne, J. R. (ed.) (1992) *Multicultural Autobiography: American Lives*, Knoxville: University of Tennessee Press.

Pennybacker, M. (1997) 'Fiction in Hawaii', *The Nation*, 7 July, pp. 33–6.

Philip, M. N. (1993) *She tries her tongue, her silence softly breaks*, London: The Women's Press.

Phillips, M. (1998) 'At home in England', in Wambu (ed.), pp. 426–31.

Pieterse, J. N. (1995) 'Globalization as hybridization', in Featherstone, Lash and Robertson (eds.), *Global Modernities*, London: Sage, pp. 45–68.

Plummer, K. (1995) *Telling Sexual Stories: Power, Change and Social Worlds*, London: Routledge.

Pratt, M. L. (1992) *Imperial Eyes: Travel Writing and Transculturation*, London: Routledge.

Readings, B. (1991) *Introducing Lyotard; Art and Politics*, London: Routledge.

Ricoeur, P. (1991) 'Narrative identity', in Wood (ed.), *On Paul Ricoeur*, London: Routledge, pp. 179–99.

Ricoeur, P. (1995) 'The creativity of language', in Kearney, *States of Mind: Dialogues with Contemporary Thinkers on the European Mind*, Manchester: Manchester University Press, pp. 216–45.

Rosaldo, R. (1989) *Culture and Truth*, Boston: Beacon Press.

Rushdie, S. (1982) *Midnight's Children*, London: Pan Books.

Rushdie, S. (1991) *Imaginary Homelands*, London: Granta.

Rushdie, S. (1992) *Satanic Verses*, Dover, Delaware: The Consortium Inc.

Said, E. (1986) *After the Last Sky: Palestinian Lives*, New York: Pantheon.

Said, E. (1993) *Culture and Imperialism*, London: Chatto and Windus.

Schamus, J. (1994) Introduction in Lee (1994).

Shapiro, M. (1997) *Violent Cartographies: Mapping Cultures of War*, Minneapolis: University of Minnesota Press.

Shohat, E. (1993) 'Notes on the "postcolonial"', *Social Text*, 31/2: pp. 99–113.

Shohat, E. and Stam, R. (1994) *Unthinking Eurocentrism*, London: Routledge.

Singh, A., Skerrett, J. T. and Hogan, R. E. (eds.) (1994) *Memory, Narrative, and Identity: New Essays in Ethnic American Literatures*, Boston: Northeastern University Press.

Syal, M. (1996) *Anita and Me*, London: Flamingo.

Tan, A. (1989, 1990) *The Joy Luck Club*, London: Minerva. First published in the USA 1989.

Taranger, M-C. (1991) 'Une mémoire de seconde main? Film, emprunt et référence dans le récit de vie', Hors Cadre, 9.
Taussig, M. (1986) Shamanism, Colonialism, and the Wild Man, Chicago: University of Chicago Press.
Todorov, T. (1992) The Conquest of America, New York: Harper Perennial.
Tölöyan, K. (1991) Preface. Diaspora 1 (1), 3–7.
Tomlinson, J. (1991) Cultural Imperialism: A Critical Introduction, London: Pinter.
Trinh T. Minh-ha (1990) 'Documentary is/not a name', October 52, Spring.
Trinh T.Minh-ha (1991) When the Moon Waxes Red: Representation, Gender and Cultural Politics, London: Routledge.
Trinh T. Minh-ha (1989) Woman, Native, Other: Writing, Post-coloniality, and Feminism, Bloomington: University of Indiana Press.
Tyau, K. (1996) A Little Too Much is Enough, London: The Women's Press. First published in the USA 1995.
UNESCO World Culture Report (1998).
Venn, C. (1999) 'Narrating the postcolonial', in Featherstone and Lash (eds.), Spaces of Culture: City, Nation, World, London: Sage, pp. 257–81.
Virgin Film Guide, 5th Edition (1996) London: Virgin Books.
Wah, F. (1996) Diamond Grill, Edmonton: NeWest Press.
Wambu, O. (1998) Empire Windrush: Fifty Years of Writing about Black Britain, London: Victor Gollancz.
Werbner, P., and Modood, T. (eds.) (1997) Debating Cultural Hybridity, London: Zed Books.
Wilson, R. (1994) 'Goodbye Paradise: global/localism, Hawaii, and cultural production in the American Pacific', New Formations, 24, Winter, pp. 35–50.
Wong, M. G. (1995) in Pyong Gap Min.
Wong, S-L. C. (1992) 'Autobiography as guided Chinatown tour? Maxine Hong Kingston's The Woman Warrior and the Chinese-American autobiographical controversy', in Payne 1992.
Yamanaka, L-A. (1996) Wild Meat and the Bully Burgers, London: Minerva.
Yocum, D. (1996) 'Some troubled homecomings', in Chambers and Curti, pp. 221–7.

Index